PRAISE FOR
BEAUTIFUL UNION

"One of *the* books for our time. An essential read. It expertly captures the beauty of orthodox Christian sexuality in a way that is thoughtful, well researched, well written, and deeply compelling."
—JOHN MARK COMER, founder of Practicing the Way
and author of *Live No Lies*

"How do we allow Scripture to shape our vision for our bodies and relationships? How do we engage the larger culture with care, nuance, and theological astuteness? These are questions the church desperately needs guidance in, which is why I'm grateful for Joshua Butler and this book. Josh offers rich and accessible theology, humor, and wonderful storytelling to help us to see the grand vision for our bodies and sexuality. This book covers much ground while never sacrificing depth. I highly recommend it."
—RICH VILLODAS, lead pastor of New Life Fellowship
and author of *Good and Beautiful and Kind*

"The timeless biblical truth of God's story of sex has been lost in our modern era. However, the sexual confusion and pain of our day demand that we return to this brilliant narrative, embracing not simply biblical rules for sex but God's heart for our sexuality. Josh Butler has done a masterful job of explaining this profound mystery in understandable language, unlocking healing, redemption, and clarity."

—Dr. Juli Slattery, president of Authentic Intimacy
and author of *God, Sex, and Your Marriage*

"*Beautiful Union* is simply astonishing. Every chapter is full of mind-blowing biblical insights, jaw-dropping theological connections, and a profound reframing of the contentious dimensions of sex. It's the Protestant magnum opus on sexual ethics we've been waiting for and one of the most important books I've ever read. With pastoral care, theological precision, and worshipful joy, Butler brings refreshing clarity to a culture (and sadly, a church) increasingly confused about the meaning, purpose, and ethics of sex. I rarely use the word *masterpiece* in describing a contemporary work, but it's absolutely fitting here."

—Brett McCracken, senior editor at
the Gospel Coalition and author of
Uncomfortable and *Hipster Christianity*

"*Beautiful Union* offers a vision of sexuality that is timely, winsome, and powerful. Josh weaves together beauty and neighbor-love, rooted in Scripture and biblical values, giving new windows and fresh language that resonates with pastors from a wide variety of church traditions in our network."

—Dennae Pierre, director of the Surge Network
and co-director for City to City North America

"Josh Butler has done it again. He has a way of taking the things I've been trying to think through and giving words and clarity to those issues and concerns. Thank you, Josh—you just made my preaching and leading easier. This is the cultural clarity we've all been waiting for."

—ALBERT TATE, lead pastor of Fellowship Church
and author of *How We Love Matters*

"What a timely and much-needed book! *Beautiful Union* powerfully shows how sex was intended to be a window into the beautiful dynamics of God's love for his people, while also speaking personally and tenderly to the painful emotions, internal wrestling, and broken circumstances that can surround sex and intimacy. Whether you are married or single, this is a must-read that will give you clarity on the meaning and purpose of sex."

—KRISTIN NAVE, creator of SheLovesBible and
co-director of Abiding Free Ministries

"One of the best books I have read on anything in the last year, *Beautiful Union* combines a biblical theology of marriage with a compelling piece of sexual apologetics, and it does so with a pastoral warmth and sparkle that few books on this subject attempt, let alone achieve. Indispensable."

—ANDREW WILSON, teaching pastor of King's Church London
and author of *God of All Things*

"*Beautiful Union* is a gem! With the mind of a scholar and the heart of a friend, Josh Butler reveals God's view of sex in a way that few people can. With wit and wisdom—and a lively prose that makes the book hard to put down—Josh creates a stunning picture of God's beautiful design for sex that is both theologically rich and profoundly practical."

—PRESTON SPRINKLE, PhD, president of the
Center for Faith, Sexuality, and Gender

"*Beautiful Union* by Joshua Ryan Butler is a marvel. Its simplicity is its profundity; its truth is its love. I finished these pages in tears, my imagination renewed and expanded to consider the pursuing, self-giving love God has shown to his people through Christ. Read this book to understand the meaning of bodies in sexual union. But read this book for another reason too: because you want to hear the voice of the Divine Lover calling you home."
—JEN POLLOCK MICHEL, author of *In Good Time*

"Sex might be the number one reason many people in the West have left the church or at least begun to doubt the goodness of God's Word. But if you look deeper, you'll find signs that the sexual revolution has failed its promises of liberation. In our lifetime, you might even see large numbers turn to Christ because of the church's view of sex. If that happens, books like Joshua Ryan Butler's *Beautiful Union* will probably play a key role. Hand this book to skeptics. Teach it in premarital counseling. You'll love how he uses biblical theology to reveal God's good design for sex."
—COLLIN HANSEN, editor in chief at the Gospel Coalition

BEAUTIFUL UNION

BEAUTIFUL
UNION

HOW GOD'S VISION FOR SEX
POINTS US TO THE GOOD,
UNLOCKS THE TRUE, AND (SORT OF)
EXPLAINS EVERYTHING

JOSHUA RYAN BUTLER

MULTNOMAH

To my grandparents, Michael and Elida Valdez,
for being an icon of Christ and the church.

ORDER OF CEREMONY

III. A Greater Vision

Dearly Beloved,

I want to welcome you to these pages. Yes, *you.* Whether you're single or married, the cynic or the romantic, happily in love or heartbroken and lonely, or somewhere in between. You are welcome here. This book is for you.

You might be wrestling with desire or reeling from the impact of divorce, married in bliss or married and barely hanging on, loving your body or feeling trapped inside it, drowning in five kids or isolated in an apartment by yourself. You might be a twitterpated teenager, a widow in grief, or haunted by the one who got away. I'm so glad you're here; this book is for you too.

Perhaps sex and romance are a source of pain, frustration, confusion, or anger. The abuser who inflicted himself upon you like a storm and whose memory still haunts you today, the attractions that got you called names and kicked out of your home, the addiction wrapped in secrecy and shame that you've tried to break but just can't shake, the stillborn child whose anniversary all these years later still brings you to tears. I'm for you; this book is for you too.

We are gathered here today, invited by Christ to discover ourselves as his beloved.

While I may not know you, I do expect I know some things about you—things that we share. I expect your life has been personally impacted by many of the things we'll discuss. I expect that you know, deep down, in your very flesh and bone that *you were made for more.* More than an aimless sexual searching. More than a dead-end marriage. More than *whatever* you've endured. *You were made for more.*

As we discuss the grand narrative that is above and under and behind and all through each of our stories, I expect you'll feel something come alive within you. Something big. Something beautiful.

So let me say right up front what I hope comes clearly through on every page of this book: *You are loved.* By God. By me. Everything—*everything*—starts with that. Ends with that too.

I'm glad you're here. And it's my prayer that by the end of this book, whether we agree about everything or not, *you'll* be glad you've been here too.

With love in Christ,
Josh

INTRODUCTION

Of Trampolines and Icons

"**M**y parents got a trampoline!" Elijah excitedly exclaimed. It was second grade, and I was visiting my best friend's new home for the first time. "No way!" I responded. "Let's go see it."

I followed his lead, as we searched through bedrooms, opened closet doors, and looked behind living room couches. We were on the hunt for any sign of that trampoline's blue matted borders, short stubby legs, and black interior net. I *loved* trampolines. I was thrilled at the prospect of taking flight to new heights on one for grown-ups.

"Where is it?" I asked.

"I'm not sure."

"Well, have you seen it?"

"No, not yet."

My confusion must have shown. "Well, if you haven't seen it, how do you know it's here?"

Elijah explained that his new bedroom was located directly beneath his parents' bedroom.

"Sometimes at night," he said, "my parents pull out the trampoline. I can hear them bouncing around on it . . ."

This is a book about that trampoline. We never did find it. Elijah was convinced his parents packed it up each night, after using it so enthusiastically. Somehow they managed to store it away, hidden. We remained enchanted by the mystery.

In the years to come, however, this mystery cleared up. We grew older, and it dawned upon us what the bouncing above his bedroom was all about. We discovered that while not strictly a piece of playground equipment, *yes*, the secret Elijah's parents had hidden in their bedroom was fun. (And *yes*, it can help you take flight, in a manner of speaking.)

Yet there is still a hiddenness, a mystery surrounding sex, that can point us to God in surprising and very life-giving ways. I've discovered in my life—as a Christian, a husband, a father, and a pastor—that what was hidden in the bedroom upstairs is a signpost of greater things. Sex tells us something. It shows us where we've come from and where we're going. In its mystery can be glimpsed the origin of our existence, the glory of our redemption, and the destiny of our world. Its mystery speaks to realities greater than little Elijah and I ever could have imagined.

Sex as Icon

Beautiful may not be the first word that comes to mind when you think of sex. Particularly the Christian vision for sex. *Backward. Bigoted. Outdated. Oppressive. Prudish. Puritanical.* These words are what many think of the traditional Christian sexual ethic today.[1] The faithful might feel they *have to* follow it, but nobody really *wants* to. Frail devotion to a list of don'ts, can'ts, and won'ts is driven by duty, not desire. And the God who made such a laundry list of buzzkill rules ain't pretty.

God might seem to you like a cosmic killjoy or a stern lecturer disappointed with your honest desires or shameful past. How could such a God care much about your regret after an unsatisfying one-night stand or your heartbreak over unrequited love? How could such a God really care about the dilemma of that unplanned pregnancy or your sobbing on the floor in the wake of a third miscarriage? What about the bland or painful sex in an un-affectionate marriage or the frustration of a "dead bedroom"?

Beautiful may not be the first word that comes to mind. But what if I told you it can be? That it even *should* be? What if I told you that, in light of the Christian gospel, your understanding of your body and of sexuality can be driven by beauty? That's the goal of this book: to restore the beauty of the Christian sexual ethic. And the first step is to learn to look *through* sex to greater things.

At vs. Through

Sex is iconic. It's designed to point to greater things. That's the central thesis of this book. What do I mean by "icon"? Historically, icons were not meant to be looked *at*, so much as to be looked *through*. They pointed to something beyond themselves.

Take *Christ Pantocrator*, for example, one of the most famous icons in church history.[2] At first glance, Jesus's face looks strange. His features are contorted; the two halves don't match. The left side of Jesus's face boasts the soft look of a shepherd: welcoming and peaceful, with a hand outstretched in the sign of blessing. The right side holds the piercing gaze of a judge: with a stern eye, pursed lips, and a raised eyebrow, holding the book of the Gospels.

The contrast becomes even more explicit in this second image, where someone has taken each half and mirrored it into a whole. *What's going on here? Did the artist make a mistake?* we wonder. *Was Jesus unable to "hold his pose"?* But the contrast between these two "sides" of Jesus is intentional, and we *lose* something when they lose their difference.

The icon is not intended to be a literal depiction of Jesus, like an Instagram selfie showing the Savior's snazzy new haircut to the masses or a photo ID to give the TSA security agent. Rather, it's a window into a greater reality. It is a picture of something larger.

Jesus holds *love* and *justice* perfectly together. Mercy and righteousness are inseparably intertwined in his identity, bound together in union through the excellency of his character and the perfection of his person. In other words, don't look *at* the icon as a photographic replica but *through* it as a window into the nature of the One it points to.

Similarly, God has designed sex to point beyond itself to greater things. In Ephesians 5:32, the apostle Paul says sexual union is a "profound mystery" because "it refers to Christ and the church." *Whoa!* That's some heavy-duty symbolism. Sex is an icon of the mystery of our salvation. (We'll explore how in chapter 1.)

At first glance, a man and woman joined together at the hip can seem clumsy and contorted (like those two halves of Jesus's face). We might wonder whether the Artist made a mistake, carving a sculpture with conflicting halves that don't quite match. Yet properly understood, sexual union is like stained glass in a cathedral: intended to give us a lens into the transcendent, and a glorious glimpse into the heart of God.

A Mega Mystery

Let's go back to that Ephesians passage. When Paul says sex is a great mystery, the phrase he uses in Greek is *mega mysterion*—literally, a "mega mystery." That's how big this mystery is; it's *mega*.

Yet while our culture has put sex in a "mega" place, it has stripped it of its mystery. As my friend Elijah and I grew older, we entered a pornified culture where everything was sexualized. Today we see this everywhere: from steamy scenes on Netflix to music videos on YouTube; from sidebar ads on Facebook to children's toys at Target; from profile pics on Tinder to racy selfies on Instagram. As everyone knows, skin sells.

We're more exposed to images of sex than ever, yet ironically—perhaps because of this—more out of touch with its deeper meaning. We've been trained by our culture to look at sex but not to look through it.

For many, sex has been reduced to nothing more than the raw, physical act. In a *Rolling Stone* interview, one kid eloquently observed how sex has simply become "a piece of body touching another piece of body—just as existentially meaningless as kissing."[3] Two bodies bouncing up against each other—meat on meat, desire on desire—nothing more. We're in danger of becoming pornified carnivores simply seeking to devour one another.

This is a smaller vision of sex, not a bigger one.

The mystery has been lost because sex no longer speaks to a greater reality in which we're found. Yet sex is a mega mystery, Paul reminds us, because it points to greater things.

Our goal is to restore the icon. We're out to wipe the dust off and let the vibrant colors beneath shine brilliantly once more.

Restoration can take some work, as any art enthusiast will tell you, but it's worth it when you uncover the treasure and see the craft of the Artist clearly again.

As we undertake this restoration project, I want to invite you to reclaim your childhood curiosity again. To become like Elijah and me all those years ago, out to search the nooks and crannies of our heavenly Father's earthly home, curious about the transcendent mysteries above that shape our terrestrial life below. For now as then, the secret of the universe is hidden just above the trampoline in your parents' bedroom.

So let's open our imaginations again to knowing what we don't know and to the possibility that God's vision just might be bigger and more beautiful than we ever dared dream.

The Game Plan

Here's the game plan. We'll start by looking at "The Beauty of Sex" (chapters 1–5), exploring not only what God has to say about sex but what sex is designed to say about God. I hope to convince you that God's vision is *way* more beautiful and compelling than anything else our culture has on offer. All would-be contenders are left in the dust.

Next, we'll move to "When God Says No" (chapters 6–10), seeing how the beauty of God's vision helps explain why some things are off-limits. We won't shy away from the tough topics in this book. We'll talk directly about divorce, premarital sex, adultery, gay sex, pornography, abortion, and more. If these are part of your story, however, take comfort: Jesus came not to beat you up over your past but to fight for your future. He's not out to imprison you in guilt or shame but to liberate you for his kingdom. Jesus came not to condemn the world but to save it, and to draw you—wherever you may be coming from—into union with him forever.

Sex can be an icon or an idol, either a window we look through to get a glimpse of the glory and goodness of God, or a mirror that reflects our selfishness, brokenness, and destruction. The point of exposing the idols is to restore us as icons.

Finally, in "A Greater Vision" (chapters 11–15), we'll expand the theological foundations that support the beautiful vision of the earlier chapters.

And what, at the end of our exploring, shall we discover? That God is love. The love of God is the endgame of this book, for it is what the icon points to. God designed sex to reveal his love for us in technicolor.

So, let's pull back the veil on the icon. Like gazing through *Christ Pantocrator,* our ultimate goal is a fresh vision of Jesus. For in the radiant light of Christ, sex becomes a window into something greater, a catalyst that can lift our gaze to the heart of the gospel and the hope of the world, like a springboard we can launch from to take flight into the heavens and ascend into the mysteries of God . . .

Like a trampoline.

PART I
THE BEAUTY OF SEX

Rediscovering the Goodness of
Embodied Life and Love

1

SEX AS SALVATION

I used to look to sex for salvation. I wanted it to liberate me from loneliness, to find freedom in the arms of another. But the search failed. My college sweetheart dumped me. I found a rebound to feel better about myself—and hurt her in the process. I then fell head over heels for the "girl of my dreams" (at the time) and spent the next five years pining after this friend who didn't feel the same.

I wanted to feel wanted, yet wound up alone.

Our culture looks to sex for salvation too. We want romance to free us from solitary confinement, to deliver us into a welcome embrace. "A nobody can become a somebody," the myth goes, "if you just find the right person." Yet the search often leads to sadness. The lover lets you down. The rapturous embrace starts to suffocate. The emotional high crashes and burns.

Idolizing sex results in slavery. You can chart up your long list of ex-lovers and join Taylor Swift in telling the newest applicant, "I've got a blank space, baby, and I'll write your name." You can find yourself in the Egypt of a new romantic wasteland, more cynical and isolated than when you first began. Yet I've discovered a crucial corrective in the gospel that can lead us out into true freedom . . .

Sex wasn't designed to *be* your salvation but to point you to the One who is.

Union with Christ

Sex is an icon of Christ and the church. In Ephesians 5, a "hall of fame" marriage passage, the apostle Paul proclaims:

> "For this reason a man will leave his father and mother and cleave to his wife, and the two will become one flesh." This is a profound mystery—but I am talking about Christ and the church.[1]

Now, the context here is marriage. "Leave and cleave" is marriage language (we'll look at this in a future chapter), and the surrounding verses are all about husbands and wives, not hookup culture. Yet that second part, about *the two becoming one flesh*, is consummation language that refers to the union of husband and wife.[2]

Paul says *both* are about Christ and the church.

This should be shocking! It's not only the giving of your vows at the altar but what happens in the honeymoon suite after that speaks to the life you were made for with God. A husband and wife's life of faithful love is designed to point to greater things, but *so is their sexual union!* We'll get to marriage soon enough in this book, but let's start with this gospel bombshell: Sex is an icon of salvation.

How? I'd suggest the language of generosity and hospitality can help us out.

Generosity and Hospitality

Generosity and hospitality are both embodied in the sexual act. Think about it. Generosity involves giving extravagantly to someone. You give the best you've got to give, lavishly pouring out your time, energy, or money. At a deeper level, generosity is a giving of not just your resources but your very *self*. And what deeper form of self-giving is there than sexual union where, particularly for the husband, he pours out his very presence not only *upon* but *within* his wife?

Hospitality, on the other hand, involves receiving the life of the other. You prepare a space for the guest to enter your home, welcoming them warmly into your circle of intimacy, to share your dwelling place with you. Here again, what deeper form of hospitality is there than sexual union where, particularly for the wife, she welcomes her husband into the sanctuary of her very self?

Giving and receiving are at the heart of sex.

Now, obviously, a man and woman both give to each other and receive from each other in the sexual act. Sex is mutual self-giving. Yet, on closer inspection, there is a distinction between the male and female sides of the equation.

The Bible makes this distinction explicit. The most frequent Hebrew phrase for sex is, literally, "he went into her" (*wayyabo eleha*). Translations often soften this for modern ears, saying he "made love to her," or they "slept together." But the Bible is less prudish than we are, using more graphic language to describe what happens in the honeymoon tent.

One Sunday morning, I learned how graphic this language can be. My friend Karen was publicly reading Scripture for our church service, and we'd recently switched to a more literal Bible translation. We were in Genesis 29, where Jacob marries Leah and Rachel, and the phrase *wayyabo eleha* shows up (we discovered) a lot! Karen has, you might say, a "Rated G" personality: very prim, proper, and polite. We all saw her cheeks turn bright red, with a lot of awkward pauses, as she had to continually read the phrase "and Jacob *went into her*" over and over again. After that Sunday, we went back to a less wooden translation, and laughed a lot with poor Karen.

The Hebrew language is onto something, however: there's a distinction between the male and female roles in sexual union.

Each brings something unique to the fusing of two bodies as one, and this distinction is iconic. On that honeymoon in Cabo, the groom goes into his bride. He is not only *with* his beloved but *within* his beloved. He enters the sanctuary of his spouse, where he pours out his deepest presence and bestows an offering, a gift, a sign of his pilgrimage, that has potential to grow within her into new life.

This is a picture of the gospel. Christ arrives in salvation to be not only *with* his church but *within* his church. Christ gives himself to his beloved with extravagant generosity, showering his love upon us and imparting his very presence within us. Christ penetrates his church with the generative seed of his Word and the life-giving presence of his Spirit, which takes root within her and grows to bring new life into the world.

Inversely, back in the wedding suite, the bride embraces her most intimate guest on the threshold of her dwelling place and welcomes him into the sanctuary of her very self. She gladly receives the warmth of his presence and accepts the sacrificial offering he bestows upon the altar within her Most Holy Place.[3]

Similarly, the church embraces Christ in salvation, celebrating his arrival with joy and delight. She has prepared and made herself ready, anticipating his advent in eager expectation. She welcomes him into the most vulnerable place of her being, lavishing herself upon him with extravagant hospitality. She receives his generous gift within her—the seed of his Word and presence of his Spirit—partnering with him to bring children of God into the world.

Their union brings forth new creation.

Body Image

We have a lot of euphemisms for sex in our culture. *Swiping right. Netflix and chill. Between the sheets.* The Bible has one too: *one flesh.* This is the most significant shorthand for sex in Scripture. Jesus uses it. Paul does too. And when they do, they're alluding to Genesis 2, the creation story of Adam and Eve (we'll look at this later). Ephesians 5 says this euphemism is ultimately about Christ and the church.

One flesh is a body image. It's unabashedly physical. Our cultural euphemisms, in contrast, speak *around* sex. *Swiping right* refers to how you meet. *Netflix and chill* to setting the ambience. *Between the sheets* to where the action takes place. Yet *one flesh* zeroes in much more directly on the center of sex itself: bodily union. Unlike that blushing sex talk your parents gave you in junior high, mumbling something about "birds and bees," there's nothing sheepish here. *One flesh* is about the merging of two separate bodies into one.[4]

This body image is a sign of salvation. God has invested it with sacred meaning. This contravenes the chorus of a recent pop song, which describes sex as forming "a monster with two heads."[5] That depicts sex as a monstrosity, where conjugal union forms a strange aberration of a creature, with parts not meant to fit together but somehow making it work.

God's vision, however, is much more like that classic song by the Postal Service, "Such Great Heights," where Ben Gibbard croons that God made us "into corresponding shapes like puzzle pieces from the clay." Our Creator has designed us, majestically and intentionally, with the ability to come together as one.

When we do, it points to something greater. The union of Christ and the church loads sexual union with meaning and power, as something beautiful and holy. Do we treat it with that reverence and awe? Or cavalierly as a personal plaything?

Whether or not you ever have sex (we'll talk about singleness in a moment, which is highly revered in the Bible), the one-flesh nature of our species' design is a sign of something much more majestic: You were made to be united with God.

Even our sexual desire can point to the gospel. As Preston and Jackie Hill-Perry observe, husbands are to love their wives "as Christ loved the church" (Ephesians 5:25):

[Christ] had to do something in order for the church to respond. I think, in the same way, the men have to show this

love and this affection for the woman to respond. . . . Christ
didn't need anything to love, to feel love, to feel emotional
for his bride. . . . Husbands are wired like that; we don't need
you to do anything. I come in the room, I come in the house,
and I see you and I want you.[6]

A husband's unprovoked desire is a sign of Christ's pre-existing
affection for his bride. Christ wanted to be with us—before we
wanted to be with him—and took the first step in movement toward
union.

This doesn't mean women are *less* sexual than men, but rather
that their sexual desire tends to work *differently* than men. To
borrow language from Dr. Emily Nagoski, men's sexual desire
tends to be more *spontaneous*, while women's tends to be more
responsive.[7] Meaning, husbands generally don't need much prod-
ding to be in the mood. (While individual experiences vary, on
average men initiate sex more often than women.)[8] Wives, on the
other hand, usually prefer to be romanced toward the bedroom.

Why did God make it this way? Christian sex blogger Sheila
Gregoire has a theory, observing how men can often climax
quickly through intercourse alone, while women generally require foreplay and external stimulation:

That means for women to feel pleasure, men have to slow
down and think about their wives. Sex is best when it isn't
just "animal" style, where you simply have intercourse with
no foreplay, because that won't feel good for her. Men have
to learn to be unselfish if sex is going to work well for both
partners. . . . God deliberately made our [female] bodies so
that if we're going to feel good during sex, men have to take
time to serve women.[9]

A wife's desire points to the gospel as well, in other words. Her
desire to be romanced is iconic of the church, which has had the
flames of our desire stoked by the passion of Christ's sacrificial
devotion toward us.

This means a husband who just wants to use his wife for selfish pleasure or his own personal release is not only bad at sex; he's failing to image Christ well. A woman's need for foreplay to enjoy full sexual satisfaction is a sign of our affections being warmed as the bride of Christ by his amorous advances and pursuit. Similarly, a husband serving his wife in the bedroom can be a sign of Christ's initiation with his church in salvation, cultivating our responsive affection toward him.

The one-flesh union of bodies is iconic of the giving and receiving at the heart of salvation. Sex is a sign of the life you were made for with God. You were made to receive his generous selfgiving, to experience his extravagant pursuit of you in this divine romance. You were made for an extravagant response of worship, giving yourself back to him in affection and praise. You were made to encounter the divine embrace in this beautiful union.

Tragic Inversions

This architecture of sex helps explain some tragic inversions. Take rape, for example, the most extreme inversion of generosity. Rape (and all forms of sexual violence, abuse, or exploitation) turns *giving of* the self into *taking for* the self. It converts generosity into a form of theft, breaking down the door uninvited, and barging into the home to ransack whatever it wants. The intruder leaves the object of their lust ravaged in their wake.

Sexual violence and abuse shatter the icon of sex in the most despicable way, replacing an image of Christ with the idol of self in its place. It is violent burglary of the highest order, a horror that rightly stands under the judgment of God.

Such acts assault the image of God in the person violated, impacting their dignity in a traumatic way that can scar them for years to come. Sexual assault violates the safety, beauty, and faithfulness sex is designed for in marriage, turning the beautiful into something brutal, intimacy into invasion. Because sex is designed for something so powerful, its abuse can wield that much more damage. As C. S. Lewis remarked, love "is a stronger angel, and therefore, when it falls, a fiercer devil."[10]

Christ confronts rape. At the cross, he stands in solidarity with the survivor through his suffering. As his own body is ravaged and the spear pierces his side, he identifies with the sexually assaulted in the brutality inflicted upon them. Through the power of his resurrection, Christ offers his hand to lift up the abused from the trenches, raising them with him from the depths they were submerged beneath, in the power of his grace.

Exalted in blazing glory, Christ confronts the abuser with his victory over their villainy, holding power to judge them unless they are willing to confess their wickedness and fall upon his forgiveness, to be run through by the sword of his mercy that has power to transform and make new.

Rape corrupts the character of the icon.

Prostitution, meanwhile, is the most symbolic inversion of hospitality. It's worth recognizing that those involved in prostitution are often pressured to do so by circumstances beyond their control, and this is not strictly comparable to the sins of rape and other sexual violence that I just described. While still a violation of the icon of sex, we'd do well to remember the warmth and compassion with which Jesus related to and ate with women who today would be described as "sex workers."

Yet prostitution welcomes a "guest" while charging admission. It turns what ought to be an exchange of pure gift into a transaction. It makes a person a product. Selling sex rents out a holy place, converting the sanctuary into a transit station, a bus depot for the traveling stranger on their way to the next stop. It forgoes covenant for compensation, turning the communion of persons into a commodity for profit. Hustling accommodates users who only want an individual for what they can get from him or her, before moving on.

Today, many call it sex work rather than prostitution, with the goal of dignifying it as a legitimate means of employment. The term *sex work*, however, itself reveals the nature of the problem:

Grace has become a work. The sacred gift of mutual self-giving has shifted to a profession undertaken for a paycheck. While sex has always involved an exertion of energy, you now sweat for a salary.

This is why, in biblical imagery, the prostitute is a prophetic parody of the people of God, why the whore of Babylon is the corrupt counterpoint to the bride of Christ.[11] When we forsake our first love and wander from the One we were made for, it's as if we're selling ourselves out to the highest bidder.

We grieve the tough circumstances that pressure many into the sex industry. We empathize with, care for, and stand alongside those who are victims. We should confront pimps and johns when they manipulate, exploit, and prey upon people in desperate straits. But we are right to feel that something deep is violated in the act of prostitution itself, for it disfigures the hospitality that is iconic of the gospel, within the secure communion of God's faithful love.

Gender Dynamics

It's worth noting the gender dynamics of rape and prostitution. Rapists are nearly universally men, while prostitutes are predominantly women. This is to be expected, if rape is an inversion more particular to the male side of the equation and prostitution to the female side. Rapists use violence to "give"; prostitutes take money to "receive." (Of course there are exceptions to this rule, but in general the principle holds true.)[12]

It's also worth observing that less extreme inversions exist too, more subtle distortions that may not land you in jail but can wreak havoc on a marriage. The *self-giving* of generosity can turn inward to *self-gratification:* using your partner as a means to an end, objectifying them to fulfill your own wishes and desires. Men have an infamously stronger tendency to struggle with this one: focusing more on pleasing themselves in the bedroom, leaving women feeling used in the process. (Pro-tip for the husbands:

Slow down! It's not a race. The goal is not to go from 0-to-60 in 4.2 seconds; you're not a Maserati.)

When Jesus says to be a servant, and that it's better to give than receive, this applies in the bedroom as much as anywhere.[13]

Hospitality, on the other hand, can turn inward to an *unwelcoming* posture: refusing to receive the other's presence, declining to prepare a space for them, shutting the door on intimacy and locking the bolt behind you. Over time, the warmth from the honeymoon can become a churlish cold shoulder. Women are known for having a stronger tendency to struggle with this one. (It's usually not the guy going, "I have a headache"!)[14]

Obviously, guys can be inhospitable too, and gals can be self-gratifying. These are averages, not universals. It's worth observing, however, that these famous dynamics between men and women relate to the icon.

Christ and the church are the model. Not only for marriage but even for sex. They reveal that sex is designed for mutual self-giving, characterized by generosity and hospitality. Inversely, sex sheds light on the nature of the gospel: the giving and receiving, intimacy and warmth, joy and delight we were made for with God.

The Nature of Grace

Sex helps explain the nature of grace. Some people struggle with the concept of grace: Did God choose me, or did I choose God? Am I an active agent in my salvation, or simply a passive bystander? The problem, I'd suggest, is we often have a *mechanical* vision of how grace works, rather than an *organic* vision.

Take driving a car as an example of a mechanical vision: Only one person can sit behind the steering wheel, accelerate the gas, hit the brakes—operate the machine. Meanwhile, the passenger is a sedentary tourist, watching the scenery pass by out the window.

Watch what happens, however, when we shift to an *organic* vision, like sex: "Did he sleep with her, or she sleep with him?" *Yes!* The answer, of course, is yes. Both statements are true; both people are involved. The physical union happens *through* the will of both parties, not *against* the will of one (assuming the act is consensual).

Yet while each party participates, they are each involved in a different way. This difference is significant and beautiful. The groom *enters into* the bride with his presence, while the bride *receives* the presence of the groom within herself. Classically, these were referred to as the *active* and *passive* roles in conjugal union. Don't read too much into this language—women are obviously *active*, and men *receive*, in sex—yet it gets at something real that's present in the physiology of our "one-fleshness."

The distinction is iconic. It is not accidental that Christ is described as Bridegroom, rather than simply Spouse. Christ has the active role in his union with and salvation of his beloved, giving himself generously to the church. This is not to communicate more value to the role of husband but to highlight an iconographic reality. We have the passive role in salvation, receiving him with hospitality as his bride. While our role may be *passive*, however, it is also *participatory*. Similar to how the bridal role in bodily union is passive (at a deep conjugal level) while also actively participatory (at a broader surrounding level), so also our relation to Christ is receptive but not idle.

We work with Christ, as he works in us.

Two Dangers

This confronts two historic dangers in the grace conversation. On one side, there's what we might call the "Just lie there and take it" heresy: where we're just lethargic observers, watching from the outside-in, entirely uninvolved in this thing that is happening to us. This false view of grace squashes human agency, making it hard to understand biblical injunctions to run the race well, and to work out our salvation with fear and trembling.

This call to salvation becomes like the advice British mothers reportedly once told young women on their wedding nights: "Lie still and think of England." Duty without delight.

Grace doesn't *annihilate* agency, however. It *activates* agency. Properly understood, God's indwelling presence *liberates* our affections and desires from the destructive power of sin, *freeing* our personhood to now live for God. The grace God gives is not some *stuff,* like motor oil to help your car run more smoothly on its own. No, the grace God gives is his very *self,* his Spirit, the presence of his love poured into your heart, that warms your affections and re-animates your life through giving and receiving, through reciprocal, welcome, and loving union with him.

God's grace *within* us frees us to give ourselves fully to the God who is *for* us.

On the other side, with grace, there's what we might call the "Go become the groom" danger: God is out there waiting for you to rise up, get your act together, and impress him. You gotta get Jesus's attention, so put on the makeup and high heels and go out to win his affection.

This is upside down. It valorizes human agency, letting it stand prior to and autonomous from God's gracious presence and affectionate pursuit. It's not on you to initiate and penetrate the divine life with your own active effort, in hopes that maybe he'll receive you. The gospel says: *No!* Christ has the active role in salvation. God has come for us in Christ, has initiated with us to make us his own, not when we are at our best but when we are at our worst.

I'd suggest this illuminates why, in cultures around the world, it is generally considered the groom's role to pursue, court, and woo the bride. The groom's pursuit is iconic of the gospel, a picture of Jesus coming after us. Now in practical terms, of course, this isn't a hard and fast rule; it's more than okay for a girl to ask a guy out and "initiate" in a relationship. (Ruth pops the question with Boaz and is a hero for it.)[15] But generally speaking, we're drawn to the guy laying it all on the line to go after his girl. This archetypal pursuit echoes the cosmic story of the world, of the Christ who's come to lay down his life for us and win our affection as his bride.

Jesus is the Pursuing God (hey, I know a guy who wrote a book on that, wink wink).[16] The gospel is not about you going out to find God; it's about God who's come to find you—and be with you forever. It's not about you trying hard enough, working long enough, or jumping high enough to get his attention. It's saying yes to the One who's gone all the way to hell and back to win *your* affection.

That's the nature of grace.

Single Like Jesus

At this point, O thoughtful reader, you're likely asking, *Wait a sec. What about singleness?* This is such an important point, I want to pause and address it directly. Does all this emphasis on sex and marriage throw shade on singles as living a "less than" life? *By no means!* In fact, quite the opposite.

Jesus was single; Paul was single. So if you're single, you're in good company. Jesus lived the most fully human life ever, and he never had sex.[17] This means you don't need sex, romance, or marriage to have all the meaning and fulfillment in the world.

The New Testament elevates singleness as a vocation equal (if not preferable) to marriage. You can experience life in God's kingdom, Paul suggests, with even fewer distractions than married life can bring.[18] When the church is functioning as it ought, Jesus says, you can experience rich relationships that go deeper even than biological family.[19] Celibacy has a deep and respected status in church history, for both men and women.

On a practical level, this means singleness and marriage are not better or worse. They are merely different. Navigating them demands a willingness to surrender in various ways throughout our lives, and this is deeply personal and individual, lived out in the context of our community and our unique journey with Christ.

But here's the point, particularly if you are single: You can have the reality without the sign. You get the movie (God's way of life and love) without having to sit through the sneak preview (sex in covenantal relationship). You can experience union with Christ—the very thing marriage was designed to point to all along—in intimacy and power. I like the way celibate pastor and author Sam Allberry puts it:

If marriage shows us the shape of the gospel, singleness shows us its sufficiency.[20]

In other words, marriage provides a picture of our union with Christ, giving us categories for its sacred nature, intimate depth, and all-of-life scope. Singleness, meanwhile, unveils how this union with Christ is enough to meet our deepest longings and fulfill our heart's greatest desire. You don't need human romance to experience the more transcendent and beautiful union you were made for with God.

Maybe you did not choose singleness. Maybe your journey has felt lonely, even painfully lonely. If so, I'm sorry—God sees the difficult road you've been on and is there to walk with you. My hope is this encourages you with the deeper beautiful union you were made for that is there for you in Christ.

Here's the point: Marriage and singleness can both be *good*. Which one is good for each of us is part of our individual story and discernment process. Marriage pictures Christ *and* the church; singleness relies on Christ *as* the church. What does this imply? That the greatest resource for a more exalted vision of Christian singleness is—ironically—a *higher* view of marriage, not a *lesser* one. They rise or fall together.

Some Christians want to take marriage down a notch to bolster singleness, but this is misguided. You don't need to *reduce* marriage to *elevate* singleness. It's not a zero-sum game. Properly understood, they mutually benefit one another. An iconic vision bolsters singleness by exalting union with Christ, the reality which fulfills both vocations together.

Jesus is both the Great Bachelor and the Glorious Groom. Jesus *gave up* sex and marriage (on a horizontal level), in order to *give his life for* his bride (on a vertical level). Jesus bypassed the sign in order to obtain the reality it pointed to. Singles can follow in Jesus's footsteps.

Singleness can be prophetic. Our culture wrongly sees sex as necessary for human fulfillment, a means of a sort of personal salvation. As historian Carl Trueman observes, nobody needs to be told the movie *The 40-Year-Old Virgin* is a comedy:

> The very idea of someone reaching the age of forty with no experience of sexual intercourse is inherently comic because of the value society now places on sex. To be sexually inactive is [in the eyes of our culture] to be a less-than-whole person, to be obviously unfulfilled or weird.[21]

The problem is this: Jesus is a forty-year-old virgin! Or, at least, he was a thirty-three-year-old one. This may sound like heresy in our culture today, but the King of the universe didn't need sex to have a meaningful life . . . and neither do you. You don't need romance to fill that hole inside your heart. You don't need that other person to complete you. You can live the fullest of lives in the kingdom of God.

You can be single. Like Jesus.

The Heart of Salvation

Union with Christ is the heart of salvation. This is the greater reality sex symbolizes. Sometimes we've made salvation more about other things, like going to heaven when you die. But we don't use Jesus to get to heaven; Jesus is how heaven has come to us! Others make salvation more about fixing things on earth. But the deepest fracture to be fixed is our distance from God's life-giving presence.

Jesus is the center. He is where the heavens have opened, blowing wide the dam to bring the floodwaters of God's presence rush-

ing back into earth. Receiving him is how you have access to the
life of God, here and now. Union with Christ can turn your mourning into dancing and deserts into gardens.

This is the New Testament's dominant language for salvation:
union with Christ. The phrase Christ "in you" shows up all over,
in places like these:

> Do you not realize . . . that Jesus Christ is *in you?*
> (2 Corinthians 13:5)

> If Christ is *in you*, although the body is dead because of sin,
> the Spirit is life because of righteousness.
> (Romans 8:10)

> Christ *in you*, the hope of glory. (Colossians 1:27)

Similarly, our being "in Christ" shows up 242 times.[22] At first
glance, that may sound like it contradicts the one-flesh image
(isn't the picture of Christ *in us*, not the other way around?). But
the phrase speaks to our corporate identification with Jesus.
Think of it like marriage, where a wife traditionally took on the
last name of her husband and entered into his family.[23] If the uniting of bodies in conjugal union speaks to Christ "in us," then the
broader uniting of lives together in marriage speaks to us "in
Christ."

With that in mind, consider victorious proclamations like these:

> *In Christ Jesus* you who once were far away have been
> brought near. (Ephesians 2:13, NIV)

> There is therefore now no condemnation for those who are
> *in Christ Jesus.* (Romans 8:1)

> If anyone is *in Christ*, the new creation has come: The old
> has gone, the new is here! (2 Corinthians 5:17, NIV)

Christ is *in us*, and we are *in Christ*. Christ *in us* speaks to his
indwelling presence that unites us to him, while us *in Christ* speaks

to our corporate identification with him. This is what it means to be a Christian—Christ in you; you in Christ—the language of a surprising, beautiful union!

It might surprise you to know the word *Christian* appears only three times in the New Testament—usually on the lips of outsiders.[24] That's because when it comes to insiders, the New Testament simply talks about being united to Jesus. When you drill down to the deepest core of what it *means* to be a Christian, it's union with Christ.

The heart of salvation is in the body of Jesus.

In Defense of Romantic Worship Music

Now, the church as bride is a *corporate* picture. Jesus is not a polygamist, with billions of brides around the world. Paul doesn't say the one-flesh mystery refers to Christ and his *churches* but rather to Christ and the church. I am not the bride; you are not the bride. *We* are the bride. The exalted King doesn't have a harem, each competing to get some time on his calendar. The church has a collective identity, united in the power of his Spirit, with a cosmic unity as the people of God.

Yet Jesus does come to make his home in each of us personally, to indwell us with his presence. This means there's a proper place for intimacy, affection, and devotion in our life with God.

Some critique worship songs that sound too intimate. My friend Sarah became a believer and called this "Jesus is my boyfriend" music. "It sounds like someone took a Katy Perry pop ballad," she said, "and simply replaced all references to the guy she liked with the word *Jesus*." I laughed. And asked why this was disconcerting. "It just sounds disrespectful," she explained, "to the greatness, transcendence, and *bigness* of God!"

"I get the critique," I told her. It's true, some lyrics can be overdone or cheesy. My pushback, however, was this: Jesus isn't our boyfriend; *he's our husband!*

There is a scandal of intimacy to the gospel. It's scandalous that the almighty, transcendent Creator has drawn so close: taking on skin and soul for our salvation, bearing our sin, and rising whole to dwell with us forever. God's goal is not just to hang out *with* us but to dwell *within* us. Not just to make us his buddies but his *bride*. This should liberate our hearts with adoration, affection, and praise.

Sex as icon puts a fresh spin on what it means to "receive Jesus." In some circles, the phrase has become so ubiquitous as to become a cliché: *Have you received Jesus into your heart?* But it is a powerful phrase worth retaining—for it speaks to the heart of the gospel.

Christ *has* come to dwell within our hearts as his people, renewing our greatest affections and desires from the inside out with his love.[25] Sex as icon adds another layer of symbolism: corporately, the church receives Christ into her *gut*, or loins, a biblical image for a place both intimate and vulnerable, the seat of strength and vigor, and the center of procreative power.[26] Christ's indwelling presence reaches within even these foundational depths for us as his people, and he makes us fruitful.

The church is the bride of Christ. There is a proper place for devotion, desire, and yes, romance, in our worship of Christ as his church. Whether you're a man or woman, single or married, this image communicates the closeness God has designed us for with him. Our union should move us to shout together the grace of the God who has taken up residence within our lives as his people, who has shaken us from the inside out, and who is revolutionizing our lives in intimacy and power. The one-flesh icon reveals a truth much greater.

We were made for union with God.

2

WHY SUNSETS ARE BEAUTIFUL

Our neighborhood comes out at sunset. We live near Hole-in-the-Rock, a beautiful red rock formation in Phoenix. Sometimes I hike there during the day, and the scenic vista is virtually always empty. But come back as the sun is going down, and the site vacant of visitors just a few hours earlier is now flooded with friends walking and laughing, lovers holding hands, families enjoying a picnic, and the drifting, distinctive smell of a certain herbal substance now legal in Arizona.

Our family has taken to these regular evening hikes. We've found the whole town emerges to bask in the glory, when day and night merge in their regular rendezvous as one.

Why are sunsets beautiful? What is it about that moment when day and night collide that draws lovers out to walk in the splendor? Sure, we can scientifically dissect it: Light rays from the sun scatter, enter our atmosphere, and ricochet from airborne molecules until reaching our retinas. But to reduce it that way is to ravage the beauty. To grind it down to its components is to obscure the drama it bears witness to. Under a microscope, you can miss the forest for the trees.

Zooming out, however, a wider view can help us reclaim the mystery we need to wander in wonder again. To see how it all fits, to recapture the beauty.

I want to introduce you to an ancient vision, more poetic in nature. A romantic perspective of nature. It lets us in on a secret: The reason the collision of day and night is so beautiful is the same reason sex is so powerful.

It's when two become one.

Made for One Another

Man and woman are introduced on the opening page of the Bible. "Male and female he created them."[1] What's often missed, however, is that they are not the only such pair. They are introduced within a constellation of patterns, a structure of creation, ever present around us.

Genesis 1 introduces us to three other major mated pairs: heaven and earth, land and sea, night and day. Together, these pairs structure creation. Heaven and earth provide the vertical dimension (*up and down*). Land and sea frame the horizontal dimension (*side to side*). Night and day establish the temporal dimension (*time*).[2]

While each component is majestic on its own, guess where the most beautiful places in creation happen? *Where the two become one.*

Where the Action Is

Let's start with *land and sea*. Rugged terrain and billowing waves are impressive all by themselves, but something magical happens when these two forces collide. As philosopher Peter Kreeft observes:

The shore is the most popular place on earth. Waterfront property is the most expensive property anywhere in the world. Because that's where the sea and the land meet. That's where man and woman meet. The land without the sea is kind of boring; desert. The sea without the land is kind of boring. "When are we going to land the ship?" But the place where they meet? That's where all the action is. And that's where we want to be.[3]

Now, I'd push back on Kreeft's claim that each is boring on its own. There's a romantic beauty to the desert, and sailors write sonnets about the wonder of the open sea. But still, he's onto something.

There's just *something* about the beach. We're drawn to this place where land and sea merge. Its aesthetic is magnetic. Tourists shell out top dollar for the hotel room with an oceanfront view, whether on the sun-kissed beaches of California, the stormy coasts of Ireland, or the international resorts of Thailand. The coast is a star witness to the marvelous power of diversity-in-union.

We're drawn to this merger like a magnet. Coastlines are the largest example, where colossal continents tangle with their tectonic match in oceanic bodies of water. Yet this magic also works on smaller scales: cabins built on lakes, oases in the desert, and cities that sprout along rivers. Indeed, the first civilizations of humanity all began along the water!

Life emerges where stream and soil collide.

Beauty does too. As author Brett McCracken observes, when river and rock caress, something majestic happens. What are canyons but rock carved out by water? What are waterfalls but water traversing rock?

Water and rock together are nature's most beautiful artistic pairing. Water can erode and mold and smooth rock. Rock can guide and contain and filter water. Their wrestling is necessary and good, and it creates beauty. . . . Whether glaciers or cascades, snow-capped mountains or geysers, the

places where water and rock meet are where painters, pho-
tographers, tourists, and lovers flock.[4]

We're *drawn* to these intersections. The mingling of their material elements is a mutually formative marriage: They shape one
another and evoke wonder. The convergence of land and sea, like
the union of man and woman, has the power to both form *beauty*
and generate *life*. It is at these "edges" where two different sys-
tems touch that the productivity and diversity of life are mas-
sively higher.[5] We are right to congregate around the cathedral
of their splendor, for they are holy spaces with a powerful allure.
They are, as Kreeft puts it, where the action is.

The Most Popular Moment

Now let's move to *day and night*. Sunset and sunrise are spellbind-
ing. Something mesmerizing happens in that magical moment
when day and night meet up for their twice-daily tryst.

The colors of their union explode through the atmosphere.
I've come to think of this radiant explosion as something like an
orgasm across the sky, an expression of holy delight emerging
from diversity-in-union. You might initially flinch at such a description as crude, but I'd suggest that's because our culture has
come to have a "crude-ified" understanding of sex, shaped more
by the pornified pursuit of self-interested pleasure, rather than
the mutual delight of a covenant pair bound with and for one
another. We might think of sexual union as vulgar or crass—but
that says more about *us* than about sex.

If sex is given by God, as a sacred window into the structure
of creation, then the point is not to sexualize creation so much as
to "creationize" sex, to frame it within God's holy design for the
structure of our world. Sunset is that moment, then, when the
sphere of energizing light penetrates the border of the horizon
and sinks into the womb of darkness, erupting forth in a volcanic
explosion of glorious colors streaming across the sky, like sparks
of euphoria flying from lovers in ecstatic embrace.

Shakespeare saw the romance in sunrise. "What light through yonder window breaks?" Romeo declares. "It is the east, and Juliet is the sun!"[6] This is perhaps the most classic love scene in all of literature. The master playwright identifies Romeo with the night, concealed in the shadows beneath Juliet's window, arriving in anonymity from his risky journey in the dark. Meanwhile, Juliet is an ambassador for the sun, whose splendor outshines the lunar Rosaline (a competitor Shakespeare identifies with the lesser light of the moon). When Juliet steps forth on the balcony, her daylight rising upon his darkness, the glory radiates like the presence of the sun at dawn.

Shakespeare sets this iconic coming together of the star-crossed lovers against the symbol of sunrise. In the splendor of the moment, they pledge their love, join hands, and hatch their plans to marry.

The Mountaintop Experience

Finally, we come to *heaven and earth*. Ancient peoples looked to mountain peaks as sacred space, where land and sky touched. In the Bible, some of the holiest encounters with divine glory occur on the heights. Jerusalem sits atop Mount Zion, Moses meets with God on Mount Sinai, Elijah's fire falls from heaven on Mount Carmel, Jesus glows radiantly on the Mount of Transfiguration, and the Garden of Eden rests atop "the holy mountain of God."[7]

Mountains kiss the sky.

We still love the mountaintop experience. Climbers hike the summit for a taste of transcendence. The weary and disillusioned look to the apex as a place to gain perspective, a site for spiritual retreat. Mountaintops are a metaphor for high points and moments of clarity in life, and for good reason: They're epic.

I grew up in the shadow of Mount Hood, and she's spectacular. Her heights are visible for hundreds of miles around, cascading upon the horizon in any direction you go. She's a favorite getaway for Oregonians all year long—whether skiing, hiking, or sharing a romantic dinner at Timberline Lodge. We're still drawn to these altitudes where alps and atmosphere collide.

Heaven and earth are about more, however, than just soil and ozone. In the Scriptures, they speak to God's space and ours. Just like you can't see air but need it to survive, so we can't see God but also can't live without him. His heavenly breath is threaded through our earthly cloth. "In him we live and move and have our being," the apostle Paul proclaimed.[8] The Author of Life underwrites our earthly stories on the foundational parchment of his heavenly presence.

The universe hangs on God.

More profound than the mountaintop, then, are the magical moments when—in *this* sense—heaven and earth collide. Jesus taught his followers to pray, "Your kingdom come, your will be done, on earth as it is in heaven."[9] When we join in this prayer, we are seeking the collision of heaven and earth, the merger of God's sphere with ours, the coming together of Creator and creation.

When heaven breaks into earth, the Divine Presence penetrates our physical existence with the power of his transcendence. This is holy space. Beauty erupts; new life emerges. The encounter is marked by joy. The wedding of heaven and earth is the kingdom of God, where the King and his bride shine far and wide. Their beautiful union gives rise to a glorious splendor, with a life-giving abundance that follows in their wake.

So what does this have to do with sex? Everything.

All Is Full of Love

Love is the meaning of the world. This is the secret sex reveals. Creation was made for diversity-in-union, and so were you. You were made by love, in love, and for love—the love of your Creator. The world around you bears witness. Do you believe that? How would it change your life if you really did trust this was true?

You don't need to have sex to experience this, but sex points toward this experience of being loved you were meant to have.

God brought you forth in all the diversity of your being, to be united with him in this affection that floods the world. Every sunset is a reminder.

Sex is sacred, because it is a sign that reveals this deep structure and purpose beneath the world. It's like a key that unlocks the truth of creation, opening us up to the mystery of the universe.

Do you treat sex as sacred, with the respect it deserves? Or are you using it selfishly—trading love for lust, virtue for vice? Defacing the icon is like taking a bulldozer to Michelangelo's *David*, the masterpiece of an artist. Don't dishonor something beautiful. It might feel like you're going against the tide of culture when you approach sex God's way.

But you're going with the grain of the universe.

Some say the world is meaningless. A random accident. That the sun will burn out one day as we descend into frozen darkness. Don't believe it! Nobody believes such things at sunset. We're too enchanted by the glow as day melds with night, in the afterlight of a universe filled with glory.

"All is full of love," in the immortal lyrics of Björk. You live in a world made by love and for love. God not only loves the world; God loves *you*. So much so, John 3:16 tells us, "that he gave his only Son" to rescue you from darkness and heal all creation.

This can be hard to remember when you turn on the news and see wars and rumors of wars. When your friend stabs you in the back and you're left betrayed, isolated, and alone. When the diagnosis comes back and your mortality crashes through the front door like a battering ram.

Do you know what I recommend doing in such times? Go outside. Look up to the mountains—or hike one, if you can. Walk by the water, soaking in signs of life. Stand and gaze like a child upon the sunset and let the rhythm of creation remind you in your bones that the sun shall rise again.

Creation has a structure and stability that speaks to God's great love for you. Even through the storm, you can be confident your Maker shall carry you through.

Best for Last

Back to Genesis now, where the Creator has saved the best for last. The theater of creation is now ready, the stage set for man and woman to step into the spotlight and begin their great drama. The Grand Artist has used broad brushstrokes thus far to cover his canvas of creation with mountains, rainforests, and oceans. But now, at the climax of Genesis 1, the switch is made to a fine detail brush as he moves in close for the apex of creation: *us*.

> So God created mankind in his own image,
>   in the image of God he created them;
>   male and female he created them.[10]

Man and woman join the complementary pairs of creation. Humanity, in the beautiful and perfectly balanced diversity of male and female, is placed like a crown on the pinnacle of creation, our size significantly outmatched by our importance. We alone are made in the image of our Creator, but we are also a microcosm of creation itself. We reflect in our very being the nature of the world God has made, as a fourth and final complementary pair. We are made with and for one another.

For the beauty and life of the world.

Together, male and female are a microcosm of the world that surrounds us, a world of diversity-in-union. Hand in hand, we jointly display the divine design of creation. As the renowned biblical scholar N. T. Wright puts it:

> The man and the woman together are a symbol of something which is profoundly true of creation as a whole. . . . The coming together of male and female is itself a signpost pointing to that great complementarity of God's whole creation, of heaven and earth belonging together.[11]

Together, man and woman are a tiny template for our terrestrial home, a window into the wonder of our enchanted world, a pint-size portrait of heaven and earth. Male and female are, together, an icon of creation.

What Is Sex?

In this way, sex becomes a window into the structure of creation. What do I mean here by *sex*? Two things. First, our sexed identity as male and female. Sex isn't just something we *do*, it's someone we *are*. Embedded in our body, threaded through our DNA, imprinted in the fabric of our being, is our identity as woman or man.

Now, I must be very clear here. You don't need to *have* sex in order to bear the image. You *are* sexed as an image bearer, whose diversity as male or female (or as one of the relatively few people with an intersex condition)[12] bears witness to the beauty of the whole. Just by *being*, you are an actor in this great, beautiful dance. Your very body tells a story larger than yourself, a story of love and belonging in the infinite presence of an eternal Creator.

Our bodies are sacred. God has designed them in his image, to preach something about our Maker and the world he's made. This means, if you want to get a robust reflection of the divine image, you need both women and men. A room of only men, or only women, will not give you the full display. What does this mean? That the foundational diversity of humanity, as male and female, is important.

We need each other.

The second thing meant by *sex* here is what most of us initially think of: afternoon delight. Sex is both a noun *and* a verb. When the two become one, their convergence is a holy place, with the powerful potential to bring forth both beauty and life. When a man and woman come together in this way, bringing their diversity into union, their interlocking bodies are embedded within an intertwined universe. Swirling around us are heaven and earth, land and sea, night and day.

Sex is, in both senses, an icon of creation.

A Global Chorus

Christianity is not alone—a chorus of global voices sings of sex as a window into creation. Take *yin and yang*, for example, China's symbol for diversity-in-union. This classic image represents the essential pairs of nature, like male and female. The white half is *yang* (associated with masculinity, heaven, and light), while the black half is *yin* (associated with femininity, earth, and night). Each side contains a dot from the other, to show their identities are intertwined.

"They embrace and contain each other," scholar Tsui-Ying Sheng explains.

> Though yin and yang look like opposites, they can't exist independently. . . . If there is no yin, yang can't appear alone. Likewise, if there is no yang, yin won't exist. That's the thought of coexistence, complementarity, and reciprocity. They form a perfect unity with two in one.[13]

The larger circle surrounding them represents how both are integral to the wholeness of society and nature. *Yin and yang* is not a Christian concept, and there are certainly places where the gospel confronts some of its undergirding philosophy.[14] Yet the point here is simply this: The foundational concept for one of the world's largest cultures also sees male and female as a window into the nature of our surrounding world.

Other global traditions speak of Mother Earth and Father Sky. In a Hindu marriage ceremony, the groom declares, "I am heaven, you are earth," while the bride responds, "I am earth, you are heaven."

While the Bible doesn't tie masculinity to sky and femininity to land in the same way, it's easy to see why an agricultural society would. The earth receives heaven's presence through rays of sun that warm her surface and nurturing rain that sinks within, as the seed penetrates the soil from above. Life is nurtured and grown within, hidden in the darkness of her womb below, until the crops are ready to emerge.

When the time has come, the harvest bursts up from the clay, into the open arms of the awaiting atmosphere. Heaven and earth share these "children"—with roots below and head above—that their mutual embrace has brought into existence.

Again, the point is not that these traditions are compatible with Christianity in every respect, but simply that male and female have been recognized for millennia, by societies around the world, within a broader pattern of nature that brings beauty and life.

It's striking how nearly universal this theme is. It's usually rare to find such common ground among radically diverse traditions. Yet this global chorus of witnesses backs up the symphony of Genesis 1. Their harmony sings of man and woman made with and for one another, within a complementary structure of creation.

Diversity-in-Union

Let's sum this all up. Sex is diversity-in-union, grounded in the structure of creation. In the chapters to come, we'll see how this sheds light on the problem with things like divorce, adultery, premarital sex, same-sex sexual activity, and pornography. For now, however, let's rest in the beauty of this design.

God loves taking the two and making them one. This is present in the very structure of our bodies and the world that surrounds us, pointing—so close to us that we can take it for granted—to a larger logic, a larger life given by God.

God loves doing this, I believe, because God *is* diversity-in-union. As we'll see in the next chapter, the Father, Son, and Spirit are an eternal communion of holy love. God is Trinity, existing from before the foundation of the world in the perfect harmony of glorious relationship. In God, distinct persons and perfect unity both flourish. The Trinity is not some weird math equation but a wondrous proclamation: We are created as relational beings made by a relational God![15]

Jesus is also diversity-in-union. The phrase describes the greatness of our Savior, who gathers the greatest of polarities— divinity and humanity—and binds them together in his very person. As we were falling into the cavernous chasm of sin, death, and the grave, the Son of God grabbed hold of our humanity and pulled it like Superman to his mighty chest, assuming the frailty of our life into the indestructibility of his. Our great mediator is *both* the flesh and bone of earth *and* the radiant fragrance of heaven. Both Creator and creation are joined together forever in Christ. The two become one in his flesh.

And we become one *through* his flesh. The church is diversity-in-union: We are one body with many parts; one kingdom comprised of every nation, tribe, and tongue; one Spirit orchestrating a variety of gifts. We are sinners and saints, the respected and rejected, peasants and presidents—and every manner of person in between—gathered through grace alone.

Add to that, sex looks not only back to creation but forward to the kingdom. The end of the world is a wedding in Revelation 21–22, when heaven and earth come together and Christ and his church are united forever. Their marriage will generate both beauty and life, as God brings their diversity into union.

So, you see, *diversity-in-union* is central to the heart of the gospel and the hope of the world. It speaks to creation, salvation, the Trinity, Jesus, and the church. It proclaims like a trumpet: The end is love, for God is love. Sex is a signpost of this story. It preaches that our destination is union with God.

A beautiful aspect of my hometown is how close the city is to nature. Mount Hood is one hour east; there you can ski, hike, and climb. Cannon Beach is one hour west, for surf, swim, and sand. On weekends, the freeways are jam-packed with people heading in both directions. And those who stay behind? You just might find them in Forest Park at the end of the day for a sunset picnic.

We're drawn to these places where two become one.

There's something majestic in the merger of these mutual spheres. Whether or not a person believes in God, when we see the beauty of nature, we feel the glory in our gut. Even atheists go for romantic sunset walks on the beach. Our jaw rightly drops in the presence of such grandeur, for our Creator has made these matches to be mesmerizing and has designed us in a way that reflects the radiance of his world that surrounds us.

Sex displays the Creator's heartbeat for creation. When the two become one, the heat they generate in the bedroom is lit like a spark from the divine flame that burns through the center of the universe. For those attuned to the gospel story, a couple's affection pulls back the curtain on the theater of history for a sneak preview, a prophetic foreshadowing, of the consummation of all things in the wedding at the end of the world.

So the next time someone asks why sunsets are so beautiful, you can tell them they are prophets proclaiming a greater reality.

We are made for diversity-in-union.

3

LOVER, BELOVED, LOVE

My wife, Holly, and I spent three months in Africa. We lived with a local family—in a house with twenty-one people—grandparents, aunts and uncles, relatives visiting from afar. We were unofficially adopted as daughter and son. Theirs was an expansive circle of love.

The hospitality was amazing! The food was simple but ever present. Children from the neighborhood came in and out, finding it a place of safety, refuge, and rest. Their home was a place where everyone had a spot at the table, where you knew you were loved.

While there, we often saw this African statue, from the Shona people of Zimbabwe.[1] It depicts the family as diversity-in-union. Father, mother, and child are three distinct persons, each with a unique identity of their own (the father is not the mother, the mother is not the child, and so on). Yet they share one substance of flesh and bone, their lives cut from the same cloth (or, better yet, carved from the same stone), united in the very nature of their being. This is a window into a powerful truth.

The family is an icon of the Trinity.

Can something so simple as the family, hidden right beneath our noses—like those statues in a crowded African marketplace—actually speak to this deepest mystery of the God at the center of the universe?

Karl Barth, the most influential Protestant theologian of the twentieth century, and Pope John Paul II, the most significant Catholic theologian on matters of the body and sexuality, both say, "Yes!" They saw the image of God as a communion-of-persons, reflected uniquely in the life of the family.

We've seen how sex is an icon of the nature of salvation (Christ and the church), and the structure of creation (heaven and earth). We now turn to the family—generated by sexual love—as an icon of an even greater reality: the identity of God.

Communion-of-Love

Lover, Beloved, and Love has been popular language for the Trinity throughout church history. The Father is the Lover, the Son the eternal Beloved, and the Spirit the unbreakable bond of Love between them.[2] The family is designed to reflect this love of the Trinity in a way unique from any other kind of love in all creation. The family is made to be an icon of the most powerful truth in the universe.

God is a communion-of-love.

Love Is Triune

Wherever love exists, Saint Augustine observed, three things are present: the lover, the beloved, and the love itself. The *lover* is the one who loves, the *beloved* is their object of affection, and the *love* is the bond that exists between them. If you love coffee, for example, then *you* are the lover, the *coffee* is your beloved target of morning devotion, and the *love* is the magnetic bond that draws its warm, savory goodness like a tractor beam toward your lips. With ristretto as with romance . . .

There's a triune shape to love.

Now, the *lover* is always a person. People love things; things don't love people. You can love your espresso, but you'll be waiting awhile if you're expecting your espresso to love you back. With God, the *Lover* behind all creation is not a divine thing—like an abstract force or cosmic power—but rather a person. The Father is the Giver of Life, and a lover of the life he has made.

Love is most powerful, however, when the *beloved* is also a person—not a thing. My fondness for my wife runs *a lot* deeper (hopefully) than for my latte. Why is this? Love can be reciprocated; a person can love you back. Reciprocal love is the root of deep friendships, strong parent-child relationships, and healthy marriages. When it comes to God, the *Beloved* is not a thing but a person: the Son who loves his Father, delights in his affection, and eternally reciprocates the love he receives.

Now, here's where we run into a problem. While *lover* and *beloved* can both be people, *love* itself is always a thing—an abstract force or impersonal bond between them. Or, at least, *almost* always.

This is where the family becomes interesting. When husband and wife come together, the love that arises between them can become tangible in the person of the child. The child is not a "thing" but a person, who joins them to participate as a member in their circle of love.

The couple's marital love is expansive, encircling another within their embrace of affection. The child is not added from the outside in but emerges organically from the inside out, sharing their parents' flesh and bone. Think of that African statue, with father, mother, and child knit together in the substance of their person and facing one another in love.

Similarly, with God, *Love* is not a thing but a person. The Spirit is the Love of God, the third person of the Trinity, who proceeds from the first and second persons as the bond of affection between them, sharing their divine substance and sharing in their communion.

The family makes love uniquely personal.[3] Not only the lover but also the beloved and even the love itself are persons, all the way around. This reflects something of the Trinity, as a tri-personal communion-of-love.

Made to Belong

Can you imagine living in perfect love? A circle of giving and receiving? Knowing and being known in secure relationship? Nothing to prove, no one to impress. Not needing to earn an identity or perform for your value and worth. Rather, receiving your identity as a gift from outside yourself, in an unbreakable communion of mutual self-giving. You were made for this reality. You want this love. You need this love. You were made for this kind of love.

You were made to belong.

God designed the family to reflect something of his divine love as Trinity. Where each person outdoes the other in seeking to lift up and shine a spotlight on each other.[4] Like an African artist sculpting that statue to depict a human family, so the Grand Artist sculpted the human family to embody something of his own existence as a communion-of-persons and to reflect that love into the world.[5]

Of course, families are broken. Perhaps you're the child of divorce. Or experienced abuse growing up. Or never knew your father. My friend Jamie grew up the child of alcoholics and tells tales of how the chaos and dysfunction shaped her to this day. Sin is real; the tragedy of the Fall has impacted us all.

Yet this love is still for you. The family is a sign that, even when broken, points toward the greater reality of the Trinity. And the love of the Trinity is unbreakable. Secure. Foundational. From eternity, God has existed as a life-giving communion-of-love. And you're invited, in Christ, to enter this divine embrace. To be filled with the Spirit (*within* you), united to the Son (*before* you), and celebrated by the Father (*over* you).

To be welcomed home where you belong.

There's healing in this love. However broken your family, however deep the wounds you carry or far astray your story has taken you, this divine love runs deeper and reaches farther. Yes, healing takes time. Sanctification is not an overnight process. The experience of belonging takes a while to work its way from your bones through your marrow, from the inside out of your heart to your behavior. Yet this love is powerful and knows how to do its work if you'll let it.

What would it look like to live in the eternal love of the Trinity? Children who grow up with loving parents are more confident, stable, secure. How would it shape you to be cared for and guided not simply by a loving parent but by your heavenly Father? What lies do you currently believe that would shatter if you invited him to speak his truth over you? What would it do to the way you think of yourself?

The icon of family invites you to live into such love, knowing you were made to belong.

Exchange of Love

No recent theologian has been more influential in reflecting on the significance of the body and sexuality than Pope John Paul II. His *Theology of the Body* contains powerful insights on God as a communion-of-love, and the family as a window into the triune identity of God. Author and speaker Christopher West, an influential "translator" of the pope's thought for a popular audience, helpfully summarizes some of his insight in this regard:

God imprinted in our sexuality the call to participate in a "created version" of his eternal "exchange of love." In other words, God created us male and female so that we could image his love by becoming a sincere gift to each other. This sincere giving establishes a "communion of persons" not only between the sexes but also—in the normal course of events—with a "third" who proceeds from them both. In this way, sexual love becomes an icon or earthly image in some sense of the inner life of the Trinity.[6]

That's a big quote; let's break it down.

First, God made "male and female" with an ability to "image his love" by "becoming a sincere gift to each other." This means when a man and woman give themselves fully to one another as a sincere gift—in covenant sexual love—this giving of their person is more than simply having sex, they are imaging divine love. Our culture does not have a particularly deep imagination for the sacredness of sex, but we should. This is one of the great contributions Christianity can give to a sexually confused culture. There is *meaning* to it all. It is pleasurable but about so much more than pleasure.

Next, this mutual self-giving establishes a "communion of persons," not only between them but with a "'third' who proceeds from them both."[7] The child is not a visitor knocking on the front door to request admission from the outside but rather emerges organically from within as the fruit of their love. The child shares in their parents' nature and substance, proceeding from their being and reflecting their image back to them.

By "normal course of events," the quote acknowledges the painful reality of infertility (which we'll look at more later). Yet sexual love is, by divine design, naturally oriented toward the generation of life.

In all this, sexual love thus becomes "an icon or earthly image" of "the inner life of the Trinity." That term *inner life* refers to God as he is in eternity (what is theologically called the *immanent*

Trinity), as compared to God in his relationship to the world (or the *economic* Trinity). In other words, sexual love is designed to let us in on something central to the deepest heart of God—not only what God *does* but who God *is*.

Like a trampoline that catapults us to a higher plane, sexual love is an earthly image of a heavenly reality.

This works, of course, by analogy.[8] God is not the same thing as a literal human family. (That's what the quote means by "in some sense.") There are differences.[9] Yet while God is not exactly like a human family, God has designed the family to reveal something true of himself into the world. While the things of this world cannot contain God, they can speak of him. God is strong as a lion and cares for us as a shepherd, even if not the same thing as either. The family is like a living, breathing statue, crafted by the Grand Artist as a created version that is imprinted with a divine likeness.[10]

This "earthly image" speaks to a heavenly reality: God is a life-giving communion-of-love.

Flesh and Bone

The family is an icon of the Trinity. This can raise some important questions, which we'll address in chapter 12 ("Triune Symphony"). But let's tackle an important one here.

Can the family really bear witness to the *oneness* of the Trinity? We tend to see "family" today as autonomous individuals who often live in separate cities and maybe get together once or twice a year for holidays. Talk of the Trinity as family can sound like tritheism: three different gods with distinct agendas who occasionally come together to form the one God. The family has a much stronger unity than this, however.

Families share flesh and bone.

The Nature of Kinship

One flesh refers to sexual union, as we've seen. *Flesh and bone* is a related phrase, which refers to the family generated by sexual union. Check out these examples, where people are said to share flesh and bone with their relatives:

> Laban discovers Jacob is his nephew, and cries out, "You are my *bone and my flesh!*"[11]

> Abimelech reminds his extended family to support him: "Remember also that I am your *bone and your flesh.*"[12]

> King David addresses the elders from his tribe of Judah: "You are my brothers; you are my own *bone and my flesh.*"[13]

Now, *flesh and bone* is similar to *one flesh*, but it's not referring to sex. Uncle Laban's not trying to sleep with his nephew (*phew*); he's simply saying they're family. Abimelech's not trying to get his relatives into the backseat of his car (again, *phew*); he's just calling on their familial loyalty for help. David's reminding his kinsmen of their biological connection as a tribe.

Some misuse "flesh and bone" language today. Proponents of same-sex or polyamorous marriages, for example, have argued from passages like these that one-flesh language was never about sex at all, only kinship.[14] All you need is covenant—the promise to care for each other as family—to become flesh and bone.

With all due respect, however, this simply shows how far we've come from the ancient understanding. Ask any indigenous person and they'll tell you: The reason Uncle Laban and Jacob share flesh and bone is because (*drumroll please . . .*) their ancestors became one flesh. You and Billy Jo Bob are cousins because (*you guessed it . . .*) your grandparents got it on.

One flesh generates *flesh and bone*. The two phrases are related, yet distinct. *One flesh* is about sexual union; *flesh and bone* is about the kinship relations that arise from that union.[15] (We'll look at adoption later, which I, as an adoptive parent, care greatly about.)

Kinship is not *instead of* sex; it's *because of* sex. That word *kinship* actually comes from a root that means "to beget, give birth to."[16] *Kindergarten,* a German term that comes from a similar root word, means, literally, "children's garden." So there's more going on with kinship than just vows of commitment.

We use similar language today: Your kids are your *flesh and blood*. (We simply swap *blood* for *bone*.) Families share flesh. Brotherhood is built by bonds of bone. Relatives are like Red Cross donors: They share blood. Descendants derive DNA from a common family lineage; Ancestry.com is making a killing off it.

Families share an organic union. Their members are made of the same stuff, sharing one substance (flesh) and nature (human). This is iconic. *Substance* and *nature* are the same categories historically used to describe the oneness of the Trinity, whose persons share one substance and nature. Now, family members have multiple wills, whereas the Trinity has one (every analogy breaks down at some point). But the Bible has a much stronger conception of the family's unity than Western individualism does. (We'll look at this more in chapter 12.) This aspect of the analogy is not a weakness but a strength.[17]

The biological family is one. Again, in a future chapter, we'll look at the power of adoption, which is indeed truly powerful, makes one truly family, and is also iconic of the gospel.

Passing On the Image

Pets are the new children. Cats and dogs now outnumber daughters and sons in major cities around the country—including San Francisco, Nashville, and Seattle.[18] As psychologist Jean Twenge, author of *Generation Me*, observes, the little beasties have perks:

> Pets are becoming a replacement for children. They're less expensive. You can get one even if you're not ready to live with someone or get married, and they can still provide companionship.[19]

Move over kid; the Corgis are in town.

Our parental instincts are still strong, even if their object has shifted species. And it is taking us to some odd places. Pet strollers and doggie backpacks are popular to carry your furry bambino around. An attachable nipple allows you to feed your cat from your "breast." There's even a prosthetic Licki brush you can hold between your teeth, to bond by "licking" their fur (watch out for hairballs!).

The "pet pampering" industry brings in over ten billion dollars a year, with couture clothing, gourmet food, and more.[20] A viral Pinterest post stands up to the haters: "Don't say I am not a Mom just because my kids have four legs and fur. They are my kids, and I am their mom."

Now, pets are great. I have no desire to dog on the fur babies. And family is more than just biological (as the power of adoption, and identity of the church, make clear). My question is simply this: How are children different from pets? The answer may seem obvious, but it's actually profound.

Children are your flesh and bone.

Children share a couple's substance and nature, extending their flesh and bone into the world—and into the future. As the media theorist Neil Postman famously put it, "Children are the living messages we send to a time we will not see."[21] Children are postcards to the future, expanding a couple's circle of affection forward in time and outward in space, in expansive embrace.

Families pass on more than just flesh and bone; they also pass on the image of God. After God created Adam "in the likeness of God," we're told that Adam knew Eve and "fathered a son in his own likeness, after his image, and named him Seth."[22] *Wait a sec—did you catch the repetition?* Yep. God fathers Adam in his image, then Adam fathers Seth in his image. We bear the image of God; our kids bear the image of us.

Sex is how the image gets passed on, biologically speaking.

Have you ever noticed how children look a lot like their parents? "Your daughter's got your nose and her jawline," friends tell my wife and me. "Your son's got her cheeks and your hair." We're still awestruck at these little human reflections of ourselves staring back at us.

Children bear the image of their makers. They inherit our DNA, genetics, facial features, and more. Even their grandparents' features show up—which used to freak me out. (*Oh no! I'm raising a mini me version of my dad.*) As pastor Peter Scazzero quips, "You may have Jesus in your heart, but you have Grandpa in your bones."[23]

Yet Genesis is saying something more. Children not only receive the image *of* their parents; they receive the image *from* their parents—the image of God.[24] You not only get the likeness of your mom and dad as makers; you get the likeness of your Maker. *One flesh* impresses the divine image upon your flesh and bone.

Beautiful union creates an image of God.

Love Is Expansive

The love of God is expansive, generative, life-giving. That's what this aspect of the icon reveals. God is outgoing, delighting to welcome you in. Like that African home with twenty-one people welcoming Holly and me into their family's embrace, our heavenly Father makes space for you to find your home in the very life of God. The Trinity extends the circle, in Christ and through the Spirit, to wrap you into the divine embrace of your Creator.

You might feel orphaned and alone, like there's no place for you. Maybe the social circles you want into have been closed, lofty, restrictive—like cliques for the elite who can climb the social ladder high enough to enter. Yet Christ has descended to meet you in your isolation, to fill you with his Spirit and draw you up into the eternal love of the Trinity.

You can find your family in God. "God's love has been poured into our hearts," Paul tells us, "through the Holy Spirit who has been given to us."[25] I love that image. The Father and Son send their Spirit to share their love with us, spreading their divine affection abroad in our hearts. The Spirit doesn't just tell you *about* God's love but fills you *with* God's love—by filling you with himself.

The Spirit, who is Love, brings forth the fruit of love in us. "The fruit of the Spirit is love, joy, peace," and more.[26] The first fruit is love because it's the root from which the other fruit springs. *The greatest of these is love*, because its Source springs eternal. Like gives birth to like. Love's children share a family resemblance. The divine virtues that flow from Love are reproduced in us.

God's love is *fruitful*. And this is the pattern for us too.

You were made to live a fruitful life. Even if you never have children, this aspect of the icon is for you. Jesus didn't have kids and lived the most fruitful life in history. Some of the most life-giving people I know are childless.

Yet the procreative nature of sex points to a powerful reality: Union gives birth to life. Your union with Christ is designed to bring forth new life into the world, to extend the hospitality of God, and to expand the circle of love.

This helps explain why infertility can be such a painful experi-ence: A couple's desire to expand their circle of affection, to bring forth children as the fruit of their love, is good—even iconic. We'll look at this more later, but it hurts when fruitfulness is frustrated by the Fall.[27]

God has designed the family to be a communion-of-love, a window into his eternal life as God. God does not just *have* love; God *is* love. The Trinity is the foundation for this gospel procla-mation. God's love is *holy*—it is other, set apart, different than—because God is the triune Creator, and we are creation. Yet God has given us the family as an earthly image of his inner life as Trinity—as Lover, Beloved, and Love.

Father, mother, and child are three persons sharing one sub-stance, imaging the triune life of God.

Echo of Joy

We tend to think of *orgasm* as a dirty word—the crass punch line to a joke, with red-cheeked adolescents giggling in the back-ground. Yes, it's appropriate this moment of ecstasy is private: intended for the intimacy of lovers in embrace, shielded from the eyes and commentary of the outside world. Yet at the risk of sounding sacrilegious, let me suggest that the reason the orgasm should be kept private is not because it is crude but rather for the opposite reason: because it is holy.

Orgasm, ideally, occurs at the height of physical union. Its ecstasy is shared between lover and beloved, at the climactic point where they can bring forth love. The *unitive* and *procreative* dynamics of sex are most powerfully charged in this consummation of one flesh toward the generation of flesh and bone. All three persons are proleptically present in the moment of union: with the second ready to proceed forth from the first, carrying his life within her, and the third ready to proceed forth from them both, conceived through their union.

Oneness is charged to bring forth the three.

The chief characteristic of this climactic moment? Joy. Ecstatic joy.

The word *ecstasy* comes from a root that means "going outside oneself." The lover is *outgoing* in this ecstatic moment: giving himself fully to his beloved, to share his life with her and impart his presence within her. The beloved is similarly *outgoing*: embracing him from outside herself to receive his life within her, sharing her life with his in mutual self-giving. The couple is *outgoing* together: bringing forth the fruit of their love shared between them as an object of their mutual affection, who arises to rejoice as a participant in their communion.

The orgasm, this suggests, is much more than simply a biological response or a pleasurable event. It is that, but it is *more* too. As a *communion-forming* event, and as such, an iconic window into the eternal joy of the triune God.[28] Our Creator was not surprised by the orgasm, as if it were some foul, dirty thing that invaded his good world. No, he created it, by his good pleasure, for our good pleasure. And it's worth considering whether this ecstatic moment in life-giving communion is itself iconic of a greater reality.

Could it be an echo of the Lover's eternal delight to generously give his life to and share his life with his Beloved? An echo of the Beloved's unending joy to hospitably receive the life of the Lover and reciprocally return such lavish affection? An echo of their mutual delight in the Love whose life proceeds from them and rejoices with them?[29]

Love. Life. Joy. These are internal to the eternal experience of the triune God. The orgasm is holy because it is iconic. It is embedded in the family's point of origination, the moment of union from which the three proceed. It marks this climax of union with joy, as the one-flesh starting point for the family as a life-giving communion-of-love.

The devil loves to throw dirt on the shiniest diamonds, to conceal the glory they're meant to display. Our pornified culture trains us to see this ecstatic moment as a self-centered act, focused on taking rather than giving, from an objectified other. But the gospel trains us to reframe sex as mutual self-giving, aimed to be pleasurable for both parties, in an "exchange of love" within the security of covenant, ordered toward the giving of life in the communion of family.

The orgasm is not crude; its ecstasy is designed by God to resound of greater things. An echo of triune joy.

4

WEDDING ON A MOUNTAIN

My grandpa is my hero. Mike Valdez bends over backward for his bride. Ever since I was a kid, my grandmother Elida has been ill: in and out of surgeries, on and off medications, up and down with chronic pain. Yet for as long as I can remember, my grandfather has faithfully cared for her: chauffeuring her back and forth from appointments, helping her in and out of the car, walking her up and down the stairs.

As I was growing up, he didn't know I was watching, but I saw him make the meals, clean the dishes, do the laundry, check in to make sure she was comfortable—over and over again, all on top of his day job. And he did it with joy. He *delights* in her. There's no begrudging spirit, no whining or complaining, no sense of dry duty or oppressive obligation. Mike serves with a smile.

She's still the girl of his dreams, and he often wonders out loud—with a twinkle in his eye and a victorious laugh—how she actually agreed to marry *him* above all those other competitors all those years ago.

This month was their sixtieth wedding anniversary. That's a rare thing these days. I grew up, like many, the child of an unhappy marriage that would end in divorce. My parents were not alone—every marriage in our proximate family (aunts, uncles, and other grandparents) crashed on the rocks of a fallen world and split apart.

But looking deeper down the trunk of our family tree, I saw a star of hope, a beacon in my grandparents' marriage of a different kind of future, a promise that a powerful alternative to the norm was possible, one where union was safeguarded through faithful, sacrificial, committed love.

Many consider Michael Valdez a hero, for a variety of reasons: his three tours in the jungles of Vietnam (where a third of his company did not return), his hard work that raised him out of poverty (and the extended family he's cared for since), his deep love for the God who saved him all those years ago (displayed in a rich devotional life). But when I reflect on the heroic legacy he's left in my life, it's his marriage that shines.

Amid the foundations faltering around me as an impressionable youth, I found myself thinking, *That's what I want someday. Not only the kind of marriage I want to have but the kind of person I want to be.* In my grandfather, and in his sacrificial devotion to his bride, I encountered a picture of something greater.

An icon of God's faithful love.

Love Is a Verb

We use the word *love* a lot. "I love this iced tea." "I loved that movie." "Oh my gosh, I just *love* your shoes!" We're like a drunk Cupid, slinging amorous arrows at everything in sight.

On the one hand, that's fine. But there's a danger to such casual usage—when we flippantly throw it around, we can gradually reduce this tremendous term to a trite symbol (like the "heart" we hit on that Instagram post that simply indicates our passing recognition that we saw someone's latest selfie). When we dumb love down, our diminished definition becomes a far cry from the character of our Creator.

Marriage is designed to display a love that is truly divine— and that can speak to us all, whatever our relationship status.

The Grammar of the Gospel

The Hebrew word for love in the Old Testament is *hesed*—and it's important. *Hesed* shows up 247 times in the Bible (that's a lot!), most significantly for God. God is praised for his *hesed* more than any other attribute in Scripture, like a recurring refrain of worship.[1] God's *hesed* is big enough to encompass all humanity, strong enough to redeem the enslaved, and wide enough to fill the earth.[2] Creation itself was founded on this *hesed*-style love, which endures to a "thousand generations" and unto "forever."[3]

Hesed is difficult to translate into English, because we tend to reduce love to feelings and emotions. But *hesed* is an action word. Its meaning is less "You make me feel good" and more "I'll be with you through thick and thin." God is regularly described as doing, showing, or keeping this loyal love to his people, with specific acts of faithfulness. Like my grandfather caring for my grandmother, it speaks to faithful action, steadfast presence, and sacrificial care.

Hesed involves emotion, but it centers on concrete action on behalf of another. Joseph asks his jail mate to show him *hesed* by remembering to put in a good word with Pharaoh when he gets out of prison. Israel's army shows Rahab *hesed* when they honor their promise to spare her in battle. Ruth shows *hesed* to Naomi, her widowed mother-in-law, by leaving her homeland to care for her. King David displays "the [*hesed*] of God" to Mephibosheth, Saul's crippled grandson, by bringing the wounded heir of his former enemy to dine at his royal table for the rest of his days (a powerful foreshadowing of what King Jesus has done for us, with our bruises and wounds, in the gospel).[4]

All these examples involve loyalty to a relationship, the honoring of a promise, in a way that is costly. This is why English versions often translate *hesed* into longer, clunkier terms (like "lovingkindness" or "faithful love") that imply action rather than simply emotion. This love is "more than a feeling," in the classic words of that song by Boston. Author Bob Goff captures the gist in his concise inspirational catchphrase . . .

"Love does."

So, when it comes to romance, this love is less like a twitter-pated teenager in the wake of a first kiss, and more like my friend Brittany's devotion to her husband, Paul, *in sickness and in health*, caring for him in the years since his diagnosis of multiple sclerosis, as his muscles deteriorated and memory faded, and he increasingly lost his ability both to work and to walk.

Or James and Sadie clinging to one another *for richer or poorer*, when his business tanked and they spent a year struggling to make ends meet and put food on the table, nurturing their children through the stress of it all.

Or Tyler and Nicole who persevered *in good times and bad*, comforting one another through the tragic death of their son, letting it press them deeper together rather than pull them apart, with bonds forged through the trenches of grief while awaiting the dawn.

These are more than random acts of kindness to strangers; they are active displays of the covenant love of God.

Marriage as Spiritual Formation

"Husbands, love your wives," Paul says, "as Christ loved the church."[5] The apostle's not asking husbands to feel fluffy emotions toward their wives; he's telling them to treat their wives with the same loyal love and sacrificial action their Savior has shown to them—like my grandpa has.

We tend to emphasize romantic love as passive. "I fell in love," you'll often hear. As the humorous quip goes, "You fall in love like you fall into a ditch—on accident."[6] The high-flying rush of endorphins that takes hold of you in a new relationship can be good, yet we too often see ourselves as merely helpless bystanders hoping to get hit by one of Cupid's arrows—and praying that it sticks.

That's a dangerous foundation to build a marriage upon. If you accidentally fell *in*, it's all too easy to accidentally fall back *out* again. God's *hesed*-style love, however, is forward moving and active, promise making and faithful. When it comes to the grammar of the gospel, divine love is more than a noun.

Love is a verb.

God has designed marriage to reflect his faithful, *hesed*-style love. What better way to learn "patience, kindness, goodness, faithfulness"—and the other fruits of the Spirit[7]—than to cram two sinners under the same roof to build a common life together? I didn't realize how selfish I was until stepping into life with Holly. I didn't recognize how unkind I could be until seeing first-hand how much my words could sting.

Marriage is a workshop in spiritual formation. God can use it to bring your imperfections to the surface and hammer them out, to form you into the image of Christ. In the furnace of covenant, the heat and pressure can be powerful: surviving on a shoestring while sleepless and exhausted, going the distance when the fears run high and the tears run dry. God can use this as a foundry for your formation, to trim off your rough edges and shape, form, and refine you—if you let him.

Our culture sees marriage as primarily about *happiness*, but God's vision is also about *holiness*.[8] Some shrink from that word *holy*, but it essentially means growing to look like Jesus. Your character can get chiseled through the drama of dirty dishes, stinky diapers, and diagnoses that come in the decades after the honeymoon.

God cares more about your character than your comfort.

Jesus is saying to those who are married, "I'm going to en-counter you here, train you here, and form you here." Your home can become like a monastery, with rhythms and practices that form you in his image. You can reflect the Savior who became a servant to joyfully care for his spouse.

The goal is to become like my grandpa, growing in your ca-pacity to love like God loves.

Making Love

Making love means something different today than it used to. The phrase has become a euphemism for sex, but originally it meant the opposite: creating the conditions for affection to grow *without* resorting to sex.[9] In courtship, for example, when a chaperone accompanied a couple on a carriage ride, her goal was to help the couple "make love," to fan the couple's embers of desire into flame.

"It is not pleasant to make love in the presence of the third person," Anthony Trollope wrote in 1869, "even when that love is all fair and above board."[10] That statement can sound risqué today, but he's not referring to voyeurism but rather to flirting while someone else is around. It's the high schooler getting sweet on his girlfriend while his mom's in the room. Awkward.

There's an important truth to this older use: Sometimes you gotta do the *actions* of love for the feelings and desire to follow. There's a joy that often follows in the wake. Research has found, for example, that when "unhappy" marriages stick together and work through it, the majority are "happy" again within five years. Those who divorce, however, do not on average become happier.[11]

Feelings can follow faithfulness.

My grandfather is one of the happiest people I know. He may not have always felt the sparks of romance, but even when he didn't, he made love to his wife—in this older, classic sense—putting in the work to serve her and stoke the flames, by laying down his life for her.

This is true for all of us. You don't need to be married to show faithful love to those around you, even when times get tough and you don't feel like it. This is the stuff deep friendships are made of. God wants to use your relationships—romantic or not—to hone you with *hesed*, to shape you in the image of Jesus.

God is faithful to you, even when you're not all that lovable. Your Savior continues to sing over you, "rejoice over you."[12] "My beloved," God calls his wayward bride, "the beloved of my heart."[13] God calls you his "favorite" (*habab*), a term of devotion that means "love" or "make love" in the original language, and became the most common rabbinic term used for the love between husband and wife.[14]

"Your Maker is your husband," the prophet Isaiah proclaims.[15] That's a shocking claim! What does it mean to be united so intimately with the Creator of the universe? Among other things, it means even if you're in a struggling marriage, even if your friends have forsaken you, even when you feel like the world is falling apart around you, you can count on his unfailing love.

He's given himself. He's *promised*.

An Epic Romance

We're weird about weddings. Americans spend more and more money on the big day (the average couple these days shells out around thirty thousand dollars), yet we increasingly see them as less and less significant: "It's just a piece of paper," one often hears.

So which is it? Our culture seems caught between glamorizing the tradition on the one hand, and gutting it of any real significance on the other. This ancient ceremony is more, however, than just a hoop to jump through to appease the parents or to get some government benefits.

Weddings—and the marriage they inaugurate—are designed to reflect God's covenant love. I like the way Pastor Ray Ortlund puts it, when he says marriage is "the wraparound concept for the entire Bible":

> The eternal love story is why God created the universe and why God gave us marriage in Eden and why couples fall in love and get married in the world today. Every time a bride and groom stand there and take their vows, they are re-enacting the biblical love story, whether they realize it or not.[16]

Weddings are a window into a powerful truth: The Maker of the universe wants to unite your life with his and live with you forever.

The most dramatic wedding ceremony in the Bible occurs on a mountain. Mount Sinai, to be exact. There are trumpets, fire, and lightning. God pulls out all the stops for this ceremony! In Exodus 19–20, God enters covenant with Israel, and the Scriptures describe it as a marriage covenant.[17] Jewish wedding ceremonies were actually modeled on this event. Let's take a closer look at the iconic scene, to see what it can teach us about the nature of marriage.

God and his bride are getting hitched.

The Goal of Salvation

First, the backdrop. "I was a husband to them," God declares, "when I took them by the hand to lead them out of Egypt."[18] God's beloved, Israel, is held captive in Egypt. Pharaoh's been like an abusive boyfriend, using Israel to get what he wants *from* her, rather than give himself *to* her. The enslaving empire he leads is described as a dragon, refusing to let her go.[19]

God's people are in chains, his beloved in bondage.

Yahweh hears her cry, however, and enters the dragon's lair. God arises to rescue his people. Like the vintage knight in shining armor, he invades the impenetrable fortress and confronts the cruel captor. The showdown ends with God striking down the tyrant, breaking shackles from his bride, and delivering her.

Once they exit Egypt and cross the Red Sea, God doesn't drop his beloved in the desert with a road map to find her own way home. God is not like Shrek, dumping Princess Fiona just beyond the dragon's drawbridge, considering the quest complete. No, the most important part is yet to come.

God's endgame is not only to get his beloved *out of* Egypt but to bring her *to* himself. Salvation is more than just liberation *from* slavery; it's entrance *into* the embrace of the King and the life-giving power of his kingdom. The goal of salvation is union with God.

So the King carries his bride into the wilderness for a wedding.

The Proposal (The Significance of Consent)

Once at Mount Sinai, God enters a covenant ceremony with his people. Three crucial elements of this scene—used in Jewish

weddings—reveal the heart of what a wedding is. First is the
proposal, which highlights the significance of consent. God asks
Israel whether she *wants* this covenant, essentially bending down
on one knee to pop the question:

> You yourselves have seen what I did to Egypt, and how I
> carried you on eagles' wings and brought you to myself.
> Now if you obey me fully and keep my covenant, then out of
> all nations you will be my treasured possession. Although
> the whole earth is mine, you will be for me a kingdom of
> priests and a holy nation.[20]

Like a proposal, God points *back* to what he has done ("I carried you on eagles' wings"), then *forward* to what he will do: She
will have a unique and cherished relationship with him ("you will
be my treasured possession"), as he commits himself exclusively
to her ("out of all nations"). There may be many fish in the sea,
but she alone will be his ("Although the whole earth is mine, you
will be for me"). This will be a monogamous relationship, where
she is set apart to the Lord ("a holy nation"). They will rule together like king and queen, as she mediates his presence to the
world ("a kingdom of priests").

Together, they will bring his kingdom to bear on earth as in
heaven. Cue the dramatic moment, all eyes fixed on the beloved
to see how she responds.

"All the people answered together": *Yes!*[21]

Let's stop here for a moment. The text emphasizes *all the people*, as with one voice. For Jewish thinkers, this consent and agree-
ment was foundational.[22] God is not coercive. He doesn't kidnap
or force his people to be with him. Rather, he invites us into union
with him.

Consent is crucial.

That may sound like a no-brainer today, but as classicist Kyle
Harper has demonstrated, it was actually a radical Christian idea
in the ancient world.[23] Back when marriages were frequently ar-

ranged by families for economic or political reasons, Christianity laid ground rules to keep daughters and sons from being pushed like powerless pawns across the game board by others. You can't be forced or pressured into marriage against your will, canon law held. Lack of consent was grounds for annulment.

This is why both bride and groom are asked, "Do you take this person in marriage?" No one else can answer on their behalf. They must commit personally and publicly to the covenant. This is also why wedding proposals are so significant: They establish consent. When a guy bends down on one knee, he's asking whether she wants to be with him forever.

True love is always consensual. You can't force someone to commit to you. Manipulation or pressure should have no part in it. Coercion might compel behavior, but it can't captivate the heart. While it's true that those abducted can develop a strange bond with their captor (Stockholm syndrome), we'd all say this is unhealthy. Healthy relationships are reciprocal.

That's why unrequited love is so painful: You can't make some-one *want* you, no matter how much you may want to.

The beauty of the gospel, however, is that God does want you. He's gone all the way to hell and back to be with you forever. Maybe you've lost in love. Maybe you're heartbroken, overlooked, or unwanted. But I've got good news for you: Christ has looked upon you and come to win your heart.

Your Maker invites you into a beautiful all-of-life union with him. The question is: Do you want to be with him? Will you give your consent? Will you be the beloved who says, "Yes!"?

We love grandiose wedding proposals. They're the videos that go viral. Back in the day, my friends and I had a competition to see who could outdo each other in how we popped the question. (I've been told I won, but that's a story for another day.)

There's a reason we love these grand gestures. They're iconic—a window into the extravagant nature of the God who carries us on eagles' wings and invites us to become his treasured possession, making our home with him as a kingdom of priests,

who mediate his presence to the world as we rule together forever.

The Vows (The Power of a Promise)

After Israel says yes, she's given three days to prepare for the
ceremony. No one is to approach or touch the holy mountain during this time. Rather, they are to consecrate themselves—like a
bride getting ready for her wedding day—for the earthshaking
significance of what's about to take place.

Similarly, in Jewish tradition, the bride and groom are not allowed to see each other—or "touch the holy mountain"—in the
days leading up to the ceremony. The anticipation builds as the
big day approaches. They use a special bath (known as a *mikvah*)
to wash for the wedding, as a sign of the holiness of what they are
about to enter in the giving of their vows.

Some think of the Ten Commandments as uptight rules and
regulations from a distant lawgiver, but Israel saw them more
like wedding vows.[24] They're pretty simple:

> Don't cheat on me with other lovers (aka false gods).
> Remember to rest so we can celebrate life together
>   (on the Sabbath).
> Don't lie, cheat, murder, or steal.
> Keep your heart devoted to me.
> Let's live together forever![25]

Vows are a vision for a life based on love.[26] Yahweh promised
his faithful love to his bride, declaring his unflinching commitment to her. Similarly, in Jewish tradition, the husband makes a
promise to his wife with a formal declaration (known as a *ke-
tubah*), a written commitment of all that he promises to do for her,
signed by two witnesses, with the consequences he'll face should
he break his side of the bargain.[27]

Israel, meanwhile, professed her devotion to God, forsaking all
others to give herself fully to the God who had given himself

fully to her. Wedding vows are the ultimate DTR (Define the Relationship). They set a common expectation for life together, with commitments of fidelity and devotion. They create a context of security for the marriage of persons, the merger of bodies, the mingling of souls—in an all-of-life union.

Vows are a promise. I've officiated a lot of weddings and noticed that when couples write their own vows, they tend to express more how they feel than what they'll do.[28] *You're my best friend. You make me happier than anyone else. I want to be with you forever.* Such sentiments are sweet but not vows.

Vows are a commitment of *hesed.* Classically, they express what you'll do ("love and cherish"), under any circumstance ("in good times and bad, for richer or poorer, in sickness and in health"), and for the ultimate duration ("till death do us part").

Such a promise is iconic of the God of the gospel, who promises to never leave or forsake us, vowing to walk with us on the highlands above and in the valleys below, pledging through it all the security of his unfailing love.

God is all in. His love is faithful, relentless, and enduring. There's nothing we can do to earn it, no distance we can run to outpace it, no hurt we can induce to break it. That's what weddings signify.

Jesus is committed, promising to be with us through thick and thin, in good times and bad, in sickness and health, till death— nay, through death—when we're raised by his resurrected arms into his presence forever.

A couple's ongoing devotion, living out their promises after the honeymoon ends, is designed to reflect Christ's unbreakable allegiance toward us. He will not run out on or betray you. You can take confidence in his unshakable loyalty and presence.

He's not going anywhere.

The Home (A Foundation for the Future)

Finally, weddings are a marker of transition. They are not a destination but a transit station, where two trails merge into a common path. From the heights of Mount Sinai, Yahweh and his bride could look back upon the old world of Egypt behind them and forward to the horizon of the Promised Land before them, where they would rule together as one.

God's covenant lays a foundation for this future. After the vows on Sinai, God gives blueprints for the tabernacle, his dwelling place where he will make a home with his people.[29] God is moving in with his bride.

Similarly, Jewish wedding ceremonies take place under a canopy (known as a *chuppah*—a cloth held up by four poles), to symbolize their new home together. The couple stands alone beneath the canopy; no other people or furniture are inside. This represents the simplicity of just these two persons who are forming the heart of this new family, to thereafter fill this home with abundance and new life.

The canopy's four walls are open, displaying a posture of welcome to their neighbors, sharing their life as a family with others. The overhead canopy also echoes God's Spirit hovering over this sacred ceremony. The wedding takes place before God and their community, as a public sign of their covenant love.

Weddings lay a foundation for the future. They reflect a God of covenant, who promises, "I will never leave you nor forsake you."[30] "There is no fear in [his] love," the apostle John proclaims, because his love is dependable, reliable, secure.[31]

You can build your life on it.

Holly and I came back from our honeymoon to a surprise: Our friends had broken into our new apartment. They cleaned and prepared it for our arrival. The place was decked out with wedding gifts—boxes of blessing from our community. We laughed as we unpacked and began undertaking a project now sixteen years in the making: building a home together.

In the years since, our home has been filled with three children, loads of friends, lots of laughter, and seasons of tears. I don't think much, if anything, from that original registry is still around. Our dishes and couches have changed. We've moved multiple times, even overseas. But through it all, one thing has stayed constant: Holly and me, seeking to build a life together on love.

I now know the secret to my grandfather's success. I understand what I was drawn to all those years ago that made his marriage so attractive, compelling, and inspiring. His marriage was a sign of something much greater: a reflection of Christ, an icon of God's faithful, unfailing, covenant love.

This love is for you. Whether single or married, Christ offers to unite your life with his and live with you forever. He will never leave you, cheat on you, or let you down. You might think God's love is fickle, dependent on how attractive you happen to look that day or how happy you wake up feeling. But God isn't like that. God's love isn't fickle; it's faithful.

He's with you when you're down as well as when you're up. He sacrificially loves you on your bad hair days, as well as your good. He's in it for the long haul. When you're married to your Maker, you can join the eternal melody that echoes down through the corridors of history, in the most repeated refrain of worship from his bride: "His steadfast love endures forever."[32]

5

BRACE TO BE BORN

I remember the birth of our firstborn like it was yesterday. Holly went into labor on September 8, 2009. Mathematical genius that I am, I realized if my wife could hold on just one more day, our daughter would have the auspicious birthday of 09/09/09. I encouraged Holly with this great vision: "Just hold her in there a few more hours!" The flash of fierce anger in her eyes let me know she did not share this laudable goal. She wanted that baby out. *Now.*

Labor is truly painful but oh so worth it.

Our daughter did end up being born on 09/09/09, but that's not why the day was so special. When I first held my daughter in my arms, her tiny finger wrapped around mine. A new chamber of my heart unlocked and opened up, one I didn't previously know was there. (I've since heard this is a common experience.) My heart filled with an immense and mysterious love, an overflowing affection, that nothing would ever be able to break. Before she could even speak, she took my breath away.

This experience was a window into God's love. Jesus says his Father has loved him from all eternity.[1] This means before God was Creator with a creation to make . . . Before God was Savior with our sin to save us from . . . Before God was King with a kingdom to rule . . .

God has always been a Father loving his Son.[2]

The love that flooded my heart at the birth of each of my children was a glimpse into the eternal love of God. You were made for this kind of love.

Procreation is an icon of God's kingdom. Sex has the power both "to unite lives and to create life," theologian Todd Wilson observes.[3] It's not only the *unitive* aspect of sex that speaks to our life with God but the *procreative* as well. Procreation means, literally, "create forth." Like sexual love, God's love is life-giving; he *creates forth* new life in us.

The New Testament uses every stage of procreation to describe the Spirit's work in our lives: conception, pregnancy, labor, birth, nursing, and child-rearing—even agricultural fruitfulness. Indeed, if you were an alien visiting our planet with no categories for birth (say your species reproduced asexually), you would be hard-pressed to understand the work of the Spirit. If marriage speaks to our union with Christ, procreation speaks to our life from the Spirit.

The Spirit of God makes us children of God.

Let's explore this aspect of sex, in order to better understand the life-giving power of God's eternal love.

Born from Above

"Unless one is born again," Jesus says, "he cannot see the kingdom of God." *Born again* has become a cliché, so we can miss its initial shock value. Nicodemus (let's call him Nic) gets the scandal, and asks the obvious follow-up question: "How can a man be born when he is old? Can he enter a second time into his mother's womb and be born?"[4] That *would* be an awkward Mother's Day conversation:

Nic: Hey Mom, Jesus says I need to crawl back in . . .
Mom: No way! You're a grown man.

Nic: But I really want to enter the kingdom!

Mom [picks up broom defensively]: It was hard enough
   getting you out. I ain't letting you back in.

Nic [pouting]: Jesus says it's the only way.

Mom [chasing him away with the broom]: You tell Jesus . . .

Jesus corrects Nic, saying: "A. That's gross. B. Your mama
wouldn't like that. C. You're missing my drift."[5] Okay, that's the
JBRV (Josh Butler Revised Version), but Nic is misunderstanding
the whole point here.

There's a wordplay happening in Jesus's teaching. "Born again"
can also mean "born from above" (both phrases are the same in
Greek). So Jesus says we must be "born from above," and Nic mis-
understands him—to humorous effect.

What does it mean to be born from above? Jesus goes on to
explain: You must be "born of . . . the Spirit."[6] The Spirit is like a
mother, giving birth to children of God. Zooming out to the rest
of the New Testament can help us understand how.

Conception (Word and Spirit)

Every stage of procreation illuminates our life from God's Spirit.
Let's start at conception, at the millisecond where life begins.
The apostle John tells us we are children of God because we have
been conceived by God:

> See what great love the Father has lavished on us, that we
> should be called children of God! And that is what we
> are! . . . No one who is born of God will continue to sin,
> because God's *sperma* remains in them; they cannot go on
> sinning, because they have been born of God.[7]

Whoa! Did you catch that? What does it mean that God's
"sperma" remains in us? The language can sound shocking at
first. Pull out your lexicon, and you'll discover it's the Greek
word for "seed." It can refer to either "the semen virile" from

which human life generates, or the agricultural seed "from which a plant germinates." So, either human seed or plant seed.[8]

Two words in English; one in Greek.

The analogy here is semen. John does not say we're "the botanical plants of God" but rather "children of God." The metaphor is not agricultural but anthropological. The rest of the letter emphasizes our identity as "little children" who've been "born of God" the Father and are now "brothers and sisters" with one another. We're one family because we're born of the same Father above.[9]

Our past conception constitutes our present identity.

Now, this is not "dirty." Semen is often a source for crude jokes in our culture. In the Bible, however, it's the source of life. It's associated with the river of life—an image for the Spirit—shared through beautiful union.[10] This points to a powerful truth: We receive life from outside ourselves.

You exist because of sex. I exist because of sex. All eight billion of us walking the face of God's green earth exist because of sex. If your parents told you otherwise, I hate to break it to you, but you weren't dropped off by a stork or delivered on the front porch by Amazon minions.

Though your imagination may bristle, your biological parents made you (back to the trampoline!). Whether in the backseat of a car, a queen bed in a hotel room, that tent in the middle of Yosemite, or a lab in Muskogee, Oklahoma—it's how the human race gets made. Whatever the simplicity or complexity of your story may be, you were begotten and birthed by two human bodies. If you *is*, you *is* because of sex.

We can't generate our own existence. You need seed and egg. Similarly, you can't work your way into the kingdom. God generously shares his life with you, through his Spirit, to make you his child. You don't need to earn it, perform for it, accomplish it. No, it's a gift of grace. And a gift our generous Father loves to give.

God gives you his character too. We won't "continue to sin," John says, because his seed remains in us. God shares the DNA of his divine disposition so that, like a child growing to resemble

their father, you will grow as a child of God to increasingly resemble your heavenly Father. This doesn't mean you'll be perfect
tomorrow; sanctification is a lifelong process. Emerging into
adulthood comes in stages. But over time, you'll grow to love
what he loves and live like he lives.

You'll image the God who's conceived you.

What does the semen represent? God's Word and Spirit. Jesus
regularly uses the term *sperma*, in its agricultural sense, for God's
Word that takes root in us and makes us "children of the kingdom."[11] God's Word is living, active, and dynamic, piercing bone
and marrow, entering the soil of our souls like seed, to generate
us from within the husk of the old world that we might emerge
as newborn children of God.

God's Spirit is also vital. "We know that he lives in us," 1 John
continues, "by the Spirit he gave us." And, "We know that we live
in him and he in us," John reemphasizes again—in case we missed
it the first time—because "he has given us of his Spirit."[12] Like a
river of life, the Spirit showers the love of God within the deepest
inner recesses of our lives, saturating our souls in his divine affection, making the seed of his Word fruitful to bring forth the new
life of God within us.[13]

Word and Spirit make us children of God.

Similar to how semen is both seed and liquid, God plants the
seed of his Word within and pours the river of his Spirit upon
the parched and barren soil of our lives. Christ impregnates the
church with the seed of his Word and the presence of his Spirit,
which conceives us within her as children of God, who grow to
emerge newborn into the kingdom. As Jesus tells Nicodemus, entering the kingdom is like emerging from the amniotic fluid of
your mother's womb. Born, again. Born, from above.

Pregnancy (Brace to Be Born)

Pregnancy also speaks to our life with God. In Romans 8, Paul
describes creation as a pregnant mother who "waits in eager expectation for the children of God to be revealed."[14] We're the kids

kickin' inside nature's belly. A mother's expectation builds as the child grows within her body. When the nesting instinct kicks in, she paints the bedroom, assembles the crib, and prepares the onesies. That's all creation: excited, eagerly looking forward to the day when we emerge from within her into the glorious light of day.

Creation is a pregnant mom.

Labor pangs are a window into the suffering of creation. "The whole creation has been groaning as in the pains of childbirth," Paul continues, "right up to the present time."[15] Labor is painful. When the water breaks and you head to the hospital, the grueling marathon begins. I knew my wife was strong but didn't realize how strong until watching her deliver our children. The suffering is real y'all. *Guys, you try pushing a cantaloupe through a slinky.*

Yet this pain has a purpose. Paul doesn't say our world's suffering is like a dude who hit his thumb with a hammer—that pain would be pointless. He says it's like a mom giving birth, and her travail is bringing something new into the world. The day is coming, Paul concludes, when "creation itself will be liberated from its bondage to decay and brought into the freedom and glory of the children of God."[16] History's going somewhere—and it's going to be glorious.

A word to the mothers: When you gave birth it wasn't just painful, it was prophetic. Your travail was a window into the suffering of creation, and the joy you encountered on the other side was a foretaste of the coming kingdom. I've never met a mother who didn't say, in the end: "It was worth it." When the baby's born, the pain of pushing through delivery fades to a distant memory. She rejoices, beholding the joy she now holds in her arms.

Similarly, God's kingdom is a celebration not only for God's children but for all creation. As mother earth gives us birth, she will share in our glory and freedom, delivering us into the arms of our heavenly Father.

God's kids will be revealed.

In the meantime, we feel the pinch of pregnancy too. "Not only the creation," Paul continues, "but we ourselves, who have the firstfruits of the Spirit, groan inwardly as we wait eagerly" for the coming kingdom.[17] That word *groan* (*stenazo*) comes from a root that means "compressed, restricted . . . to groan because of pressure being *exerted forward* (like the forward pressure of child-birth)."[18]

You're the baby being pushed through the birth canal.

Do you feel the pressure of the world around you? You might feel constricted and claustrophobic, like the walls of your circumstances are pressing in, with no apparent way out. You might feel like you've hit rock bottom at the end of a dark, damp well. Yet the gospel lets you in on a secret: *You're not at the bottom of a well, you're at the tip of a birth canal!* Cling to the Holy Spirit who's pushing you forward, and move toward the light of the coming resurrection.

Brace to be born.

Your suffering isn't pointless. The Spirit is forming you through the compression of today for the kingdom of tomorrow. The hurt you're in is forging your character on this on-ramp into new creation. "Our present sufferings are not worth comparing," Paul says, "with the glory that will be revealed in us."[19] The labor pains are worth it—not only for mom but for baby—when you come out the other side.

Into the arms of our heavenly Father.

Birth (An Icon of Resurrection)

Birth is an icon of resurrection. "God raised [Jesus] up, loosing the birth pangs of death," Peter preached to Jerusalem's crowds, "because it was not possible for him to be held by it."[20] Christ emerged from the trembling womb of the darkened tomb. The old creation was unable to restrain the righteous Savior within her belly, so he burst forth with the light of dawn to launch the new creation.

Jesus is the "firstborn from the dead," Paul tells us, and the "firstborn among many brothers and sisters."[21] Our older brother has crawled out before us, but we are coming close behind.

Jesus is born again: the first time from Mary, the second time from the grave.

Jesus is born from above: by the resurrecting power of the Spirit.

An interesting church tradition envisions Christ as "Mother Jesus" on the cross, giving birth to the church through his agony.[22] While a provocative metaphor, it is more biblically accurate to see Jesus as the child in the analogy, and the mother as creation.[23] Jesus emerges through the suffering pangs of a groaning world into the new life of the age to come.

Creation is in labor; Christ is born.

Historically, church architecture embraced this imagery. The baptismal font, for example, was frequently constructed as a womb. (This was where new believers were baptized, as a sign of their being raised with Christ.) Sometimes, the more explicit imagery of a vulva or vagina was used, from which the new believer emerged in baptism.[24]

Anglican priest Tish Harrison Warren humorously reflects, "I love to imagine that ancient Christians could say, 'Our pew is on the right, three rows behind the giant vagina.'" She goes on to observe, however, that such architecture is "pro-female and profoundly theological," demonstrating that:

> The female body was not (and is not) deemed dirty, unholy, or otherwise bad. The ancients apparently were not only comfortable with the reality of female anatomy but considered it sacred enough to actually fuse it with their very sacraments. The only way to enter the church family was through that particular vagina.[25]

The female body is iconic: It points to the maternal identity of the church, the life-giving power of the Spirit, and the hope of resurrection. For most of us, this is a radical notion. It dramatically undoes messages that can lead to bodily shame or objectification for so many women. We can find incredible freedom in the symbolism encoded in Christian theology and church history that is *so much better* and *so much bigger* than the cramped or exploitative narratives with which our dominant culture has denied the rich Christian message of worth and beauty regarding the female body.

And all of this, ultimately, is rooted in *God!* God's love is life-giving. It's generative. The Spirit delights to bring you forth as a child of God, making you a new creation. You might feel like you're dying inside, like the darkness around you is too strong. But God is a Giver of Life, whose resurrection power is available to you today. Look to the Spirit!

Giver of Life

Birth proclaims: God's endgame is not to get something from you, it's to give life to you. To wrap you into his family and share his life with you. All your activity *for* God flows out of this reality *from* God. You were made to belong, and ultimately to belong with God.

You don't need to strive to ascend from below; you were made to be born from above.

Birth is a sign embedded in the structure of creation, like the glory of sunrise. It's a sign of new life, like the fertility where water meets land. It points to something greater, like the transcendence where heaven and earth collide. It points to the life we were made for from above.

Birth is a sign of resurrection. It speaks to God's ability to bring you new life: to cleanse the cancer from your body and heal your broken bones. To cast the anxiety and depression from your troubled mind and restore your mental health. To set you free from your addiction and deliver you from your oppression. To mend your broken relationships and reunite your shattered family.

In God's kingdom, the question is not *if* you'll get healed but *when.*[26] Resurrection's coming. Sometimes, we get an advance foretaste of God's resurrection power, the "not yet" breaking into the "now." I've seen leukemia healed, multiple sclerosis cured, infertility overcome, mental health restored, and more. Really. No joke. Do I fully understand it? No. Can I promise it? No. But what I know is that Jesus is alive and exalted, powerful to bring such healing today. And even if we don't get the healing today—which is more common—these stories are still good news for us all, because they're signs of his coming kingdom.

In light of Christ's victory, the convulsions of our suffering world have become birth pangs on the precipice of our delivery into the kingdom.[27] Jesus has gone ahead of us as our forerunner, passing through the darkened vale of this world's travail into the light of new creation on the other side. In the light of his glory, we can glimpse a foreshadow of what we shall be when we emerge from the trembling world to join him.

When you're tempted to forget this, remember your baptism. This is where the waters broke, as Christ pulled you up into newness of life with him. "If anyone is in Christ, he is a new creation. The old has passed away; behold, the new has come."[28] That reality is true right now *within* you, and will be true one day *outside* you.

So when someone asks, "Where'd you get that Spirit within you, that insurmountable joy inside you, that powerful orientation to love?" you can tell them, "I was born this way."

Born again . . . from above.

So hold on to hope, even when times get tough. Your heavenly Father has conceived you in the womb of the old world, where we endure the labor pains of a groaning creation. Yet when the appointed time arrives, the mountains will bow down, the trees of the forests clap their hands, and the angels shout "Happy Mother's Day!" to the earth like a trumpet, when she delivers us as children into the embrace of our heavenly Father.

The Exodus as Childbirth

This New Testament imagery has an Old Testament backdrop. In the previous chapter, we saw the Exodus as a marriage story.

But it's also a birth story: the birth of God's firstborn son.[29] Abraham's seed has gone down into Egypt, growing large within the imperial womb. When the time for delivery has come, Israel emerges from Egypt's travail through darkness and water, as the sea parts like a birth canal to make way for their arrival. Theologians Alastair Roberts and Andrew Wilson describe the scene:

> Israel steps out from the womb through doorposts covered in blood . . . and later emerges into new life from a narrow passage through waters, which then close again behind them.[30]

Exodus is the birth of a nation.

The word *hardened* displays this birth imagery. Some people struggle with God's *hardening* of Pharaoh in Exodus, but it's helpful to recognize there are actually three different Hebrew terms here that get translated into English as *hardened*, and each word has a different resonance within the surrounding Exodus story; one is of birth.[31] This word, *qashah*, means "severe, fierce, or stiffened," like intense labor pains. It shows up in an important earlier scene, when Rachel is giving birth to Benjamin.[32] Her labor pains are so *severe*, their intensity so *fierce*, the hardening upon her body so *stiffening*, that she dies during delivery. As Israel's final tribe emerges from her womb, his mother goes into the grave.

Similarly in the Exodus, God "hardens" Egypt with *severe* and *fierce* labor pangs, as the empire *stiffens* under the intensity of the plagues.[33] Abraham's seed has grown large within her belly, but when the time has come for their delivery, Pharaoh refuses to let God's people go.[34] God's firstborn son is denied exit from the imperial womb.[35] Egypt is a recalcitrant mother, refusing to give birth.

So God induces labor.

The *severe* plagues are like *fierce* labor pangs, and Egypt groans under their weight, *stiffening* under the intensity of her suffering, until—like Rachel—the last tribe emerges from her trembling womb, and she collapses in the wake, as the waters roll back shut. Egypt's labor is an apocalypse.

In the Romans 8 passage above—where all creation "groans"

in labor—Egypt has now "expanded" to become the world, marked by slavery, bondage, and death.[36] Yet God is out to deliver his children.

Israel's birth is a new creation. Imagery from Genesis 1 is used, as God separates light from dark between Israel and Egypt (like Day 1 of creation), then parts the waters of the Red Sea (like Day 2), then "dry ground" appears (like Day 3).[37] Israel follows the light, delivered through water, leaving the darkness behind while emerging out the other side.

Israel is born again.

After exiting the imperial womb, Israel is now like an infant in the wilderness, entirely dependent upon God's daily provision. God carries them "as a nurse carries an infant," we're told, and nurses them with "honey . . . , oil . . . , curds and milk."[38] Ezekiel saw this wilderness provision as parental care for a helpless newborn.[39] Jewish commentators associated the daily manna with breastmilk.[40] God sustained Israel with such maternal care until they were ready to enter the Promised Land.

This foreshadows gospel themes too. In the wilderness of this world, God sustains us with his Word and Spirit, to grow and mature us as we prepare to enter the Promised Land of his kingdom to reign with him forever.

Children of God

When my dad first held me, I peed in his face. I don't remember the incident, but it's become folklore in our family history. Word has it he laughed. It's the only time I can imagine (thankfully) that my father could ever have found joy in being urinated on. Parenting is—even in its more challenging moments—a joy.

Parenthood doesn't stop at birth. In many ways, the job has just begun. My wife and I had to learn to change diapers, snuggle our babies to sleep, and keep them fed multiple times a day. *They just let you take these little creatures home with no instruction manual?* many bewildered parents wonder upon leaving the hospital. Children must be nurtured and raised up to maturity as adults.

Procreation's iconic nature doesn't stop at birth either. The New Testament continues to use maternal imagery to describe the church's ministry and the work of the Spirit, to raise us up as daughters and sons of God.

Nursing (From Milk to Meat)

Basic teaching is nursing. "We were gentle among you," Paul reminds the Thessalonians of his early ministry with them, "like a nursing mother taking care of her own children."[41] The apostle is comfortable in his masculinity, describing baby believers as breastfeeding on his instruction. The Corinthians were similarly "infants in Christ" when he met them, so "I gave you milk, not solid food, for you were not yet ready for it."[42]

Before Ben Stiller introduced the "Manary Gland"—an attachable breast for dads to nurse their children—in the comedy film *Meet the Fockers*, the apostle Paul had baby Christians suckling upon his basic teaching until they grew mature enough to handle more advanced instruction.

God doesn't want us to stay on baby food forever, however. The author of Hebrews chastises those who've been Christians for years but are still sucking the Similac bottle:

> Though by this time you ought to be teachers, you need someone to teach you the elementary truths of God's word all over again. You need milk, not solid food! Anyone who lives on milk, being still an infant, is not acquainted with the teaching about righteousness. But solid food is for the mature, who by constant use have trained themselves to distinguish good from evil.[43]

Over time, he's saying, God wants to move you from Gerber to grown-up food, from Christianity 101 to the meatier matters of mature doctrine, until you can train yourself with the "solid food" of "teaching about righteousness." It's appropriate for a new Christian to need the mashed peas and carrots on a spoon ("Here comes the airplane!"), but to still be there ten years later is like a teenager nursing at his mother's breast.

What?! Hebrews is saying. *You still need breastmilk, not solid food?*

Notice, the goal of good teaching is not just head knowledge but wise living—to be able to "distinguish good from evil"—not just information but transformation. Like healthy nutrition, it should nurture our mind and nourish our heart to live for righteousness.

Some are drawn to junk food: teaching that tastes good going down (telling us what we want to hear) but can damage our long-term spiritual health. The irony is we'll use demanding regimes like keto or Whole30 to care for our bodies, while subsisting on the equivalent of Snickers and Ben & Jerry's for our souls.

Mother Church

The church has a maternal identity. The famous reformer John Calvin joined a long line of Christian teachers through history who celebrated the church who nourishes us at her breast, with a hope that cannot be found away from her bosom, because she exclusively—as the covenant bride—has been entrusted with this ministry:

> I shall start, then, with the church, into whose bosom God is pleased to gather his sons, not only that they may be nourished by her help and ministry as long as they are infants and children, but also that they may be guided by her motherly care until they mature and at last reach the goal of faith. . . .
>
> So that, for those to whom he is Father, the Church may also be Mother.[44]

Mother Church is entrusted with nurturing and raising up God's children in righteousness. This means abusive Christian leaders are like bad babysitters: neglecting, mistreating, or leading God's children astray. They need to be held accountable. This also means rotten teaching is like moldy food. Heresy is poison, and teachers are held to a higher account for what they feed God's children.[45]

But if you've endured bad leadership, Mother Church can nurse you back to health. In college, I came home after a wild season—a bit beat-up and bruised—and my mom gave me warm food to eat and space to rest. She spoke truth into my life and built me back up. The church is designed to do the same thing for you.

Maybe you've been hurt by the church. I know I've been. Jesus was too. The church can be a mess. It can be hard to trust again, and there's a good place for healthy boundaries and discernment when it comes to toxic leadership. But I've also found healing in the church and believe you can too. For she is the bearer of a beautiful glory. I've become convinced that Calvin was right: This hope cannot be found away from her bosom, for she is the covenant bride of Christ and mother to the children of God.

Maybe you're a bit beat-up and bruised. But like me in college, you can find rest and recovery in the Spirit-saturated bride of Jesus, who loves us sacrificially; nourishes and nurtures us through healthy instruction, counsel, and care; and provides a place of belonging in the family of God.

Maybe you've wandered far from the faith. Paul worries he "labored . . . in vain" over the Galatians, whose turning from Christ threw him "again in the anguish of childbirth until Christ is formed in you!"[46] That's a wild image! Mom has to take an ambulance back to the hospital because her child was crazy enough to crawl back inside. (It's Nicodemus's misconception come true.)

Yet Mother Church—like Paul—cares enough about you to go through labor all over again, if that's what it takes, to raise you up strong in Christ. Most mothers I know will do anything for their children. That's an iconic window into the Spirit of God, who empowers the church in her maternal ministry to build us up to maturity as daughters and sons.

Our Father

For those to whom the church is Mother, God is also Father.[47] "Our Father," Jesus teaches us to pray.[48] Notice, not *my* Father but *our* Father. Jesus does not simply call us into a one-on-one relationship with God but into a family ruled by grace: the "household of God."[49] We are *brothers* and *sisters*—such language saturates the New Testament—who are to treat an older man in the church "as you would a father, younger men as brothers, older women as mothers, and younger women as sisters."[50] When we're born into the kingdom, we become not only subjects or citizens but siblings.

We're family because we share God as Father.

The Father invites you into intimacy. "The only person who dares wake up a king at 3:00 AM for a glass of water is a child," pastor Tim Keller observes. "We have that kind of access."[51] That's the kind of intimacy you have. You can boldly approach the King of the universe, night or day, because you're his child.

"God sent the Spirit of his Son into our hearts," we're told in Galatians, "the Spirit who calls out, '*Abba*, Father.'"[52] *Abba* is a term of intimacy, like *Papa*. In Jesus's day, it was used only by family members. Neighbors and guests wouldn't call your dad *Abba*; only family would.[53] Some have mistakenly suggested it was like a toddler saying "Daddy" (I've heard adults do awkward baby-voice prayers based off this suggestion), but it was more like when my adult Korean friends call their dad *Appa*, a term of both endearment and respect, used by adults as well as children, but only by family.

Abba isn't childish, but it is childlike.

You're in the family, Paul's saying. What does it mean to be a member of God's family? Say the word *membership* today, and many think of Netflix or 24 Hour Fitness: a club that gives you benefits. All you gotta do is join and pay your dues. Churches can sound like just one more company peddling their wares for a fee.

Notice the difference, however, when we shift to being a *family* member. Family means you belong—warts and all. You're still stuck with that awkward uncle who says all the wrong things at Christmas dinner and your sister who still owes you money, because you're bound together by blood. The church is a family bound by blood—the blood of Christ—that draws us into the home of the Father.

We are "one body," with "many members."[54] (The body was ancient imagery for families and nations, sharing a common life and identity together, under one head.) The church is a family with Christ as head, where we work together—like eyes and arms, hands and ears—and none can say, "I have no need of you."[55] We all belong.

The church is a family, not a club.

God sent the Spirit of his Son into your heart, to make you family. Jesus shares his sonship with you! He brings you into the love he's had with his Father from all eternity. As deep calls out to deep, the Spirit's cry of love for the Father becomes our cry of love for the Father. The Divine Presence stirs up our foundational longings to find their ultimate fulfillment in God.

Salvation is Trinitarian. The Spirit *within* us unites us to the Son *before* us as children of the Father *over* us. We become "partakers of the divine nature," in Peter's words, participants in the eternal communion of God's love.[56] Not little independent deities but human children born of God. Jesus shares his Father with us, pouring his Spirit into us, bringing us into the triune family.

That's what it means to be born from above—the beginning of new life, growing into the family resemblance of our Father.

PART II
WHEN GOD
SAYS NO

Living with Intention and Integrity
When It's Not Easy

6

CIVIL WAR AMPUTEES

"It could be worse," Holly said, "at least we're not amputees in the Civil War." Newly married, my wife used to bust out this funny aphorism whenever hard times hit. I was intrigued as to where the random fascination with nineteenth-century veterans came from. Turns out, she did a grade-school research project on the Civil War and was shocked by the graphic detail of one image in particular: a soldier having his leg amputated . . . in an age before anesthetic.

The image stuck and somehow helped her put things in perspective when life got tough. She couldn't imagine anything more horrible than having a part of you cut off while you're awake and aware of it.

This unimaginably painful image is, shockingly, how Jesus describes divorce—like an amputation.

Before we dive in, a word to those who've been divorced or who have been intimately impacted by divorce. You could be worried the guilt trip is about to begin. *Uh oh, he's been pretty nice so far but*

now the hammer drops. No. I want to reassure you that Jesus is *for* you. Even if you were significantly responsible for the divorce, Jesus came not to condemn but to save, not to beat you up over your past but to fight for your future, not to imprison you in regret but to set you free for himself.[1] Divorce is not a dictator that can define your identity when Jesus is your deliverer who emancipates your destiny.

A broken marriage may be brutal, but Jesus is stronger.

Yet it is worth us asking, What makes divorce so painful? Research says that divorce is one of the most difficult experiences a person can endure. The Holmes-Rahe Stress Scale, used by the medical community, ranks divorce as more stressful than going to prison, battling cancer, or even the death of a close family member. It's ranked higher than moving homes, planning a wedding, or getting fired. In fact, the only life event that outranks divorce is the *death* of one's spouse.[2]

Divorce rates skyrocketed over the twentieth century.[3] Millions of marriages now fall apart, with many children growing up in split homes. I've journeyed with plenty of the walking wounded and seen firsthand that our domestic civil wars have come at a tremendous cost and left plenty of carnage on the ground.

So again, it is worth asking: What does this tell us about the nature and meaning of sex in the historic Christian understanding? I want to suggest here that the pain is embedded in something deeper than simply its impact on us. If marriage is iconic, could it be that divorce is so painful because it preaches a false gospel? Does it hurt so much because it speaks a lie about God?

Shattering the Icon

A group of lawyers surrounded Jesus in Matthew 19 to ask a question some people are still asking today. "Is it lawful for a man to divorce his wife for any and every reason?"[4] There's a backdrop to that phrase "any and every reason." A Jewish tradition had developed that allowed a man to divorce his wife for anything. *Burnt dinner?* Done. *Put on a few too many pounds?* It's over.

This was brutal for women. They were way more vulnerable in the ancient world and had much more to lose in a broken marriage. The tradition was demeaning and unfair, and so rightfully controversial even back then. You see, another Jewish tradition held a higher view of marriage that made it much more difficult to get a divorce. It was a hot topic.

So imagine the scene: the journalists and media pundits holding out microphones to see how the young messianic hopeful responds.

Back to the Beginning

Jesus starts by going back to creation:

> Haven't you read . . . that at the beginning the Creator "made them male and female," and said, "For this reason a man will leave his father and mother and be united to his wife, and the two will become one flesh"? So they are no longer two, but one flesh. Therefore what God has joined together, let no one separate.[5]

Notice two things. First, Jesus grounds his sex ethic in the structure of creation. Sound familiar? He refers to God as "the Creator," points back to what God did "at the beginning," then refers to both Genesis 1:27 ("made them male and female") and Genesis 2:24 ("the two will become one flesh"). Jesus sees Genesis as authoritative. I love how he chides his interrogators for not knowing their Scriptures ("Haven't you read?").

Jesus says marriage is more than simply a social construct; *it's a divine gift.*

Second, Jesus affirms sex as diversity-in-union. (Hang on to that idea for later.) He emphasizes both *diversity* ("male and female") and *union* ("one flesh"). Interestingly, Jesus only needs the "one flesh" bit to confront divorce, but he goes out of his way to include the diversity of "male and female" as integral to what marriage is.[6] These are the two who can become one.

The problem with divorce, Jesus goes on to explain, is that it violates the union side of the equation ("let no one separate"). Jesus says God has embedded something in the structure of creation that divorce renders asunder. It's serious business to try pulling it apart, because "God has joined [it] together." The gravity of divorce is not only what it does to us but to the creation God has made.

Divorce shatters the icon. It displays *the wrong thing.*

God abhors the death of a marriage because it takes this window into the hope of the world and cracks it at the center, turning the image of salvation into a fractured reflection of the fragmenting reality of sin. It tears the canvas of his prophetic painting right down the middle. The trauma is not only what it does to us but what it *says* about God—the message it implicitly speaks about the nature of creation and the heartbeat of our Creator. It is a witness to a world divided.

Kids often understand this better than their parents. When Mom and Dad talk about divorce, they can tend to focus on logistics: deciding who gets weekends and holidays, determining how to cover childcare and coordinate school drop-offs, finding the best counselor, and introducing constructive activities to rebuild normalcy. But children are more perceptive. They often reach for words to describe something deeper, something tumbling beneath the surface like Leviathan.

The union that brought them into existence is unstable, precarious, dissolving. Something foundational is crumbling in the ground beneath their feet, a rupture rippling through the rafters of the ceiling overhead, a crack fissuring through the heavenly skies as the universe unravels around them.

And they're right.

If marriage is an icon of creation, a stained glass window into the cathedral of the world, then divorce displays an architecture built for collapse, a universe where detachment, dissolution, and disintegration have the last word. A house divided against itself cannot stand, and a crumbling couple images the collapse of our cosmic home. It is a blueprint for a world where division has the final say, where togetherness yields to separation, communion gives way to isolation, and we wind up alone at the end.

Divorce is an icon of hell.

If the family is made in the image of the triune God (as we saw in chapter 3), divorce also preaches the abolition of the Almighty, the instability of our Maker, the rupturing of the Trinity. It depicts not only the breakdown of creation but the unraveling of the Creator. It depicts the victory of sin and the triumph of the fragmenting power of evil, as the devil's disrupting dominion drives its way into the very heart of God.

Our salvation is insecure, divorce proclaims, for our union with Christ as his bride is on rocky footing. The wedding feast of the Lamb shall establish no final peace, we are told, for we live in a land where division has the final say. Divorce is a liar who symbolizes the greatest of horrors—the defeat of the gospel and the destruction of God.

Wedding as Welding

Jesus says *God* is the one who unites a couple ("what God has joined together"). This confronts the way we tend to think about marriage. *We're* the ones who reserve the ballroom, hire the caterer, pay the photographer, and pick the flowers. *We're* the ones who say the vows and consummate the marriage in the honeymoon suite that night. What does God have to do with it?

Yet God is actually at work in all this, Jesus says. He's the One who binds a couple, taking the two and making them one.

I've officiated a lot of weddings, and I often tell the lovebirds I'm merely a placeholder standing before them at the altar. Yes, I make the classic pronouncement: "By the power vested in me I now pronounce you husband and wife." But the power vested in me comes from above. I'm simply a representative signifying a greater reality: The Creator of the universe is the One who ultimately binds your lives, consecrates your commitment, and solemnizes your union.

God is the officiant at your wedding. Just as he brought man and woman together in the beginning, he brings us together now. The effect is true union. ("So they are no longer two," Jesus says, "but one flesh.") Like welding, God takes two pieces of iron and forges them in the fire through the furnace of his love. Once joined, they are no longer easily separated as two independent components. Rather, they are transformed through the merger of their material elements. You can no longer simply pull the pieces back apart without rupturing them; their existence has become intertwined on an existential level. Marriage is the furnace in which a couple's lives are fused together.

A wedding is a welding.

Many in our culture do not share this conception of marriage. When legendary actress Gwyneth Paltrow announced the end of her marriage to Chris Martin, the lead singer of Coldplay, she infamously described it as a "conscious uncoupling" rather than a divorce. One can empathize with what she was trying to say: They would not treat each other with cruelty and vitriol or demonize each other to their kids, as so often sadly happens. That's admirable, of course. Yet doesn't it seem there's a naïveté or denial held in the casual nature of that phrase? *Uncoupling*.

She contended divorce did not have to be a heartbreaking and damaging process, so long as you treated your former partner with dignity and respect. A marriage is not like IKEA furniture, however, that can be gently disassembled if handled with care. We can't just say, "The components will be okay if we just unscrew them carefully!" That isn't how welding works, or weddings, for that matter.

Jesus confronts misconceptions about the nature of marriage, saying the union is real—and therefore the shattering is too.

Marriage unites a couple's lives physically, emotionally, financially, generationally, and more. You're not the same person you came in as. You grow together, grieve together, build together, struggle together, and prevail together, in the context of one of the biggest promises you can make to another person. "You are no longer two," Jesus tells us, "but one."

It's laudable to treat an ex with dignity. But you can't so easily pull apart what God has joined together. Indeed, Paltrow looked back years later to acknowledge that, despite their best efforts, her divorce was the most difficult experience she ever endured.[7] The "uncoupling" was . . . something more. Jesus was right: Divorce is less like a conscious uncoupling and more like a Civil War amputation, where, through hostile internal conflict, a one-flesh union is severed into separated members. And all without anesthetic.

Unbreakable Love

You were made for a love that is unbreakable. Jesus will never leave or forsake you. That's what marriage points to. Divorce is tragic, in part, because it breaks this image of divine love that marriage was meant to display.

Maybe you've had friends walk out on you or people take advantage of you. Maybe you feel like the world has left you isolated and alone. Well, I've got good news: Jesus will never do that. When you say yes to him, his union with you is secure. He's not going anywhere. He will never belittle or betray you but rather will lift you up and embrace you as his beloved forever.

Even if divorce breaks the sign, the reality it points to is safe. Christ's union with his church is unbreakable. Heaven and earth will be united forever, and nothing—no conflict or war—shall ever tear them apart. However much the world may crumble, your future with Christ is secure.

Why God Hates Divorce

This helps explain why God hates divorce; it's because he loves the world. God famously says in Malachi, "I hate divorce." (It's important to note: God doesn't say he hates divorced people, but he does say he hates divorce.) Why does God stand so strongly against this calamity? He goes on to explain: because the person at fault "does violence to the one he should protect."[8] This is the language of injustice. God describes divorce here as violence. Those are strong words.

You were supposed to "protect" your spouse; instead you hurt them. In Hebrew, the phrase literally means "to cover with cruelty" (*wekissah al hamas*).[9] You removed the down comforter from the bed you once shared and covered them instead with cruelty. You might not be *physically* violent to your spouse, but when you break the covenant you violate them as a person and vandalize the integrity of your union.

Divorce is unjust.

Now, every couple is a two-way street, and most marital problems have some share of blame on both sides. Yet generally, divorce is more painful to the one deserted. It's easier to leave than to be left. More fun to take the money and run than to remain behind holding the empty bag. A husband who bails on his family can be having a blast with his new fling on the beaches of Cancun, while his wife makes beds and lunches for their children and tries to make ends meet all alone.

Speaking of kids, children are particularly vulnerable in divorce. Study after study confirms the weight of the blow. On average, when children's parents split, their grades suffer, behaviors worsen, and they're less likely to graduate from high school. They get sick more often and recover more slowly. Children of divorce are more likely to get addicted, go to jail, endure child abuse, or descend into poverty. Later in life, they tend to have a harder time maintaining stable relationships and are themselves significantly more likely to divorce.[10]

Now, God's grace is big and can bring healing and restoration. These are averages, not unavoidable fates. But when the foundations are shattered, children often suffer the most.

It's interesting that, just after Jesus's teaching on divorce, he famously welcomes the children to come to him.[11] Everything in Matthew's gospel is orchestrated with care, and this famous scene's placement is intentional. The Savior who stands against divorce is the same Savior who welcomes the children caught in the crossfire to find comfort and care in his embrace.

There's a tragic irony to divorce: The one most at fault is often the one least affected, while those who often experience the greatest impact are those with the least control over the outcome. Yet the Judge of all the earth sees this injustice and will hold it to account. God cares about your actions because God cares about the spouse you betray and the children you leave behind.

God hates divorce because God loves people.

Good vs. Permissible

That's not to say divorce is never permissible. Jesus says there are circumstances where divorce is permissible. Many churches have used the three *A*'s for discerning when divorce might be legitimate: adultery, abandonment, and abuse.[12]

Does this mean if you experience one of the three *A*'s, you should immediately get a divorce? Not necessarily. A guy asked me once, "So you're saying if I have an affair, I can legitimately end my marriage?" Talk about missing the point. "No," I responded, "it means *she* can legitimately end your marriage."

I later learned the reason he wanted out was because he had secretly been having an affair for months. When his wife, Angela, found out, however, did this mean she should walk straight down to the courthouse and file the papers? Not necessarily.

Just because something's allowed, doesn't always mean it's the best.

Angela saw this as an opportunity to display the gospel, to reflect a God who relentlessly pursues his unfaithful and adulterous people. This didn't mean pretending the affair didn't happen or putting a quick-fix Band-Aid on the marriage to try and prematurely get things back to normal. No, reconciliation is a process. Angela boldly confronted the sin.

A healthy approach will involve lots of truth-telling to expose the horror of what's been done, with honesty about the hurt the affair inflicted, alongside lots of hard work by the offending party to deal with the underlying issues, and respect for boundaries while rebuilding trust. If they're truly repentant, they'll be up for the challenge ahead.

But there's hope. I've walked with many who've pursued reconciliation as a way of displaying the redemptive love of Christ to one who's been disloyal to them in the most intimate way. Some of the couples I know who are the most head-over-heels in love today have endured infidelity in their past. They've experienced the power of Jesus to bring them through the valley of adultery's shadow, into the green pastures of mutual love on the other side.

And when it hasn't worked out, I've seen those who pursued an unfaithful spouse grow intensely in Christlikeness, shining radiantly with God's love even when their unrepentant spouse grew ever more hardened in darkness against them and against God.

There's a difference between something being *permissible*, and it being *good*. While Jesus says divorce is allowed in certain circumstances, and may at times be prudent, it's always a tragedy. Always. Even when it is the best thing in a bad situation. Nobody knows this better than the one who's been abused, abandoned, or betrayed—such a situation is horrible. Even when separation is the right move, divorce always sucks.

Jesus says divorce was allowed because of "hardness of heart."[13] God gave the permission slip, not because divorce is good but because people can be evil. If one of the three *A*'s has taken place, it means at least one person in the relationship has failed the other. God made an accommodation for human wickedness so the person being mistreated in their marriage would have recourse.

Yet, Jesus continues, "from the beginning it was not so." Jesus reminds us of the power of what's being broken, by drawing our attention back behind the letter of the law (in Deuteronomy) to the structure of creation (in Genesis). Jesus raises the bar, rather than lowers it, for those of us who follow him. The big question is more than what's lawful. It's what's loving.

He elevates the Christian sexual ethic to a high level. "If such is the case," his disciples say, "it is better not to marry."[14] "Yep," Jesus essentially responds. "It's a high bar."

Marriage transcends culture. Since Jesus roots his ethic in the structure of creation, his teachings go beyond Jewish law or practice to apply to us all. It's not the case that Jesus wanted to advocate for a different sex ethic but was stuck with the cultural customs of his time. No, Jesus unabashedly raises the bar in his time and in ours, basing his ideal not in an accommodation for Israel in the law but in a story for humanity in creation. We cannot pretend his purpose is anything less than universal, with implications for all of us from every nation who would follow him.

There is hope, however, for those who've been shattered by divorce—for Jesus himself was shattered to put us back together.

The Shattered One

Jesus bore the brunt of our Great Divorce. Whether in large ways or small, we've all "cheated" on the Faithful One, our revolt sparking a civil war in creation. This secession from the kingdom of God has rent the fabric of the human family, shattered the peaceful foundations of our terrestrial home, and separated us from the life-giving presence of God.

Yet Jesus was shattered to bring the human family back together. On the cross, the Faithful Groom was abused, abandoned, and betrayed for our sake. We covered him with cruelty and left him to die. Jesus came not only to raise the bar but to bear its weight on your behalf.

He bore our brutality to make us whole.

Jesus is the ultimate icon, who allowed himself to be thrown to the ground and shattered, that the civil war might be atoned for and our pieces put back together through the state of our union with him. Jesus was cut off, dismembered, and severed—without morphine—to put you back together.

Now Jesus is bringing the family back together—the human family of nations. He is restoring us not only *to* himself but to one another *through* himself. Our foundations are reestablished upon the solid bedrock of his glorious life. Jesus bore our division to restore our condition, receiving the brunt of the nations to heal creation. Our Redeemer reverses the curse and its brutal impact on all God's children, establishing peace for the household of God.

In risen glory, he delights to raise you with him. However broken your past, Jesus bends down on one knee and proposes you enter into union with him. He will never leave or forsake you. The glorious Groom lifts you up from your alienated estate to join his bride, filling you with his Spirit's indwelling presence, and welcoming you into the Father's expansive embrace, as he pulls the pieces of your rent humanity back into radiant union with God.

Jesus points back to creation to look forward to the kingdom. He reminds us where we've come from in order to fix our gaze on where we're going. For the hope of the coming kingdom is a destiny marked by faithful love, where we'll be united forever with the very life of God.

Rejoice, O bride of the King, for this union is unshakeable.

God's not going anywhere.

THE GREAT EXCHANGE

"I was ready to pull the trigger," Tony said, "when the phone rang." My friend had been on the verge of killing himself. Why? Let's back up a second.

Tony met God when he was four years old through the love of his mother. At the age of twelve, Tony realized he had a crush on one of his male friends. Over time, a mix of national culture wars, shock-jock radio, small-town prejudice, and some bad Christian teaching left Tony convinced he would lose those closest to him if they ever discovered his secret—same-sex attraction—and that God would have nothing to do with him.[1] And so, at sixteen, Tony had been sitting up sleepless at 3 A.M. holding a gun to his head.

There is arguably no conversation more controversial in the church today than the LGBTQ+ one, and many voices are holding megaphones. So before we dive in any further here, a few preliminary words are in order.

First, if you're gay, *you're loved*. Jesus is *for* you. His posture toward you is one of radical *embrace*. You are created in the image of God, with inherent dignity, value, and worth. You have gifts and talents unique to who you are, to contribute to the glory of God's kingdom and the flourishing of your neighbors. Jesus loves you extravagantly, and the Cross shows how far he's willing to go to be with you—all the way.

It's been heartbreaking to hear stories like Tony's from LGBTQ+ family and friends, stories of rotten treatment they've received, at times from the hands of self-professing Christians. Spat upon, called dehumanizing names, even kicked out of their homes. This is *not* the way of Jesus. If that's you, what you need to know is that you are not alone. That there's power in the arms of the Savior. That there are Christians who love you unconditionally. That before God, *you are not an issue to be solved but a person to be loved.*[2]

And if you're straight, don't hate. There's no place for cruelty in the kingdom, no venom in the Savior's veins. Jesus calls all of us who follow him to sacrificial love, to pick up our cross and lay down our lives for others—especially those who might disagree with us.[3] We are to be quick to listen and slow to speak, seeking not to burn people down with our words but to build them up.[4] Why? Because we follow a King who's done this for us.

When Tony's phone rang at 3 A.M., it was a friend who loved Tony and had been praying for him. He called to let Tony know God loved him, God saw him, God was for him. The caller was there to walk with Tony, to know his story, to be his friend. After putting the phone down, Tony had an encounter with Jesus that changed the course of his life, leading him to discover that God was more beautiful and restorative than he could have ever imagined.

Unraveling Creation

Friends like Tony have told me one of the most helpful things, when it comes to their sexuality, has been discovering the beauty of the Christian sexual ethic. How sex is designed to point to greater things. Not just rules and regulations for behavior but majesty and mystery for the heart. Not just what God says but how sex is designed to be a window into who God is and what God does.

With that in mind, let's look at the most famous passage in the Bible on gay sex.[5] Romans gives the longest discussion, with the most explicit detail, found anywhere in Scripture. While the passage is frequently discussed, what's often missed is how Paul grounds his argument in the structure of creation, against the backdrop of Genesis, with themes of diversity-in-union like we've seen throughout this book.

Diversity-in-union is central. If Jesus says the problem with divorce is that it violates the *union* side of the equation, Paul says the problem with gay sex is that it violates the *diversity* side of the equation. Like Jesus, he appeals to Genesis to make his case. Let's start with the verses in question, then zoom out to see how they fit within the larger context of Romans 1:

> Because of this, God gave [humanity] over to shameful lusts. Even their women exchanged natural sexual relations for unnatural ones. In the same way the men also abandoned natural relations with women and were inflamed with lust for one another. Men committed shameful acts with other men, and received in themselves the due penalty for their error.[6]

Okay. Straightforward. Women are rolling in the hay with women; men are hopping in the backseat with other men. Notice, however, the opening line: "Because of this . . ." Because of what? What's just happened earlier in the passage leading into this? Turns out, a lot.

Saturated in Creation

Romans 1 is saturated in creation imagery. We see this in three major ways. First, God is described as "the Creator," who has been revealing himself "since the creation of the world." Our problem, however, is that we have "worshiped and served the creature rather than the Creator."[7] Paul is clearly painting this picture upon the canvas of creation.

Second, Paul uses seven key words drawn directly from the first page of the Bible. When we compare Romans 1 to Genesis 1, notice the overlapping root terms that show up in both:

Then God said, "Let us make mankind [*anthropon*] in our image [*eikona*], in our likeness [*homoiosin*], so that they may rule over the fish in the sea and the birds [*peteinon*] in the sky, over the livestock and all the wild animals, and over all the reptiles [*herpeton*] that move along the ground."

So God created mankind [*anthropon*] in his own image . . . male [*arsen*] and female [*thelu*] he created them.[8]

They . . . exchanged the glory of the immortal God for images [*eikonos*] made in the likeness of [*homoiomati*] mortal mankind [*anthropou*] and birds [*peteinon*] and animals and reptiles [*herpeton*] . . . women [*theleiai*] exchanged natural sexual relations for unnatural ones . . . men [*arsenes*] also abandoned natural relations with women [*theleias*].[9]

Romans 1 echoes Genesis 1. This language is loaded. For Paul's readers, this would be like a politician saying, "I have a dream"—everybody's mind immediately turns to Martin Luther King, Jr.'s famous speech. The allusions are unavoidable; attentive readers of the Scriptures know what he's talking about.

Creation is the stage on which this dramatic saga is set, the height from which humanity is about to fall, launching our nose-dive from this exalted platform into the swirling depths below. Genesis 1 is the diving board; Romans 1 is the deep end of the pool.

Finally, there's Paul's use of the terms *natural* and *unnatural*.

The phrase here is *para physin*, which means, literally, "against nature." In the ancient world, this phrase meant one thing when talking about sex, and one thing alone: same-sex erotic behavior. There were different terms used for other sexual practices, like men sleeping with boys (*paiderastes*) or sexual immorality more generally (*porneia*). But when Jews, Greeks, or Romans used this term for sexual activity, they used it to highlight its same-sex nature.

Why was gay sex against nature? Different voices in the Greco-Roman world disagreed. Some emphasized the lack of sexual complementarity (the two bodies could not become integrally united as one). Others highlighted the inability to procreate (unlike couples who struggle with infertility, the very structure of same-sex relations was not oriented toward the possibility of children). Still others were concerned with the crossing of gender boundaries (turning a penetrated man into the "passive" partner, for example, who was entered into like a woman).[10]

What all these uses of the term had in common, however, was the underlying conviction that same-sex relations went against something in the design of nature. Whether or not Paul had all these specific arguments in mind, he is clearly referring to something within the structure of creation.[11]

This confronts a popular myth: that Paul was merely concerned with exploitative relationships, such as men with boys or masters with slaves. The text is pretty clear. Paul's use of the term "against nature" speaks here not to power dynamics in culture but design dynamics in creation. While of course exploitative sex is wrong, this, ultimately, isn't about that.

Some also claim Paul wrote from ignorance, because the ancient world didn't know anything about consensual same-sex relationships, only exploitative ones. This is a myth, however. Consensual same-sex relationships were well attested in the ancient world, even openly among emperors.[12] And Paul emphasizes the mutual desire of both participants here as willing partners.[13] He would have had plenty of terminology for rape or other abuse.

So, creation is the *backdrop* to Romans 1. What is the *structure* of the passage? That of exchange.

Making the Trade

Romans 1 is structured by three exchanges. Did you notice that word *exchange* earlier ("women *exchanged* natural sexual relations for unnatural ones")? That's actually the third time the word appears. The first two exchanges are ones we've made on God: Humanity has traded the glory of God for idols (verse 23) and the truth of God for a lie (verse 25).

It is here, on the heels of these first two exchanges, that the third arrives: Men were exchanged for women as sexual partners. Paul presents gay sex as a *horizontal* exchange that mirrors the greater *vertical* exchange we've made on God.

Three Exchanges
1. Glory of God for idols (verse 23)
2. Truth of God for a lie (verse 25)
3. Men for women as sexual partners (verse 26)

The first exchange echoes Genesis. Humanity "exchanged the glory of the immortal God for images in the likeness of mortal mankind and birds and animals and reptiles."[14] We were made to *image* God, to reflect his glory into creation (Genesis 1), yet we've swapped the Giver for the gifts, the Sustainer for the stuff he's freely lavished on us (Romans 1). We were made to rule *over* the creatures, stewarding the world God's made (Genesis 1), yet we've placed ourselves *under* the creatures, bowing down to images in their likeness (Romans 1).

The image bearers have become idol makers, Paul's saying.

The second exchange also echoes Genesis: We "exchanged the truth about God for a lie and worshiped and served the creature rather than the Creator."[15] Back in the garden, we took the serpent's shiny bait, swallowing his seduction hook, line, and sinker. We bought the devil's deception, took the tempter's temptation, and in so doing unleashed destruction into the fabric of God's good world, rupturing reality with our rebellion and tearing earth from heaven.

We've traded the Creator for creation, and it was a bad swap. We can thus think of these first two exchanges, together, as the Great Exchange: We've swapped the Giver for his gifts, God for the things of this world. This is the most significant trade, the initial break in the fabric that leads to the unraveling of all humanity that follows in the rest of the passage.

When it comes to the third exchange, it's worth asking: Why doesn't Paul use murder, rape, or greed as the illustration, rather than gay sex? Surely there are other sins more damaging, other acts that more strongly depict this disruption of humanity on a horizontal level. Was Paul just homophobic, obsessed with two dudes getting it on? No; there's a *logic* within the flow of the passage. Against the backdrop of Genesis, the third exchange is a symbol of something bigger.

An unraveling in the structure of creation.

Cracking the Icon

The climax of Genesis 1 is the classic "image of God" poem, where God *created us male and female in his own image.* The seven key hyperlink words Paul uses all come from this "image of God" section of Genesis 1. Paul zeroes in not only on the first page of the Bible but more specifically on the climactic place of humanity as image bearers within creation.

The three exchanges represent a breakdown in this epic poem, along both its vertical and horizontal axes. God above has been exchanged for things below, while men have been exchanged for women, side-to-side.

Paul uses gay sex here not because it's necessarily *more serious* than other sins but because it is a *poignant symbol* that illustrates something bigger.[16] This is vital to remember. Paul argues, throughout Romans, that all of us are on equal footing in regards to both sin and salvation. Against the backdrop of Genesis 1, his

point represents a breakdown in the structure of creation that
flows from our trading out on the Creator.

As the passage continues, this sets up the theme Paul will unpack more fully: the shattering of humanity by sin. Paul goes on
in the next few verses to lay out a laundry list of twenty-one
other sins (including murder, greed, rape . . . even talking smack
to your parents) that covers pretty much everyone.

The broader focus here is not on *some* people but *all* people, not
on homosexuality but humanity. This is clear from Paul's epic
conclusion: "All have sinned and fall short of the glory of God."[17]
That's the big picture of his argument.

Humanity is unraveling in our distance from God.

Some nuance. The emphasis here is *corporate*, not *individual*.
Paul is not saying, "Jimmy worshipped an idol, and now it turned
him gay." He's saying, rather, humanity traded out on God, and
now we're all unraveling in the process.

Also, the language used for these exchanges is plural and past
tense (*they did*), not singular and forward looking (*you should not
do*). While Paul clearly sees gay sex as outside the divine story of
sex, he's not writing *10 Rules for Life* to prescribe behavior but
rather narrating a collective history of the nations, under the conditions of sin, in which the third exchange is an illustration that
symbolizes his greater theme: We're all coming apart at the seams.

The exchanges of Romans 1 thus represent something tragic:
the cracking of the icon. Corporate humanity has been fractured
along both its vertical and horizontal axes. This disruption is
seen in the most deeply embedded diversities image-bearing humanity is designed to display: Creator and creation; male and female.

What does this mean for sex?

God Is Pro-Diversity

Sex embodies an iconic diversity that is central to God's heartbeat for the world. This includes both our sexual difference *as*
male and female, and the sexual union *of* male and female. The

biological reality of our anatomical particularity speaks, at a foundational level, to the diversity of our nature grounded in the structure of creation. Men and women are together an icon whose image-bearing bodies make a bold proclamation.

God is pro-diversity.

Rachel Gilson, a same-sex attracted author, puts it this way:

> God has designed sex to communicate about big, beautiful things. . . . God's sex ethic [isn't] primarily a bunch of "no's." God designed sex difference, and sexual union, for some very big "yes's". Yes to diversity. Yes to new life. . . . A marriage cannot rightly depict God's relationship with his people if it lacks faithfulness, or pleasure, or fruitfulness— or sex difference. The metaphor demands it.[18]

The problem with gay sex, according to Romans 1, is that it violates this diversity. When man exchanges woman for a male sexual partner or vice versa, diversity is traded for uniformity, complementarity for similarity. We replace a window into our biological counterpart with a reflection of our mirrored self.

And this is a symbol of something bigger. Same-sex sexual activity becomes a window into a world of same-with-same, rather than difference-in-harmony. Of earth above and earth below (which is a cave), rather than heaven above and earth below.[19] It is unable to bear witness to the beauty and life that mark night and day, land and sea, the complementary pairs of creation.

More significantly, it is unable to bear witness to the even greater diversity of Christ and church, the temple reality where divine and human come together. (The power of the gospel is that Christ is *not* like us, yet we are able to receive him.) Or of the Trinity, with Lover and Beloved as distinct persons in a life-giving communion-of-love.[20]

Gay sex is an icon of *anti-diversity*.

That may sound ironic at first, because when we talk about diversity today in the context of sex, we tend to think of diversity of *desire:* the unique tastes and preferences an individual might have for different types of sexual experiences and the gender or number of partners. So to speak of gay sex as anti-diverse can sound counterintuitive to modern ears.

But we are talking here about something much deeper and more concrete than our personal appetites. We are talking about a bodily diversity embedded in our blood and bones, what the philosophers might call an *ontological* diversity, a difference in our being through our particularity as sexually differentiated persons. We are talking about an order set in the fabric of creation, remember? Something able to point us to Someone larger than ourselves.

Humans are diverse in all sorts of ways, of course. Some people like spicy food, others mild. Some prefer rap, others country. Some love the outdoors, others are homebodies. We are diverse in the shades of our skin, all "precious . . . in his sight."[21] But when it comes to sex, Paul—like Jesus—draws our attention back to the most deeply rooted difference running biologically through the heart of our intertwined humanity: We are male and female. This diversity-in-union of sex is iconic. The Creator delights in the distinctions and differences of his creation.

He *delights* in you.

Another major challenge facing gay sex is that, when this difference is swapped for sameness, true unity cannot happen. The two cannot become one flesh. With the biological distinction erased, consummation in conjugal union is impossible.[22] It is not only the *diversity* side of the equation that suffers but the *union* side as well.

Is this just saying, "The parts don't fit"? No, it's saying, "They're not just parts." Our bodies are sacred. We are more than just souls that *have* bodies, we *are* bodies. We are embodied souls, and ensouled bodies. We are designed to be a temple—personally and corporately—our bodies a home for the indwelling presence of God, who delights in the diversity-in-union of his creation.

Our bodies are more than simply a vehicle for the satisfaction of desire, more than an appendage to our "true self" beneath. They *are* our *selves*, and they are iconic: designed to be a sacred signpost of a bigger story. If this sounds radical, especially in our culture, it is because it is radical.

With gay sex, the two's inability to become one flesh reflects something deeper: an inability to be a microcosm of the human social body, with its deeply rooted diversity of male and female. The two halves of the temple are unable to come together, as a tangible vehicle through which the life-giving presence of God can potentially bring new life into the world. They are unable to be a window into heaven and earth coming together, along with the other complementary pairs of nature.

Gay sex is unable to be an icon of creation.

If divorce preaches a world destined to fall apart, gay sex proclaims one that cannot come together. It is unable to participate in the icon, to bear witness to the holy realities it displays.

We would not be doing justice to Paul, however, if we stopped here. For the main point of this passage is not about homosexuality but humanity, not about *some* people but *all* people. So let's turn now to explore the significance of sexuality for Paul's main point: We're all in the same boat.

Aboard the *Titanic*

When people ask, "Do you think homosexuality is a sin?" (which as a pastor, I tend to get asked a lot), my first response is usually, "Well, I think *American* sexuality is sin." What we look to it for, how we approach it as a whole. From the proliferation of premarital sex to the prominence of adultery, from the skyrocketing rates of divorce to the ubiquity of pornography and hook-up culture, from the prevalence of sexual abuse to the plight of children in broken homes and the cries of the unborn we'll never hear.

Focusing only on gay sex is like focusing on a leaky faucet on the *Titanic:* Yes, there's water getting into the ship there, but American sexuality is the *Titanic.* We've got a breach in the hull, with water flooding in everywhere. Jesus pulls up in a rescue cruiser saying, "That ship is sinking, come over here with me."

The problem is *much* bigger than gay sex.

Getting What We Want
_____

We should all find ourselves in the sights of Romans 1. This is made clear by another feature of Paul's argument: The passage is structured not only by the three *exchanges* we looked at earlier but also by three *give-overs* that appear immediately after each of the exchanges. So there's a pattern here: We trade in on something God's given, then God hands us over to the impact of what we've chosen. Taken together, these three give-overs reveal something profound.

God's greatest judgment is often giving us what we want.

We Exchange	God Gives Over To
Glory for Idols	Impure Desire
Truth for a Lie	Shameful Lusts
Men for Women	Unapproved Mind (twenty-one examples)

The first give-over is "in the desires of their hearts to impurity."[23] That word *impurity* is associated with disease or contagion in the Bible.[24] We all have unhealthy desires—greed, rage, envy— that can unleash destruction in the community. We want distance from God, so God hands us over to our dirty desires with all their dangerous potential.

The second give-over is to "shameful lusts," a phrase with sexual connotations. *Heads up, straight people! Everyone is in view here.* If you're sleeping with your girlfriend, have cheated on your husband, or are addicted to porn—congratulations! You're part of Romans 1 too. These intimate lusts are lurking beneath the surface within us all.

The problem is rooted in *everyone*. Me. You. Them. Us.

The third and final give-over is to "an unapproved mind." There's a play on words here: The original language essentially reads, "Because they did *not approve* to retain God in their mind, God gave them over to an *unapproved* mind."[25] There's a symmetry between what we've chosen and what God hands us over to. You don't want to think about God? *Okay*, God says, *here you go!*

We're getting our wish, reaping what we've sown. And that is the point of all this. It's about sex. And it's about so much more.

What does this unapproved mind look like? Paul launches into a tirade of twenty-one dirty deeds, an all-encompassing barrage of naughtiness. I love Eugene Peterson's paraphrase, which captures the gist well:

> Since they didn't bother to acknowledge God, God quit bothering them and let them run loose. And then all hell broke loose: rampant evil, grabbing and grasping; vicious backstabbing. They made life hell on earth with their envy, wanton killing, bickering, and cheating. Look at them: mean-spirited, venomous, fork-tongued God-bashers. Bullies, swaggerers, insufferable windbags! They keep inventing new ways of wrecking lives. They ditch their parents when they get in the way. Stupid, slimy, cruel, cold-blooded. And it's not as if they don't know better. They know perfectly well they're spitting in God's face. And they don't care—worse, they hand out prizes to those who do the worst things best![26]

Sounds like an average day in America! Such things are not hard to find, whether in the heights of Washington, D.C., the halls of your local high school, or the daily parade of news on your Facebook feed.

More likely significant than the specifics of each naughty deed is their total number. Paul's laundry list includes twenty-one things (or seven times three), which is suggestive in Jewish literature of totality (where seven symbolizes completeness, and three wholeness). Paul is zooming the camera out, with this third and final give-over, to the widest possible lens. He's not giving a comprehensive list of every possible wicked deed but rather a symbolic display of the total brutality and extravagant depravity of humanity's shattering by sin.

We're all in the same boat together, Paul is saying.

And the boat is sinking.

An Aikido Move

Each give-over builds in intensity upon the previous one. The first involves *desire* (*epythumias*), a word which can be positive or negative depending on its context. The second increases to *lust* (*pathe*), a stronger word that always carries negative connotations in the original language. The third involves our *mind* (*nous*), which is more than just our brain but suggests something deep within our internal life, interwoven with the fabric of our humanity.[27]

The picture is one of humanity's affections being increasingly corrupted, enfolding us all within the wake. This is important to highlight, because it reiterates how gay sex is an important part of Paul's argument though not his main point. It is, rather, a symbolic display of something bigger that affects us all.

Paul is performing here what I like to think of as an aikido move. In aikido, a major strategy is using your partner's momentum against them. You get them charging, then leverage their own weight and strength to flip the tables on them. Paul similarly gets his audience's momentum going, with things his Jewish audience will surely find objectionable, like idolatry and sexual immorality.

You can imagine his listeners nodding their heads, "That's right, they *do* do those things." Then, once they're in motion, he swings their arm beneath his, receives their incoming weight, and effortlessly performs his aikido flip:

> You, therefore, have no excuse, you who pass judgment on someone else . . . you are condemning yourself, because you who pass judgment do the same things. . . . When you, a mere human being, pass judgment on them and yet do the same things, do you think you will escape God's judgment?[28]

This is huge. Paul's not singling out a few folks; he's doubling down on everyone—*including himself.*

All have sinned and fall short of the glory of God.[29]

This means if anyone is looking to Romans 1 for arrows to fire at LGBTQ+ folks, they should get ready to find its bullseye on their own chest. The whole purpose of the passage is not to *restrict* our sense of sin's impact on the world but to *expand* it. We're all in the crosshairs of critique here.

God loves us all, but we've all rebelled against God's love.

The good news is, Romans doesn't end here. The bar is raised not to shame you but to level the playing field and make way for grace. Sin runs deep, but grace runs deeper. Paul gets us charging to set up the glorious good news of what God's done for us in Christ. Because of Jesus, grace is available to all of us, there for the taking. When the aikido flip is finished, we're all lying on the mat defeated, staring at the ceiling, and in need of God's grace.

And God offers his hand to lift us back up.

The Same Boat

One evening, I went out with some guys from church. Talking about sexuality was not on the agenda, but the conversation soon turned there. Things got interesting quick. A friend confessed he'd recently developed a romantic attachment to a woman who was not his wife; he was worried it was about to turn into a full blown affair. Once this first domino tipped, the confessions around the table began to fall.

The next guy confessed he'd recently kissed a woman on a business trip; he needed to own up to it with his wife. Another had racked up over ten thousand dollars in credit card debt in online porn; he had yet to tell his fiancée. Another was unable to stop compulsively masturbating multiple times a day. Roughly half the men around the table were struggling with something significant and sexual in nature. And none of it involved attraction to the same sex. American sexuality, remember?

Sometimes I worry the LGBTQ+ conversation has consumed so much recent attention for churches that it can function as a distraction at best, or a scapegoat at worst, from the deeper depths of our dysfunction. It's an important topic, given the pastoral need to shepherd people well in our congregations who are navigating attraction to the same sex and to respond well to the cultural pressure of our moment and the confusion it generates for people.

Yet remember Tony? When he was twenty-three, married to the girl of his dreams and on staff at a church, his secret—same-sex attraction—came spilling out and he came close to losing it all. The lead pastor heard the rumor and called Tony into his office. "Is this true?" "Yes." "Pack up your office. You're fired."

Tony was devastated. With one painful and vulnerable admission of a fact, of a simple truth, he had lost his job and his community. This was wrong. He was living faithfully, needing friendship, community, and support. Everything Tony thought he knew about God was rattled, leading to arduous years of deconstruction.

Eventually, he would rediscover God in the beautiful mystery of the gospel, now seen with renewed faith. He's a leader I look up to and have learned much from.[30] But his tragic treatment was unnecessary. We have to do better. We *cannot* treat same-sex attraction as a "special," more serious, issue. This goes against the spirit of Romans 1; we're all in the same boat.

You need grace. We all do. You have corrupted desires; I do too. We all have "shameful lusts." All of us are invited to bring our brokenness to the only One whose sexuality is not broken, to find healing and restoration in his arms. This doesn't mean your sexual struggles or temptations will go away, but like my friend Tony, you can encounter a divine love that is stronger and more beautiful. And when God's kingdom comes in fullness, so too will the full healing of your body and your desires.

Tony now lives in the knowledge of God's love for him. He *knows* that God delights in him, in all the particularity of his story, fully aware of his attractions and inclinations . . . and seeing him as so much more. When God is the Lover of your soul, you have an affection more compelling and fulfilling than your sexual desires and temptations, whatever they may be. Rather than just "stuffing" your sexual desires, you can redirect them toward the Creator you were made for.

You can flourish without sex, in God's great love for you.

God is true beauty. Your longing for beauty is fulfilled in God. The things you might look for in the arms of another are ultimately found in your Savior's embrace. We need friends like Tony to remind us that the deepest fulfillment of our desires is found not in sex but in God.

God's goal is not just to give you rules and regulations to control your behavior but his presence to cultivate a worshipping heart. He can meet you and fill you with a presence greater than anything in all creation. So don't trade the Creator for creation; redirect your desires to the One they were made for.

Let your longing for beauty and acceptance drive you to long for him, the One in whom true beauty and belonging is found.

When I think back to that night with the guys around the table, we could all find ourselves somewhere within Romans 1. We've all participated in the Great Exchange, trading the Creator for creation at one level or another. And we all need the hope that God has brought in Christ, that can lift us up and restore us with the glory of God through an even greater exchange.

The Greater Exchange

Christ exchanged himself for us. Wherever you've been, whatever you've done, he gave himself over for you. Gay or straight, widowed or divorced, single or married, his arms were outstretched wide on the cross, where the vertical and horizontal come together, to welcome you into his embrace, to heal and restore you, and to bring back together what sin has fractured to make us whole once more.

This is the Greater Exchange.

Greater than our exchange of the Creator for creation is the Creator who entered his creation to exchange himself for us. Jesus laid down his life that we might live, and he brings the greatest diversity of divinity and humanity together in his person.

The Cross has often been called the Wondrous Exchange, where Christ takes the worst we've got to give and exchanges it for his best.[31] He takes our sin and gives us his righteousness, trades his obedience for our rebellion, swaps his perfection for our rejection. Jesus bears our poverty that in him we might become rich, tastes our evil that we might feast on his holiness, and receives the curse we've unleashed in order to bless and make us whole.

Greater than the diversity of male and female is the diversity of Christ and his church. Union with Christ is how we receive these benefits.

We may think movie portrayals of such love are cheesy, like that classic scene in *Titanic* when Leo and Kate are united at the helm of the ship, with arms stretched wide. But it's an image of solidarity, like Christ's identification with his church on the cross. And there's not a dry eye in the theater when Leo lays down his life for his beloved, lifting her up as the ship's going down, to save and restore her to wholeness again. Similarly, in the gospel, the Lover not only lays down his life for us as his beloved but is himself raised up from the icy waters, to be united in radiant life with us forever.

Jesus reveals that deeper than our revolt against God is God's revolutionary love for us. Jesus is famous for taking idol makers and restoring them as image bearers. Wherever we might be coming from, he invites us all to bring our unraveled lives and shattered pieces to him, allowing him to begin putting our pieces back together and restoring our beauty through union with him as King.

8

SEX ISN'T CHEAP

'm not too worried about a terrorist attack right now. I'm sitting in a coffee shop in Portland, Oregon, while writing this. My hometown's relatively small in population, influence, and wealth. On the national scene, we're small potatoes (sorry, Portland) . . . unless al-Qaeda's got a thing against hipsters. A major metropolis, like New York, Los Angeles, or Washington, D.C., is more likely to find itself in the crosshairs of a national enemy. Why? Valuable things are a target.

The more something's worth, the more tempting the hit. A mugger's more prone to attack a CEO with a Rolex than a homeless person with a shopping cart. My 1979 Pinto doesn't need a fancy alarm system, but your Lamborghini might. No art thief is going to break into my mom's house for my childhood watercolor paintings; you can find him outside the Louvre scheming and salivating for a shot at that Monet masterpiece.

God's enemy targets sex for a reason: its great value.

You have an enemy. He wants to distort your vision of sex and the message it carries. He wants you to think it's about selfishness rather than sacrifice, hedonism rather than *hesed*, fickle indulgence rather than faithful love. Because if he can, he can distort your vision of Christ.

A while back, we invited people to text in questions for a "Sex and Dating" event at our church. Only we made one big mistake: *We gave the wrong phone number!* It was only one digit off (our media person mistyped an "8" for a "9"), but "close" only works in horseshoes and hand grenades. One digit makes all the difference.

I imagine some poor guy on his living room couch, receiving dozens of incoming texts from random numbers with crazy sex questions: "Is masturbation a sin?" "How far is too far?" "What's the purpose of sex?" After the first one, he probably thought: *Wrong number.* Second: *What is going on?* Thirty texts later: *God, are you trying to tell me something?*

We got in touch with the guy to apologize, had a good laugh, and offered a gift card for his troubles. Once we got the number fixed though, you want to know the most frequent question that came in?

"What's wrong with premarital sex?"

Rule Keeping vs. Image Bearing

Sex outside of marriage is common. By age twenty, 75 percent of Americans have had premarital sex. By age forty-four, that number jumps to 95 percent.[1] The term *premarital* is perhaps a misnomer, as many of those hooking up have no plans of getting hitched. Are there good reasons to swim upstream against this powerful cultural tide? Does the gospel give us a more powerful motivation than simply keeping the rules?

The Sexual Prosperity Gospel

Let's first talk about purity culture. Many Christians flinch at talk of sexual purity today, because of a hangover from this recent evangelical movement. Purity culture emphasized saving sex for marriage, often holding out big promises that essentially said,

"Just wait till your wedding day, and God will bless you with a hot spouse, off-the-walls sex life, and picture-perfect family."

Journalist Katelyn Beaty helpfully refers to this as a "sexual prosperity gospel," a false teaching ensuring God's imminent reward for good behavior:

> The giveaway of any prosperity teaching is an "if/then" formula: If you do this, then you will get this. If you put a $100 bill in the offering plate, then you will get tenfold back. If you stay chaste now, then you will later be blessed by marriage and children.[2]

The problem is: God promised no such thing. Many who grew up in purity culture were let down when they did all the right things but their marriage still sucked. Or Prince Charming never came. Or they were sexually assaulted.

False expectations can lead to disappointment with God.

It's not hard to understand why youth pastors held out such promises. With the rising tide of sexual promiscuity and hook-up culture, it probably felt like a life preserver to help keep horny youth out of each other's pants. And there was some truth behind the promises: Research shows that chastity before marriage increases your odds of a lasting marriage,[3] and marriage itself has long been shown to make couples happier, healthier, wealthier, and longer lived than their peers.[4]

There's wisdom in preparing a good foundation for the future. Putting words in God's mouth, however, is always dangerous. Our Maker's not a widget machine: You can't put in x behavior and be assured to get y output. Living wisely today doesn't assure a perfect outcome tomorrow, any more than driving the speed limit means you'll never get in a car accident. These are averages, not promises—wisdom for living well, not witchcraft to manipulate the future.

Guidelines aren't guarantees, however wise some of them might be.

Consider the Wisdom Literature in the Bible. Proverbs provides guidelines for wise living that lead to good results when the moral order is working well. Ecclesiastes, in contrast, points to the tragic realities of our transient world that can hit even when you play by all the rules. Both books are true (even written by the same author, King Solomon, the wisest man who ever lived!). True wisdom holds both together.

Purity culture could also make those who messed up feel like "damaged goods," beyond repair, doomed to failure in any future relationship. This is a major problem, because it cuts against a culture of grace, pulsing with the heartbeat of Jesus. The gospel says that if you've crashed and burned in relationships, God's grace is big enough to cover your biggest mistakes and restore you back with him on the right track.

Here's the thing: The goal of sexual purity is not to *make* God love you; it's to *reflect* the purity of God's great love for you. It's not to manipulate God into giving you the spouse of your dreams but to reflect the beauty of the God who's given himself for you. The goal is not success; it's faithfulness. You may not get prosperity, but you can still live with integrity. The endgame is much deeper than rule keeping.

It's *image bearing.*

Reflecting the King

God invites us to move from rule keeping to image bearing. From simply jumping through the hoops to try and keep God happy, or to get a blessing, to rather seeking to be formed by his character and accurately bear his image to the world.

Now, image bearing doesn't mean the rules don't matter. I've heard many say, "There's no verse against premarital sex in the Bible," or "It's not that big of a deal." That's just not true. There are rules, and they're serious. The rules are there to protect the image.

The term "sexual immorality" (*porneia*) shows up all over the New Testament—and it's never good. What is *porneia*? Jews used this Greek term to summarize any form of sex that fell outside of

God's law.[5] These expectations are still in place for Christians today. Jesus gives severe warnings about sex outside of marriage, saying you're literally playing with fire.[6] The early church made clear that the Old Testament prohibitions on sexual immorality, like idolatry, were still relevant for New Testament Christians.[7]

So the next time someone says there's nothing in the Bible against hooking up with your girlfriend, ask 'em what they're smoking. Extramarital sex *clearly* breaks the rules.

Image bearing doesn't say "the rules don't matter." Rather, it says the rules are there to safeguard something deeper: the integrity of the image. And that image is you.

The icon gives us a deeper motivation for sexual faithfulness. While the rules make you aware of the boundaries at the edge, the icon invites you into the heart at the center. Give me a boundary, and I'll see how close I can get to the edge without breaking it. But give me a God to reflect, and I want to draw as close as I can to his beauty and goodness at the center—to experience a deeper union with him, and reflect him more accurately to the world.

Knowing *the image of God* is at stake—the deepest vocation you were made for, on page 1 of the Bible—can raise your stakes *higher* and motivate you *stronger*. But it also gives you deeper resources for sexual faithfulness, because it starts not with your behavior but with God's bold love. Like the moon receiving the light of the sun to reflect and display its glory, you soak in the warmth of Christ's love to reflect him to the world.

The rules might keep you from making some life-altering mistakes, but the icon can press you deeper into intimacy with Jesus.

Where's the Wedding?

We've looked a lot at the famous "wedding formula" from Genesis 2, but there's a curious question we haven't yet asked: "Where's the wedding?"

> For this reason a man will *leave* his father and mother and *cleave* to his wife, and the two will become one flesh.[8]

There are no vows, no rings put on fingers, no drunk uncle making that awkward toast at the reception. Couldn't this classic wedding formula be a little more explicit about, you know, the wedding?

The magic's actually in that "leave and cleave" phrase. It's covenant language.

God's people are called to "leave" all other gods and "cleave" in covenant to God alone. *Leave* (*azab*) is a strong word in Hebrew, that can literally mean "to forsake or abandon." When entering the covenant, Israel was called to abandon all other allegiances, forsaking all other gods, to ditch the idols in the dumpster and wrap her arms around God alone.[9]

Cleave (*dabaq*) is another covenant word, which means "to cling, hold fast, or be united to." God's people were regularly reminded to *cling* to God in the covenant, like a wife holding fast to her husband.[10] Israel committed in her covenant vows to "loving the LORD your God, walking in all his ways, and *holding fast* to him."[11] The covenant bond was to be marked by faithfulness, commitment, and permanence.

Inversely, God declared he would never "leave" or forsake his covenant bride.[12] God is always faithful, even when we're unfaithful. God clings to us in covenant. There's nothing you can do to make God break his promise to you. When you hold fast to him, you find he's already been holding on to you.

Okay, two observations. First, this wedding formula is iconic—*from the very beginning!* It's like the opening of a novel, when a theme is established that will develop and blossom as the story unfolds.[13] Genesis 2 is setting you up to understand God's covenant relationship with his people in the story that follows.

Marriage points to the life you were made for with God.

Second, the word order is significant. "Leave and cleave" comes before "one flesh." Covenant comes before consummation; commitment precedes copulation. The generosity and hospitality of sex are designed for the security of covenant. When God takes the two and makes them one, it's way more than their genitals he has in mind. The uniting of bodies was intended to be embedded within the uniting of lives.

So say "I do" *before* "Let's do it."

This is iconic. God commits to us before he unites with us—and calls us to do the same. Christ is not just out to *sleep* with his church but to *marry* his church! Wedding your spouse before bedding your spouse images God's covenantal love.

God's vision is for an all-of-life union, marked by faithfulness, commitment, and permanence. The problem with premarital sex is that it violates this covenantal love of God.

Premarital sex preaches a false gospel. It reflects a God who is not all in, who is not fully committed to us. It images a Christ who is unwilling or ashamed to proclaim his devotion to us before the watching world. It fails to reflect God's faithful, relentless, and enduring love, and the security of our life in his divine embrace. It's wrong not just because it breaks a rule but because it fails to accurately image God.

Again, the point of this divine decree is not to spoil your fun or make you feel bad about yourself. It's to help you participate in the great story of our Creator's own relational and self-giving life. Sex outside of marriage confuses or distorts that story. It warps our lived experience of the covenantal character of our King, corrupting the majesty the icon is meant to display. God's not holding out on you; he wants nothing to hold you back.[14]

Jesus is committed to us, and our love lives are meant to reflect that.

The "Leave and Cleave" Gospel

How did Jesus leave his father and mother and cleave to his bride? Ephesians 5 applies the *whole* wedding formula from Genesis 2 to Christ and the church: not just the "one flesh" portion but the "leave and cleave" portion as well. This is a powerful shorthand for the gospel.

Jesus left his Father's throne above to pursue his bride in faithful love. This is the Incarnation: The divine Son of God assumed the fullness of our humanity, taking upon himself our flesh and bone, setting out to find his bride in the distant land and make his home with us forever.

Jesus left his mother, Mary, at the cross, to consummate the covenant with his bride.[15] This is the crucifixion of Good Friday: Jesus uniting with us in the fullness of our condition—in sin, darkness, and death—to raise us with him forever. With his dying words, Jesus cries out, distant from the face of his Father, and departs from the presence of his mother.[16]

Jesus left his Father and mother to pursue his bride.

Jesus cleaves to us in death. On the eve of his crucifixion, he declared, "This is my blood of the covenant,"[17] identifying his death as that which will seal his covenant with us. This shows how far Jesus is willing to go to be with us—to hell and back—and how serious the depths of his commitment are, giving over his life for his beloved. Jesus commits himself to us for eternity through his death and resurrection.

Jesus commits to us, then unites with us. His final words upon the cross, as he prepares to give up his spirit and bow his head, are, "It is consummated."[18] Saint Augustine pictured it this way:

Like a bridegroom Christ went forth from his chamber. . . .
He came to the marriage-bed of the cross, and there in
mounting it, he consummated his marriage. And when he
perceived the sighs of the creature, he lovingly gave himself
up to the torment in place of his bride, and joined himself to
[her] forever.[19]

We are united through his death. This is the one-flesh moment that seals the covenant. This may sound spooky, but don't get creeped out—it's not necromancy. It's the deeper reality sex points to.

La petite mort ("the little death") is the famous French term for the orgasm—in which the lover gives of themselves so fully to the other that they must "let go," in a certain sense, of themselves on their own terms. The famous Renaissance poet John Donne likened sexual ecstasy to a love-death. Donne went so far as to say nothing was truly possible in love without a type of death, a giving over of the self to consummate union with the other.[20]

Jesus unites himself to us through his death and resurrection. On Good Friday, the glorious Groom clings to us as bride in the fullness of our condition. On Holy Saturday, we lie together that we might rise together, from the slumber of the grave. On Easter Sunday, we are like Sleeping Beauty, raised by the kiss of his presence that finds us in the darkness and breaks the long-standing spell. We awake to reign with him in his kingdom, happily ever after.

Cross and Resurrection.

Christ and church.

One flesh.

The early church fathers loved to observe how the whole Adam and Eve story of Genesis 2—not just the wedding formula—foreshadows the gospel.[21] Remember how God put Adam to sleep, pulled flesh and bone from his side, and formed Eve as his bride? Similarly at the cross, God puts his Son to sleep (a new and better Adam), pulls flesh and blood from his side (as the centurion's spear pierces his dead body), and builds us from this as his bride.

As the second-century theologian Tertullian put it:

Adam's sleep was [a type] of the death of Christ who had slept in death. Eve coming from Adam's side is a type of the Church, the true mother of all the living.[22]

The creation of Eve is a prophetic picture of the church. Like Eve from Adam, we are made *from* Christ and *for* Christ. Baptism proclaims we were united with him in his death to reign with him in resurrection. The Eucharist regularly reminds us it is his body that makes us a body, his blood that has made us his bride. We are bone of his bones and flesh of his flesh, one flesh with him, built from his body as his bride.

The risen Christ awakens to rejoice over us, like Adam rising from his sleep to celebrate Eve. Jesus's song echoes in our ears like the lyrics of that ancient poem:

> This at last is bone of my bones
>   and flesh of my flesh;
> she shall be called Church,
>   because she was taken out of Christ.

> We are called church for we are taken from Christ.
> "Leave and cleave" foreshadows the gospel.

Cheap Sex

But despite the highness of this calling, sex has become cheap. While promiscuity has been prominent throughout history (just read Chaucer or *The Decameron*), there's something unusually drained of any semblance of the sacred in our time. Though sometimes touted as "liberation," I would argue this is a smaller, more constricted, and less pleasurable vision of sex, not a bigger, freer, or more positive one.

Market Disruptors

Practically speaking, at least two market disruptors have "lowered the cost" of sex. First, porn. Today's high-resolution pornography is more realistic (a far cry from Grandpa's rumpled *Playboy*), more accessible (as close as the phone in your pocket), and more novel than ever (with an endless stream of genres that cater to every possible fantasy, and even a few impossible ones). All this has led to an epidemic of sexual addiction, rewiring the brains of an entire generation and deteriorating actual romantic relationships.[23]

The availability of porn drives down the cost of real sex in society because a cheap substitute is on offer that costs nothing (except one's long-term health and spiritual and mental wholeness).[24] You can satiate sexual desire with a virtual experience that simulates the real thing. Sort of, at least. You not only don't need to get married; you don't even need to put in a few dates. You can find release with the click of a button.

A second market disruptor, birth control. Modern contraception is an invention on the level of the printing press, and it has radically altered how we approach sex, romance, and marriage today. The Pill, IUDs, condoms, and more have essentially removed children from the equation. For the first time in history, couples can reliably make love without concern for making babies.

Sex has been severed from procreation; union divided from multiplication. You can hook up without the fear of getting knocked up. I'm not saying contraception is always off-limits; it can be used to wisely steward the size of your family.[25] But historically, part of the logic against premarital sex was the risk of getting pregnant. Reliable birth control, for better or worse, changed that risk.

Many assume the Sexual Revolution instigated the rise in premarital sex, as if a bunch of hippies chanting "free love" at Berkeley in the 1960s was the sudden catalyst that converted the mass public. But the ideological revolution rested on a technological foundation.[26]

Notice how these market disruptors sever sex from its natural relationships. Porn severs sex from the unitive dimension: its intimate relationship to another flesh-and-blood person (you can now "have sex" with someone who's not even in the room). Birth control severs sex from the procreative dimension: its organic relationship to children in the generation of life.

If sex is designed to form a communion of persons, then porn severs sex from the person of the spouse, and birth control from the person of the child. If the family is an icon of the Trinity (as we saw in chapter 3), then this disruption is actually a dismantling of the icon, a separating of beloved from lover and from the love that arises between them.

On a deeper level, we've severed sex from its most important relationship: the divine dimension. It's not only the relationship market that's been disrupted but God's iconic design. Sex is designed to display the character and purposes of God into the world. Sex has become cheap, because it no longer speaks to a greater reality in which we're found.

The triune reality of God.

You were made to belong, in a secure communion of persons. In Christ, you are the beloved of God. Jesus does not use you to pleasure himself from a distance, leaving you open to the exploitation of pornographers and the lusty gaze of others. No, Jesus commits himself to you and unites himself with you in the intimate security of sacrificial, faithful love.

Also in redemption, you are children of God. Your heavenly Father delights to share his life with you, to bring you forth in fruitful love. He does not begrudge your existence, does not see you as an inconvenience, does not ask you to perform to prove your worth before he'll embrace you. No, God's love is generative. He gives himself to you in life-giving, unbreakable love.

If sex is truly about greater things, like Christ and the church—and it is—this makes it invaluable. And priceless things are worth protecting.

Guard your vision of sex. Don't let the Enemy have this treasure God's given you. Hold on to it like it has holy value, for it does. This is for all of us. If you're celibate, your union with Christ can motivate your faithfulness and fulfill your longing. If you're married, it can carry you through rocky seasons with your spouse when you're tempted to look elsewhere.

God has invested sex and marriage with a meaning greater than all the money in the world, for it points to him. The goal of sexual faithfulness is not to make God love you; it's to reflect the faithfulness of God's great love for you.

It's bearing the divine image.

Extramarital sex images the Enemy. Satan abhors covenant; he lives for himself. He's not committed to you; he's out for his own interest. He'll use you to get what he can from you, then when he grows tired of you leave you in the dust.

God is committed to you. You can count on his love. Whether you're single or married, widowed, divorced, or celibate, your sexual faithfulness is a way to reflect his divine faithfulness. His love is, to quote *The Jesus Storybook Bible*, "a Never Stopping, Never Giving Up, Unbreaking, Always and Forever Love."[27] *That's* the kind of love marriage is designed to point to and sex find itself within. It's about so much more than rule keeping; it's about bearing the extravagant image of God.

It bears repeating: The goal of your sexual purity is not to make God love you but to reflect the purity of his great love for you. God wants something better for you, because God *is* something better for you. Turn from the ways of the Enemy and live in the light of God's love.

CHEATING ON GOD

"Can you come over?" Jessica asked. "Mark's been having an affair." Holly and I sped over right away. We found our friend sitting cross-legged on her front lawn, sobbing. She said she'd been there for hours, unable to move. She'd discovered texts that revealed the bitter truth: Her husband had been cheating on her for months with a woman from the office. The betrayal cut deeper than any pain she'd ever known. We sat, wrapped our arms around her, and wept with our friend.

The weeks and months to come would be a grueling journey of grief and tears, of confrontation and separation, of explaining to the children and figuring out the future. I've walked with many couples through the valley of infidelity's shadow and can say not many things in this world are worse.

Adultery is *brutal*.

The problem is not only what it does to your spouse, as horrible as that is, but what it says about God. Adultery images a God who is unfaithful—and that is simply not true. If premarital sex violates the covenantal nature of God's love (by refusing to enter covenant), adultery violates the faithful nature of God's love (by breaking the covenant one has entered).

It's a problem of image bearing. Infidelity infiltrates the icon, disfiguring and distorting the divine reflection of faithful love (*hesed*) at the heart of the One it was meant to represent. It cuts against the grain of the universe, reflecting a false god. It preaches a false gospel, betraying the divine character embedded in the icon of marriage.

To lie with another is to lie about God.

Corrupting the Covenant

The word *adultery* comes from a root that means "to alter or corrupt," and this is an apt description for the impact of an affair.[1] Adultery corrupts the covenant, altering the integrity of the relationship. It's thus no surprise that, when it comes to our relationship with God, the prophets' most popular picture for sin is adultery:

- "I have been grieved by their adulterous hearts, which have turned away from me," God confides in Ezekiel, sounding like a heartbroken husband, "and by their eyes, which have lusted after their idols."[2]
- "Like a woman unfaithful to her husband," God says through Jeremiah, "so you, Israel, have been unfaithful to me."[3]
- "You burn with lust among the oaks and under every spreading tree . . ." God says through Isaiah of child sacrifice. "Forsaking me, you uncovered your bed, you climbed into it and opened it wide."[4]
- "A spirit of prostitution leads them astray," Hosea laments of the people's idol worship. "They are unfaithful to their God."[5]

The list could go on. Worshipping other gods is more than a misdemeanor.

Idolatry is adultery.

Idolatry as Adultery

God uses pretty graphic imagery to describe humanity's cheating ways. Israel entered forbidden alliances with pagan nations, "whose genitals were like those of donkeys and whose emission was like that of horses."[6] This is shocking, bestial language: The idolatrous empires are like ejaculating stallions, corrupting the integrity of Yahweh's bride.

Israel "lusted after" Babylon, sending flirtatious signals until the empire "came to her, to the bed of love, and in their lust they defiled her."[7] "You longed for the lewdness of your youth," God says of her amorous advances with Egypt, "when in Egypt your bosom was caressed and your young breasts fondled."[8]

Similar language could be used today. When the church conforms to the idolatrous ideologies and wicked ways of the empires that surround us, when we abandon faithfulness to Christ for the cheap thrill of cultural assimilation, we are cheating on God.

Not only idolatry, but also injustice, is adultery. "How the faithful city has become a whore," Isaiah cries aloud about Jerusalem, "she who was full of justice! Righteousness lodged in her, but now murderers."[9] God's bridal city has become like Gotham—filled with bribery and corruption, violence and thieves—and the prophet denounces this as infidelity.

We are to be marked by justice and faithfulness.

God wants you to reflect the goodness of his character to the world, to shine as his beloved bride. When you and I persist in unrepentant sin, God depicts himself like Jessica sobbing on the front lawn. When we continually corrupt the covenant, he says he's heartbroken over our betrayal.

Have you ever experienced betrayal from a friend? Been stabbed in the back? It hurts. The closer the relationship, the deeper the wound. That's the sentiment your Creator wants you to tap into, to understand the weight of your infidelity against him.

When you think of sin, what image first comes to mind? I

think of *rebellion:* a political image that speaks to our insurgency against the rightful King of the earth. Or *disease:* a physical image where sin infects humanity like a virus, corrupting our condition and leading to death. One theologian chose *vandalism:* a social image, where wrongdoing attacks human flourishing and the public life of the world.[10]

All these images are true. Yet the Bible makes a different picture most prominent: adultery. More than any other image, infidelity is the most frequent depiction of sin. It's an intriguing image, for it speaks to a betrayal of trust—intimate and relational. It involves giving yourself to another, in departure from the One you were made for. While wickedness can take on many forms, and evil is ineffable and difficult to describe, at the core our crime is adultery.

Sin is cheating on God.

Stages of Grief

When Jessica uncovered the affair, she had to go through stages of grief. First, she practically wanted to *kill* Mark. The anger was intense. Her volume was *loud*—and appropriately so—in their conversations. He had wounded her so deeply; she needed him to know how badly it hurt, wanted to protect herself from the vulnerability of being hurt again, wanted to get through to him.

Next, she wanted to leave. He'd spoiled everything. Could she ever trust him again? Where would she go from here? What would this mean for their kids? Their finances? Their future? She needed space to sort through everything. It felt hopeless.

Then, eventually as time passed, like glimmers of light through dark storm clouds, she began to consider the possibility of staying. Was reconciliation possible? What would true repentance look like for him—not just words but actions? What would he need to do to rebuild trust in the months to come? What boundaries would she need in place in the meantime? Could her heart handle healing from a cut so deep?

Now, I'm not saying this is the only way to deal with infidelity on a practical level. Every couple must navigate their personal situation, and the factors can be complex. But in terms of her emotional journey, interestingly, God shows similar stages of grief. The famous incident of the golden calf (Exodus 32–34) is depicted as an affair on the honeymoon. It occurs just after the wedding on a mountain that we looked at in chapter 4. Israel has *just entered* covenant with God, just said yes to the wedding vows, committing to "no other gods." Then, as God's giving the blueprints for his home with his bride (the tabernacle), the Hebrew people melt down their gold into a cow and bow down to the ritzy bovine in a festival of idolatrous debauchery.

They're still on the honeymoon! It's as if God zipped down to the hotel bar for a bottle of champagne, then came back to the suite to find his new bride in bed with a bellhop. We can be so quick to betray God. The divine response is fascinating:

1. *I want to kill them!* (Exodus 32): God is angry.
2. *I'll just leave them!* (Exodus 33): God considers calling it quits and walking away from the whole thing.
3. *Okay, I'll forgive and go with them* (Exodus 34): God remembers the significance of his covenant, forgiving and going with them.

This looks *a lot* like the stages of grief I've seen Jessica and other friends go through (like, shockingly similar). It's as if God knows what our typical process is like—and legitimates it. It all highlights the importance of the relationship, the value, ultimately, of the union that's been violated.

God is jealous for his spouse. He wants all of us, not just part of us. The reason he tells us not to worship idols is "for I the Lord your God am a jealous God."[11] God's unwilling to share you with another. Moses goes so far as to connect jealousy to God's very identity: "Do not worship any other god, for the Lord, whose name is Jealous, is a jealous God."[12] *Whoa!* That's intense:

God's name is Jealous. Like that classic Gin Blossoms song, "Hey Jealousy." Jealousy is not just an attribute of God; it's an identity.

God's jealousy does not contradict his love; it flows from it. It's because God's crazy about you that he's unwilling to share you with the seductive lovers who will alienate you from him and lead you to destruction in the long run. It's because God's love is faithful that he desires our reciprocal faithfulness within the intimate security of covenant.

If you're married, it's appropriate for you to be jealous for your marriage. If you're single, it's right to get mad when you experience betrayal from a deep friend. It's godly to be angry when a covenant has been violated. Don't short-circuit or rush through this part of the process. Give yourself time to experience this range of emotions.

Hope in Betrayal

Hope is present, even in betrayal. Though God considers leaving in Exodus 33 (stage 2), he ultimately decides to stay in Exodus 34 (stage 3). The God of the gospel is the Faithful One who pursues an unfaithful spouse. Jesus has stuck with us as his adulterous bride.

The most beautiful picture of this in the Bible is the book of Hosea, where God calls his prophet to marry a prostitute. (*Hey Hosea, I've got someone I want you to meet . . . Surprise!*) Hosea marries Gomer, and no matter how many times she runs into the arms of other men, God has him pursue her and bring her back to himself.

What's God up to? Hosea's marriage is a prophetic picture, an icon of God's unrelenting commitment to us. God's the holy one; we're the harlot. God is faithful, even when we're unfaithful.

Maybe your marriage crashed and burned over mistakes you've made. Maybe you've lost friends you've wounded. Maybe you're racked by guilt and regret, with things you'd do anything to take back. The aftermath can feel like an arid wilderness of your own making.

If so, hear God's words in Hosea to you as his bride:

Therefore I am now going to allure her;
    I will lead her into the wilderness
    and speak tenderly to her.
There I will give her back her vineyards,
    and will make the Valley of Trouble a door of hope.
There she will respond as in the days of her youth,
    as in the day she came up out of Egypt.[13]

I love that image: The Valley of Trouble will become a door of hope. God can walk us through the valley of the shadow of the mess we made and bring us out the other side—as through a door—into lush vineyards. God can turn our deserts into gardens, where good things are restored in place of the barren wasteland of before.

God can take the wreckage of infidelity and turn it into a place where he speaks tenderly, drawing us to himself. God brought us "up out of Egypt" before, and he can do it again. He can bring you out of the captivity you brought in. He can romance you in the "wilderness," a place where everything else is stripped away except your utter dependence on him.

When God says, "she will respond," that word *respond* can also be translated *sing*. God can get us back to a place where we *sing* again. It may seem impossible now, but his grace can restore us, leading us to the joyous celebration of worship.

Confronting the Double Standard

Adultery reinforces the central theme of this book from one more angle: Sex and marriage are iconic of the life you were made for with God. The horizontal and vertical are intertwined. Cheating on your spouse is so bad, in part, because it distorts the divine reality marriage is meant to portray. It's not "just" a mistake. Things are shaken at their foundation by certain sins, and this is one of them. Yet redemption is real, and God is famous for taking cracked icons to restore them as full-throttled image bearers of his divine grace and love.

One of the things I love about the Old Testament is how God confronts the double standard. In ancient societies, husbands were often excused for being—or even *expected* to be—promiscuous. (*Boys will be boys!*) Wives, on the other hand, were held to stricter standards and severely chastised for cheating.

There was a logic to the double standard, even if it is unfair. Men couldn't get pregnant. But if another guy knocked up your wife, this could bring unwanted children into your lineage and jeopardize the stability of your family tree and the economics of the whole neighborhood. An invasion of her gynecology was a possible intrusion into your genealogy—and beyond.

For Israel, however, the core problem was rooted in something much deeper than an unwanted pregnancy. The foundational issue was an image-bearing one: God was in a covenant relationship with his people marked by loyal love. Unfaithfulness violated the divine character of *hesed* that marriage was meant to display.

God is a husband who doesn't cheat.

A Crime Against God

Ancient societies saw adultery as primarily a crime against the husband. Israel, in contrast, saw it as first and foremost a crime against God.

- Joseph resists the seductions of Potiphar's wife, exclaiming, "How then could I do such a wicked thing and *sin against God?*"[14]
- God warns King Abimelech not to sleep with Sarah, explaining, "It was I who kept you *from sinning against me.*"[15]
- When King David is exposed for violating Bathsheba and murdering her husband, Uriah, he cries out to God, "*Against you, you only*, have I sinned."[16] (Obviously, he sinned against Bathsheba and Uriah too; the point is the divine weight of his offense.) David's injustice against them was treason against God.

Notice: All three of these examples are men, and powerful men at that. The Bible is full of #MeToo-like confrontations—such as Judah the powerful patriarch exposed by Tamar as the scoundrel fooling around[17]—calling out mighty men for sexual indiscretion. Men in ancient Israel were to be held to a higher degree of responsibility than those of the surrounding nations.

Don't just take my word for it. Anthony Phillips, an Old Testament scholar, notes how "Israel's law of adultery rested on a distinctive principle found nowhere else in the ancient Near East," that adultery was "a crime [against God] and not just a civil offence."[18] The Bible's legal code stood out, Richard M. Davidson observes, "in treating adultery as primarily *a moral crime against God* and not merely a personal injury to the husband."[19] This allowed the Bible to do something distinct for women: critique the double standard.

Growing boys are admonished in Scripture: "A man who commits adultery has no sense; whoever does so destroys himself."[20] The cheater was considered a fool. "Can a man scoop fire into his lap without his clothes being burned? . . . So is he who sleeps with another man's wife; no one who touches her will go unpunished."[21] He should expect to be held to account. If a couple was caught in adultery, the consequences of the Law were to be applied to "both of them," not just the woman.[22]

Go God! Your Maker doesn't play favorites; he stands up for women. Jesus cares about the more vulnerable partner in the relationship. Maybe you find yourself vulnerable in a difficult relationship. It can feel like all the cards are stacked against you. But the Maker of the universe is on your side—and when he's got your back, who can ultimately stand against you?[23]

A power dynamic was also behind the double standard. Men generally wielded greater muscle mass (physical power), held the family checkbook (economic power), and schmoozed with the neighborhood movers and shakers (social power)—all on top of extra legal rights (judicial power).[24] If his wife mustered up the courage to confront his cheating, he could easily intimidate her to "put her in her place." Tragically, many women are still caught in adulterous or abusive relationships from similar power dynamics.

Against this backdrop, it is significant that God has *by far* the greater power in his relationship with us, yet he uses it to faithfully serve us rather than manipulate or exploit us. God is all-powerful, ever-present, and all-knowing—we are *way* more vulnerable in the relationship in every conceivable way—yet God uses his power to sacrificially care for us and lift us up.

If you've had people misuse their power against you, one reason this can be so devastating is it misrepresents God. It can distort your image of who God is. Jesus wants to heal your misconceptions. He laid down his life for you—the King of the universe, the most powerful being in all creation, taking the form of a slave and hanging upon a cross, revealing a beauty at the heart of the gospel.

God is the Faithful One.

Healing the Heart

God is out to restore those who've committed adultery too. Jay Stringer, a leading Christian therapist focused on sexual brokenness and addiction, observes how unwanted sexual behaviors—like porn and extramarital affairs—arise from deeper, unaddressed parts of our story: like rejection, trauma, and abandonment.[25] His groundbreaking research, with over 3,800 men and women, revealed that what we're looking for in sex is much more than sex. This means that, in order to find freedom, you need to encounter God in the unique reasons that bring you to sex in the first place.

Your sin is, strangely enough, an opportunity for curious self-reflection. *What's driving me to this behavior? What am I searching for when I knock on the door of this particular brothel?* If you listen to your struggles, they have much to teach you about the absence you're craving from the presence of God. They uncover an opportunity for faith, for trust, in God's gracious presence toward you.

I met with Mark, Jessica's husband, in the months after the affair. Through counseling and prayer, he began to realize how his actions related to deeper parts of his story: his childhood, where sexual prowess was a sign of what it meant to be a real man; his insecurities, where he found himself in midlife wondering whether he'd really accomplished anything worthwhile; and his wounds, where he wanted to feel desired by someone new with the rush of fresh emotions that entailed.

This by no means excused his behavior, but it helped him better understand the things he was seeking to fill in the wrong places. In a deeper sense, he realized that what he was really searching for was God. As Bruce Marshall, the old Scottish novelist, put it, "The young man who rings the bell at the brothel is unconsciously looking for God."[26]

God cares about the fullness of your story. He's not just out to control your behavior—sexual or otherwise—but to meet you in the deeper areas of your desire. He wants to cut your self-destructive actions off at the root, by planting his gracious presence in your heart.

God loves you. You can bring the *real* you to him, warts and all, with all your broken desires. God is faithful even when you've been unfaithful. He's for you and committed to you even if you've made mistakes, with a rock-solid commitment stronger than yours to him. His goal is to heal your heart.

Even if you've never had an affair, there are all sorts of ways you can cheat on God. Yet the good news of the gospel is that Jesus raises the bar not to condemn you but to reveal your need for grace. He replaces the double standard with his divine standard, in order to meet it himself on your behalf. He bore the weight of your offense on the cross, in order to set you free.

In the light of Christ, even our adultery reveals how deeply loved we are—and can send us back to the arms of our Lover.

Jessica eventually reconciled with Mark. She knew she had permission to leave the marriage, but she saw it as a unique opportunity to image God. God had pursued and forgiven her; this was a chance to pay it forward. Jessica was like Hosea, represent-

ing the God of the gospel: the Faithful One who pursues an unfaithful spouse. A choice like that is not best for everyone, but in
Jessica's case, the *choice* returned her agency and she was a prophetic picture of the love of Jesus, who has stuck with us, his
adulterous spouse.

It wasn't easy. Mark had to show true repentance, confessing
his sin before her and other close friends, ending the affair and
taking concrete steps to rebuild trust, taking practical steps like
giving full access to his phone and email to establish transpar-
ency, going to counseling to work through his junk, and respect-
ing her boundaries while they worked through everything to
rebuild from the rubble.

But today, they are happy. God has brought them back to a
place where they can sing again. Some of the most in-love couples I know have endured through the trenches of adultery to
come out the other side stronger than ever. Infidelity doesn't
have to have the last word, because in marriage as with God . . .

Redemption is *real.*

A Better Hosea

Jesus is a better Hosea, who relentlessly pursues us. It doesn't
matter how far gone we think we are. When we encounter the
unfailing love of God in Christ, life is transformed and restored.
Christ fulfills the promise of this ancient prophet, spoken so long
ago, that one day the King would renew the everlasting covenant
with his beloved:

"In that day," declares the LORD,
  "you will call me 'my husband';
  you will no longer call me 'my master.' . . .
I will take you as my wife forever;
  I will take you as my wife in righteousness and justice,
  in love and compassion.
I will take you as my wife in faithfulness,
  and you will know the LORD."[27]

Christ brings us to a place where we no longer call him "my master" but "my husband," where our relationship with him is no longer characterized by *duty* but rather by *devotion*, not by *obligation* but by *affection*. As the church you are his bride, whom he has taken as his wife forever, in a divine marriage characterized by faithful love.

You were made for God. He is the beauty you are looking for, the deeper source of fulfillment you are longing for. The solution to your insecurity is finding your security in his divine embrace. The healing for your wounds is found in his arms, where you are known as his beloved, called his own forever, sung over with holy affection, and invited into the reciprocal embrace of worship.

In Christ, you can encounter the One your restless heart was made to rest in.

He can teach your heart to beat again, can bring you from death to life. He can overcome your weak-willed and wandering lusts with a greater affection. The things you've lost can become the spaces in which you're found. His goal is not to snuff your desires but to reignite deeper desires within you, drawing you into the transcendent realities the signs were meant to point to all along.

You can become a picture of his faithfulness. A testament to divine love that brings beauty from the ashes. Like Jessica's tears on the front lawn that desolate afternoon, your sorrow can begin to water the wilderness to become a seedbed of renewal, where he draws you up away from the things that enslave you and into the abundance of life with him.

You can hear him sing over you once more, "You are my beloved, and I am yours."

Forever.

10

WELCOME THE CHILDREN

———————————

We got the call on a Tuesday. A newborn was waiting for us at the hospital. We had tried for more children after our daughter was born, but to no avail. So we decided to step into foster care, to become a temporary home for a child in need. As we held James in our arms, he quickly captured our heart. We were now his foster family. Little did we know that two years later he would become our son. That's the power of adoption.

Too many children today face abandonment, abuse, and neglect. Children are an icon of God's kingdom, we saw earlier, but the alternative kingdom of darkness tears too many children down through no fault of their own. Procreation speaks to the life-giving power of God, but the death-dealing power of the Enemy is at work too. We were made to belong in family, but too many children are isolated and alone. This is not the way it's supposed to be.

It's no surprise, then, that God is all about adoption. God is "a father to the fatherless," the psalmist sings, who "sets the lonely in families."[1] This means adoption is not just something God recommends; it's something God does. It's a window into his redemptive response to a fallen world.

Adopted in Christ

Adoption is an icon of the gospel. Check out this majestic doxology—a hymn of praise to God—that opens Paul's letter to the Ephesians, centered around our adoption in Christ:

> Praise be to the God and Father of our Lord Jesus Christ, who has blessed us in the heavenly realms with every spiritual blessing in Christ. For he chose us in him before the creation of the world to be holy and blameless in his sight. In love he predestined us for adoption to sonship through Jesus Christ, in accordance with his pleasure and will—to the praise of his glorious grace, which he has freely given us in the One he loves.[2]

Notice how God adopted us. He "chose" us. God was not forced to take you in: his heart not guilt-tripped by a social media campaign; his arm not twisted by an extended family member; his will not coerced by the Department of Human Services. No, God chose you because he wanted you.

Notice *when* God chose us: "before the creation of the world." God saw the train wreck coming and still planned to embrace you on the other side, to restore you by making you his own.

God did all this "in love." Our heavenly Father *delights* to bring you into his family. We are welcomed by divine affection, "in accordance with his pleasure and will"; it brings him *pleasure* to bring you home. When we enter his living room, he doesn't just give us the scrappy leftovers but rather flings open the fridge and blesses us "with every spiritual blessing in Christ." All that belongs to Jesus is now yours—you're now part of the family.

Our heavenly Father lavishes the best he's got to give. On *us*.

Adoption to Sonship

The phrase *adoption to sonship* is one word in Greek (*huiothesia*) that combines "son" (*huios*) with "to place, appoint, or establish" (*tithemi*). In other words, adoption involves *placing* a child in a family, *appointing* them as a daughter or son, and *establishing* them with permanence. This was a legal term in Roman culture, where adopted children held all the same rights as a biological heir.

That's what God has done for you. He's placed you in his family, appointed you his child, and established you with the same blessing and privileges of his only-begotten Son.

You are truly his kid.

Adopted children inherit the farm. In the ancient world, they were not second-class citizens but full-fledged members of the family. This is important to me, as an adoptive father, because it means my adopted son is not *partly* my son, not *halfway* my son, but *fully* my son. Any less would diminish the icon, corrupting our vision of the gospel. We are fully accepted in Christ.

If you've *been* adopted, you might question whether you're a legitimate part of your family. It's helpful to remember that Jesus was "adopted" too. Joseph was not his biological father (given the virgin birth), yet Joseph raised him as his own. Furthermore, Jesus *needed* Joseph to be his father—truly his father—in order to be the Messiah. The Messiah had to come from the line of David, in order to fulfill the promises.

Check this out: Jesus is the son of David *through the line of Joseph!*[3] Did you catch that? Even though Joseph is not his biological dad, the Gospels make clear it is because Jesus is "the son of Joseph" that he can truly be the Messiah. He's grafted into Joseph's family tree.

Adoption works. Your salvation depends on it. For all of us who are in Christ, you are truly a daughter or son of your heavenly Father, grafted into his family tree. You can take confidence in your identity, inclusion, and belonging. He has brought you in and established you, permanently, as his child.

There is nothing that can take away his love for you. No mistreatment from a parent, no lie from the Enemy, no power of hell, can separate you from your belonging in the family of God.

God's not out to simply make you a better citizen; he's out to make you family. "God sent his Son," Paul tells the Galatians, "that we might receive adoption to sonship."[4] The goal of the gospel is our adoption. Jesus was adopted by his earthly father, so that you and I could be adopted by his heavenly Father.

God sent his Son to make us sons and daughters.

Adoption vs. Birth

Adoption is different from biological birth, however. This difference is worth reflecting on.

Adoption is always a response to some kind of tragedy. *Always.* Is the adoption tragic? No! It's to be celebrated. But the circumstances that made it necessary always contain some difficulty or loss. The creational ideal is being raised by the parents whose union brought you into existence. The circumstances that create the need for adoption—whether abandonment, abuse, neglect, or the untimely death of a parent—are horrible. Adoption may be a *redemptive* response, but it is a response to a tragedy.

Does that mean this is a "second best" form of family? *Not even close.* But we need to be clear-eyed about it. Adoption means that there is—always—something extra that must be navigated in the relationships within the family.

This also means adoption is unique as an icon of redemption. While natural birth is embedded in the structure of creation, the need for adoption only arises because the world has been torn apart by sin. It is thus a window into the reality of the Fall. We are all orphaned, destitute, and alone—in one way or another—alienated from our existential belonging and transcendent purpose, in our broken world.

There are two lessons we can learn from adoption about our salvation. First, recognizing your tragic backstory gives you permission to grieve. As my son gets older, I fully expect he will have questions about where he came from. Indeed, at nine years old he already has. He will likely desire to try and connect more with his birth parents. Rather than being defensive (*He's not your dad! I'm your dad!*), my wife and I are committed to supporting him through this process.

Too often, adopted children are expected to pretend everything's great and just be glad they got a family. As Rev. Keith C. Griffith observes, "Adoption loss is the only trauma in the world where the victims are expected by the whole of society to be grateful."[5] Yet adopted children need permission to grieve.

Similarly, in our spiritual life, some Christians feel they just need to put a happy face on, spout some clichés, and polish their performance to prove to the world they're worth God's affection. But all of us have some form of tragedy in our backstory. We live in a fallen world. You've been through hell, literally. That pain doesn't just go away overnight. Growing accustomed to life in God's family is going to be a long road, a process. God welcomes all your emotions along the way. He's there to wipe your tears, hear your aches, and care for your heart.

A second lesson we can learn from adoption is that we all have sacred roots in creation that go deeper than the Fall. It's important to honor a child's biological parents, recognizing them as a sacred part of the child's story, to be treated with dignity and respect.[6] With adoption, it can be easy to demonize a birth parent when you witness the impact of their actions: the scars on a child's body, their whimpers as they dream in the night, the wounds in their heart. Yet that parent is still made in the image of God, and the child is still made in their image—as their flesh and bone, who came into the world through them.

How you talk about them matters.

Similarly, for all of us, our stories didn't start at the Fall. Your origins are in creation. Some Christians have too low a view of themselves, as despicable worms who accidentally slipped by God's radar on mistake. But God's story doesn't start with sin and rebellion, it starts with our creation in the image of God. You have dignity, value, and worth that nothing can take away. No matter how broken you are, there are deeper foundations in your bones sovereignly ordained by God.

You are not a mistake, no matter how many mistakes you've made.

Birth is in the order of *creation;* adoption is an icon of *redemp-*

tion.[7] It bears witness to God's redemptive response to our alienation under the tragic conditions of sin. We have been embraced in Christ, out from the wreckage of our war-torn world and into the arms of our heavenly Father.

A few years after our son's adoption was finalized, his birth mother got clean and sober. We have been greatly inspired by her; she worked hard to get healthy. We also worked hard to build a strong relationship with her, even in the earlier years when she was struggling. Eventually, I had the honor of officiating her wedding and providing premarital counseling. She now has more children of her own, and we consider them part of our extended family.

We *love* her.

She loves Jesus and walks with him too. The gospel is big enough not only for children who need adoption but for parents who need healing and restoration. In that respect, she and I are both in the same boat. We've both been welcomed into the family of God.

The Horror of Abortion

There is still one practical desecration of the icon left to discuss: the killing of the unborn.

When people ask whether I'm *pro-life* or *pro-choice*, I like to respond, "I'm pro-grace."[8] In our politicized culture, some can pit pro-life as being for the *baby* against pro-choice as being for the *woman*, yet the gospel is for both. Before we go any further, know this: If abortion is part of your story, Jesus is for you. The Son of God loves and gave his life for both. There is healing in his grace for both.

Yet this grace flows deep into a valley where even angels fear to tread. If children are an icon of the kingdom, then abortion represents the greatest tragic horror—the death of the new creation.

Becoming a Person

Imagine a terrorist attack wiped out the entire populations of New York, Los Angeles, and Chicago. Then add the other fifty largest cities of the United States. That's how many children have been aborted in America since 1973.[9] *Sixty million* people are missing, who would otherwise be walking our streets, contributing to our culture, and living alongside us as neighbors.

Yet are the unborn even people? Many object to referring to them as *persons*. This is the central philosophical question in the abortion debate. As Justice Harry Blackmun put it in the monumental *Roe v. Wade* decision,

> The word "person," as used in the Fourteenth Amendment, does not include the unborn. . . . If the suggestion of personhood is established . . . the fetus' right to life would then be guaranteed.[10]

What we call people matters, especially if we refuse to call them people. Dehumanizing speech can be a precursor to genocide. Nazi propaganda portrayed the Jewish people as vermin. The Tutsis of Rwanda were labeled "cockroaches" in preparation for their extermination. Studies have found that associating racial minorities or women with animals makes it easier for people to commit violence against them.[11]

Language matters.

The term *fetus* is technically accurate for the unborn (it literally means "offspring"), yet many in our society associate the term with a clump of tissue or inanimate cells, easy to discard.

It is easy to think of a fetus as a *thing* rather than a *person*.

It's worth recognizing that the New Testament uses the same word for a child *inside* the womb as *outside* of it. When Mary visits Elizabeth to celebrate their pregnancies, Elizabeth exclaims, "The baby [*brephos*] in my womb leaped for joy."[12] John the Baptist throws a party inside his mama's belly in the presence of Jesus the fetus. *Even the unborn can recognize Jesus and jump for joy!*

Shortly after, the author of this gospel, Luke, uses the same word to describe Jesus, now outside the womb, as "a baby [*brephos*] wrapped in swaddling cloths and lying in a manger."[13] Later again, Jesus famously welcomes the children [*brephos*] to come to him, describing the kingdom as belonging to "such as these."[14] Luke was a doctor—and he saw children as children. Whether jumping in mama's belly or bouncing on the Savior's knee.

So when does personhood begin? *Life* begins at conception; every serious scientist agrees with this. A new organism is formed when the male sperm combines with a female egg. This embryo has all the inherent potential to develop into a full-grown person. So the unborn are clearly *alive* and *human*.[15] The question is when they become a *person*.

Philosophers and legal theorists have proposed dozens of possible criteria for when personhood begins: when the fetus feels pain, or exhibits neural activity, or begins to communicate. Increasingly, influential thinkers are pushing the criteria even *past* birth. As Christian philosopher Nancy Pearcey observes, noting an argument advanced since the 1970s:

James Watson, co-discoverer of the DNA double helix, advocates waiting three days after a baby is born before deciding whether it should be allowed to live. The rationale is that some genetic defects are not detectable until after birth. His colleague Francis Crick agrees: "No newborn infant should be declared human until it has passed certain tests regarding its genetic endowment and if it fails these tests, it forfeits the right to life." Peter Singer [a leading Princeton bioethics philosopher] says even "a three-year-old is a gray case." After all, how much functioning does a toddler have?[16]

These are extreme examples. Yet they show such ideas being advocated not by crackpots in the basement but by influential leaders in the ivory tower. More so, they illuminate a trajectory underlying all abortion: personhood as a status to be achieved, rather than a gift to be received.

This provokes a deeper question, relevant to us all: Is our worth something to be earned by our accomplishments or received in love? Do we believe our existence is justified by works or grace?

Abortion is an icon of works religion.

An Icon of Works Religion

Abortion is a window into a world where one's existence must be justified by something you have done or become. Where your status as a person must be attained by your ability or achieved through your performance. You must prove to the world, *I deserve to be here.*

Whatever criterion one uses to establish personhood, the mere fact that criteria is now imposed means a revolutionary shift has been made from the icon. Our existence is no longer received as gift, springing forth from the union of our parents in love. Rather, we are a clump of cells that must strive to attain an identity on our own, to justify our existence through our internal resources. We must reach a certain bar to become worthy of welcome and acceptance.

This is a departure from a uniquely Christian conception (pun intended) of personhood. The early Christians were noted (and reviled) by the classical world, particularly the Romans, for their practice of rescuing and adopting unwanted babies who had been left to die of exposure, as was a common practice.[17] To welcome the difficulty of raising an abandoned child was a deep statement of value and love that was countercultural—and is, sadly, becoming so again.

The cultural mindset of "worth" behind abortion affects us all. It can be seen in the skyrocketing anxiety and depression of youth, clamoring on social media to stand out as unique, or prove you have a life worth living. It can be seen in the rat race and consumerism of modern society, striving to be secure, recognized, and affirmed at the mercy of a cutthroat world ready to drop the guillotine once you no longer make the cut.

Yet you were "fearfully and wonderfully made," the gospel whispers, before you ever gave your permission. You were "knitted . . . together in [your] mother's womb," when you'd done nothing to prove your worth. Even if a mother could forget her child, the Maker of the universe says, "I will not forget you! See, I have engraved you on the palms of my hands."[18] That's a powerful image: *carved into the palm of God's hand.*

God's got you as a tattoo.

If the family is an icon of the Trinity, then abortion depicts the killing of the Spirit—terminating his procession in the communion of God. If birth is an icon of salvation, then abortion represents a refusal of the renewal brought about by grace.

The devil hates grace. "You are of your father the devil," Jesus—grace incarnate—tells those who seek to kill him. "Who's your daddy?" Jesus is asking. "The heavenly Father who gives life to the world, or the ruler of this age who seeks to steal, kill, and destroy?"[19] The devil's a deadbeat dad: Once you become an inconvenience, he'll walk away. Or kill you. Abortion reflects his character, so if you look in the mirror and see the Enemy's features staring back at you, it might be time to ask the heavenly Father for an adoption.

Speak of the devil, Jesus's primary term for *hell*—*Gehenna*—was infamous for child sacrifice. It was a valley located just outside Jerusalem's walls. In the Old Testament, the people would walk outside the city, light the fires, and burn their children upon the altar, in worship to bloodthirsty gods.[20] The prophets railed on this horror. The valley came to symbolize the broader idolatry and injustice of God's people, representing just how far gone they'd become. If you could do that to a *child*, to *your* child, something had gone very wrong.

Yet the prophets held out hope. One day God would return to

establish his kingdom, justice would reign from Jerusalem, and the rebellion would be kicked outside the capital walls—back into *Gehenna*, where it came from. The insurgency's spiritual arson would be sent back where its destructive flame had first been unleashed—where the children had been killed.

Hell is an abortion clinic.

The Symbolic Order

Abortion violates a symbolic order. If the Spirit is the river of life, abortion is a slash-and-burn policy against the harvest emerging upon the banks of the kingdom. If union with Christ generates a new existence, abortion symbolically executes the fruit of salvation. If birth is an icon of our coming deliverance, abortion depicts the termination of a believer in the womb of the old world before our emergence into the light of new creation. The intentional termination of a pregnancy can shatter this icon of future hope.

Our annihilation is depicted in theirs.

Not everyone is happy with this symbolic order. In his book *No Future*, queer theorist Lee Edelman argues against such a future orientation for sexuality. He sees Christian social teaching and Western law using "the fascism of the baby's face" to uphold a whole moral order. We should reorder sex around the *present*, he argues, and resist any claim children would make upon the nature of our sexuality. Any time that moral order is invoked, Edelman rallies his followers to respond

> by saying explicitly what Law and the Pope and the whole of the Symbolic order for which they stand hear anyway in each and every expression or manifestation of queer sexuality: F— the social order and the Child in whose name we're collectively terrorized; f— Annie; f— the waif from *Les Mis*; f— the poor, innocent kid on the Net; f— Laws both with capital ls and small; f— the whole network of Symbolic relations and the future that serves as its prop.[21]

That's a lot of expletives. And anger. Directed at children.

Edelman says explicitly here what our culture practices implicitly: When life-giving love loses its outward-facing orientation toward children and the future, it curves inward in self-serving narcissism shut within the hedonistic confines of the present. What he says is a clear and consistent statement of values—horrible values. We exchange the welcome embrace of the newborn into our family for a string of expletives cursing their claim upon our existence.

Yet to my eyes, the very symbolic order Edelman finds so repulsive is shockingly beautiful. It is stunning, profound, glorious. Union gives birth to life. Far from "no future," we have a future. There is hope because our union with Christ shall defeat the death drive of sin, drawing us forward into God's future and carrying us across the threshold of his kingdom.

We shall emerge from the womb of this darkened world into the embrace of our heavenly Father, inhaling the fresh air of his new creation. God has given us a powerful symbol to represent all of this: the hope and newness of a baby's face.

New life. New creation.

Daughters and Sons

Adoption is one way to fight abortion. Bringing our chapter full circle, I love this quote by Mother Teresa. Imagine the scene: an elderly nun in Washington, D.C., hunched over a podium at the National Prayer Breakfast, standing before the president and American leaders in the halls of power, to speak about her work in Calcutta, India:

We are fighting abortion by adoption—by care of the mother and adoption for her baby. . . . Please don't kill the child. I want the child. Please give me the child. . . . We have saved over three thousand children from abortion. These children have brought such love and joy to their adopting parents and have grown up so full of love and joy.[22]

This is the voice of the family of God, welcoming at-risk children into loving arms. This is pro-grace, emphasizing care for the mother as well as the child. Women and children facing difficult circumstances should have a flood of support from their church and community.

Churches do help in all sorts of ways. Pregnancy resource centers across the country help women make an informed decision, while offering resources and support. Practicing Christians are more than twice as likely to adopt than the general population, and significantly more likely to foster.[23] More than 40 percent of churches provide support groups for adoptive and foster families, and many churches also support with household help, travel costs, and other financial support.[24] Such work embodies the heart of God.

Adoption is a picture of God's grace. It restores identity, security, and belonging. It's received as gift, not won by achievement. You were not made to work *for* love but *from* love. There's nothing you can do to earn God's love, yet God delights to give it. If abortion symbolizes works religion, adoption is an icon of grace.

This grace flows freely because, in a dark irony, the Son of God was murdered in the womb of the old world. The Cross is, from this angle, an abortion. The Father of Lies and Mother Earth's children conspired to put the righteous Son to death within her blood-soaked soil. "You killed the author of life," the gospel proclaims, "but God raised him from the dead."[25] Our heavenly Father endured the aborting of Jesus's life at our hands, yet raised him that such killing might no longer have the last word on his story—or on ours.

The good news of the gospel is that, no matter what you've done, God's grace is big enough to cover it. Jesus's victory is strong enough to wash away your most stubborn stains. Perhaps you feel guilty for a difficult decision you made in the past, perhaps even a terminated pregnancy. God's grace is big enough for this too. Through the power of the Cross, Jesus brings you acceptance rather than accusation, renewal in place of regret. His

Spirit washes you to walk in the light of new creation, clothed now in glory.

Our heavenly Father embraces you as his daughter or son and throws a party for you in his kingdom. We are each welcomed as his child.

PART III
A GREATER VISION

The Biblical Story of Our Beautiful Union—
and What It Leads Us to Discover

11

SPLITTING THE ADAM

So far, we've seen how God's vision for sex is beautiful, how the life of the Trinity is impressed upon ours, how despite the complexities of our fallen world we can still glimpse the profound *goodness* and *glory* of that design in our real daily lives. We've also looked at some of the most controversial difficulties surrounding sex, relating them to the icon to help us navigate them with love and integrity, in faithfulness to Jesus.

In this final section of the book, I want to lay a thicker theological foundation for the beautiful vision thus far. In many ways, we've saved the best for last. We're going to look at how the grand narrative of the Bible points us, through key passages and stories, to what the iconic vision—not only for sex but for all of life—has *always* been about: *beautiful union.*

And we're going to begin this book's ending all the way back at the beginning—with Adam.

Splitting an atom is one of the most powerful forces known to man. It's what makes nuclear energy tick and atomic bombs go *boom!* The alchemy works by chain reaction. Scientists shoot a neutron into the nucleus of an atom, which causes the atom to split off three of its own neutrons. These neutrons then fire into surrounding atoms, causing them to split off their own neutrons as well. The process is known as *fission:* if *fusion* binds two elements together, *fission* splits (or fissures) them apart. In the chain reaction that follows, the one splits into three, three splits to nine, nine to twenty-seven, twenty-seven to . . . and the results are explosive.

Let's look at an even more powerful chain reaction. Genesis 2 recounts the parsing of a different kind of "atom." (Pardon the dad joke; I come by it honestly.) While our modern atomic version can incite catastrophe, ending lives, tearing down buildings, and leading to generations of contamination and fallout, this ancient chain reaction works in the opposite direction: generating life and building up humanity like a temple, to be indwelt by the presence of the living God. And the primordial event that kicks off the whole process?

The splitting of the *Adam.*[1]

We're All Connected

God makes Adam and Eve differently—not just *anatomically* different but using a different *process.* Adam is made from the ground; Eve is made from Adam. Why the difference? Wouldn't it be easier to use the same construction method for both? The difference is actually significant.

Let's start with Adam. God first forms Adam's body, then fills it with his breath.

Then the LORD God formed a man [*adam*] from the dust of the ground [*adamah*] and breathed into his nostrils the breath of life, and the man became a living being.[2]

The Creator's bare hands burrow like bulldozers into the dirt, shoveling up soil like a child building sandcastles at the beach.

There's a primordial play on words here. The Hebrew word for "ground" is *adamah*. So, God forms *the adam* from *the adamah*. The earthling is made from the stuff of earth.

Adam's anatomy is sculpted like a Rodin masterpiece, his frame chiseled and carved. Yet his limbs lie limp and still, a lifeless body. So, like an EMT medic, God kneels down to give divine CPR, breathing "the breath of life" into his lungs. As Adam's body fills up like a balloon, his eyes blink open—awakening to behold the face of God.

Adam is an icon of heaven and earth. Body from below; breath from above. He is a living temple, made of soil and spirit, formed from creation and filled by Creator. Humans are "beloved dust," as my friend Jamin Goggin likes to say.[3] Our feet are firmly grounded in the humble soil from which we come, our head held high sustained by the dignifying wind of God's presence.

We are earthen clay animated by heavenly breath.

Adam has intimacy with God, communion with his presence. Yet there are no other humans. Adam is alive, but Adam is alone.

So God makes for him a bride.

Enter Eve. She is built from Adam. God causes the man to enter a "deep sleep," knocking him out with some celestial anesthesia in preparation for divine surgery. God then pulls flesh and bone from his side to construct the woman as a corresponding counterpart. They awaken to behold one another in joy. And the rest, as they say, is history. This part of the story reveals something profound.

We're all connected.

One Human Family

There is an organic unity to the human race. That's why it's significant that Eve is made from Adam, rather than made separately. The point has nothing to do with her value or importance (in fact Adam is fundamentally incomplete before Eve comes along. *Take that, men!*). It's so much bigger and more beautiful than that. The point is that from our foundational beginnings, our humanity is intertwined, our lives woven together.

After this origin story, every man will be pulled from a woman (his mother), and every woman originate from a man (her father). As the apostle Paul puts it in 1 Corinthians 11, "For as woman came from man, so also man is born of woman."[4] Men and women are made not only *for* one another but *from* one another.

The sexes are intertwined.

Every guy on earth spends his first nine months in Hotel Mama, receiving life from her umbilical cord and being built up by her body, until ready to burst forth from her womb into the world. Every girl is planted by the seed of Big Papa, originating from his existence and carrying his genetic quirks and filial features forward into the future. Woman comes from man; man comes through woman. We are all of Adam; all of Eve. *Every one of us.*[5]

What lesson does Paul glean from this? "Woman is not independent of man, nor is man independent of woman."[6] We are *inter*dependent—not independent—creatures. You need both sexes to exist, literally. Without your mom and dad, you wouldn't be here. We need each other. Our lives originate from prior union, emerging from the merger of the sexes. Your existence is bound up within the broader communion of our ancestral family tree.

Do you see yourself as intimately connected to your family, community—even the human race? Or do you see yourself as an isolated, autonomous, separate individual? You are not an island. You can say, alongside the poet John Donne, "I am involved in mankind."[7] This is biologically bound up in your very nature. You are not independent; you are interdependent. You were made *by* communion and *for* communion. Your existence is existentially intertwined with those around you, even unto the furthest ends of the earth.

"The whole tree is contained within the seed," the proverb goes, and all humanity is *in* Adam.[8] Adam is depicted here as the primordial seed, planted deep within our generational soil, whose substance will eventually give rise to an international family tree. Since Adam was crafted by the hands of the Creator, Paul is sure to emphasize our foundational source: "Everything comes from God."[9]

Adam, in the biblical imagination, is like an original batch of Play-Doh, from which Eve is first pulled as spouse, and then—through their diversity-in-union—all their children will arise. This Play-Doh expands and grows throughout history, our lives stretched and pulled from this original "source material" to arise into existence. Sex is the vehicle through which we spread.

So, this "splitting of the Adam" sparks a chain reaction: Eve is split from Adam, then their union splits out three, the three split out nine, the nine split out twenty-seven, and so on down the line. The chain reaction of humanity has begun.

Men Are from Fiji; Women Are from Hawaii?

Humanity shares a primordial union. Let's imagine an alternate creation story, to contrast more clearly what Genesis is saying. Imagine God made two separate individuals—we'll call them Jimmy and Jenny—on two separate islands. Jimmy he makes on Fiji; Jenny he makes on Hawaii. Jimmy he makes from tree bark and sand; Jenny he makes from grass and coconut shells. Different locations; different raw materials. Independent persons.

Eventually, God builds a canoe to carry them across the water. Jimmy and Jenny get introduced and fall in love. When they first meet, however, they have no common background, no shared history, no intrinsic connection or prior relation to one another. They are alien strangers, building bonds from scratch. This is the "Men are from Mars, women from Venus" trope (only here, men are from Fiji and women from Hawaii).

This would be a creation story of primordial individualism. Here, the individual exists independent of others, separate from community, with a completely autonomous starting point for identity and relationship. This would be a fitting creation story for American individualism, underscoring our culture's understanding of what it means to be a person.

Genesis, however, is a story of primordial union. We share a common origin. Adam rejoices over Eve, "This is now bone of my bones and flesh of my flesh."[10] He's essentially saying, "We're made of the same stuff, you and I, inside and out!" ("Bone" is a Hebrew way of summarizing the *interior* of the person, and "flesh" the *exterior* of the person.)[11] Adam recognizes their common substance of flesh and bone, sharing the same fibers of being and fabric of existence.

Too often, a theology of the sexes starts with our differences, the ways man and woman are distinct from each other. These differences are important, as we'll see below, but it's important to recognize that Scripture starts with our sameness. This is not Jimmy made of sand, and Jenny of grass. No, we are both made of flesh and bone, breath and blood. We are both *human*.

Adam's poem keeps going, to make the same point from another angle: "She shall be called 'woman' [*ishah*], for she was taken out of man [*ish*]." There's a play on words here. *Taking an ishah* is a common Old Testament phrase for "taking a wife" (the expression shows up nineteen other times in Genesis alone).[12] So the Adam and Eve story gives an ironic backdrop to the phrase, with the sense of: *The man will take a woman to himself, because the woman was taken from himself.*

We share not only one substance ("flesh and bone") but also one name ("*ish*"). The Hebrew word *ishah* contains within itself the root *ish* (similar to our English word *woman* containing the word *man*). Though men and women have differences, Genesis is saying, we share a foundational identity in our joint humanity.

Humanity is *one*.

Sex is iconic of this *unity* of the human race. Two-become-one is a window into the broader diversity-in-union of humanity, how we're all connected. Within the multicolored tapestry of the international social body, the threads of women and men interweave to mutually reinforce, beautifully build upon, and together compose the fabric of the whole.

This means that you are inextricably connected to an eighty-nine-year-old Chinese grandmother living in Beijing, to a twenty-four-year-old migrant worker in the fields of Nigeria, and to my daughter and sons here in Phoenix, Arizona. You are integrally connected to the human family tree through the sexual union of your ancestors who have brought you into existence. Fight it though you may, your origins betray your reality. You are part of the human communion. Our lives are all connected, across space and time, arising against a backdrop of union.

All humanity is related; we are flesh and blood. Men and women are, together, a window into the interdependent nature of the human family.

Sex is an icon of one family of humanity.

Together a Temple

There's a strange detail I passed over earlier. God builds Eve from one of Adam's ribs. Why a *rib*? My friend Savdy, a young Cambodian leader who really wants to find a wife, jokes about running around Phnom Penh calling out, "Who has my rib?!" It's a funny image, but is there significance to this particular body part?

The Hebrew word is *tsela*, and it simply means "side." It's an architectural word, used primarily for the side of buildings. (Think the "ribs" of the Taj Mahal, for example.) *Tsela* shows up over forty times in the Old Testament, and every other time it means "side"—not rib.[13]

So, why translate it rib? Probably because it's weird to envision God splicing Adam down the side like a cucumber. But let's see how the passage reads with "side":

> So the LORD God caused a deep sleep to fall upon the man, and while he slept took one of his *sides* and closed up its place with flesh. And the *side* that the LORD God had taken from the man he built into a woman and brought her to the man.[14]

The picture here is less like God pulling a brick out of one building to construct a whole new building around it with other outside materials, and more like God removing a wall from one side of a home to convert it into a duplex with mirroring sides. Eve doesn't just have a "little piece" of Adam buried somewhere deep within her foundation; she's formed *from* him, constructed with the same materials.

Adam recognizes this when he sees her, saying, "This is now bone of my bones and flesh of my flesh." She's made from his same stuff, sharing the same substance. They're compatibly crafted to stand side by side with each other.

A Holy Place

Now, here's where it gets really interesting. Guess where this word *tsela* primarily shows up? The temple. Virtually every other time *tsela* appears (like, 95 percent of the time), it's for the temple (or the tabernacle, which preceded the temple).[15] It's used to describe the two halves of the tabernacle and the architecture for the temple. It's also used to describe the holy things within the temple, such as the two sides of the ark of the covenant and the two halves of the altar. *Tsela* is a temple image; that's its dominant association.

Tsela is what my friend Tim Mackie from *Bible Project* calls a hyperlink word.[16] When you're reading online and double-click a hyperlink, it takes you to other articles that load the term with more meaning and background. Similarly, when you click on *tsela*, the hyperlink takes you to a flood of temple imagery, with literary threads and allusions that mutually reinforce and build upon one another.

So what's the significance? Adam and Eve are compatibly crafted as two halves of a temple. They, together, are a *holy place*. Sex is where they reunite as one. They become a vehicle for the life-giving presence of God.

This means sex is holy ground.

Are you treating sex with the respect it deserves, as something with sacred value? Or are you treating it as a personal plaything, to simply get what you can out of it? Has romance become a mirror that reflects back your own self-centeredness and vice? Or is it a window through which is visible the glory of God and goodness of his character?

Don't desecrate the icon. Treating sex too cavalierly is like taking a sledgehammer to the temple or bringing idols into its holy place. You might be tempted to think the goal of sex is nothing more than your personal pleasure, but God is calling you to approach it with reverence and awe, as a means of reflecting the beauty of his purposes for the world.

Sex is holy because it points to greater things. Our Creator has ordained this as sacred space—a sign of the intimacy and union you were made for with God.

This doesn't mean you need to be married to be holy. We saw above how Adam is designed as a temple, an icon of heaven and earth, all on his own. And we are all part of the corporate temple of humanity (whether or not you are a husband or wife, we are all someone's child).

Yet there is something holy about sexual union. God "splits" the human temple into two halves—man and woman—able to come back together. God "closed up the place with flesh," signifying Adam and Eve are each distinct people with their own personal identity—a mini-temple on their own. But they have a shared wall, so to speak, corresponding to one another in such a way that they can rejoin back together.

Man and woman are, not only individually but together, a temple.

Russian Dolls

Hold on to that temple theme. Over the next few chapters, we're going to see this theme expand. (*The temple is loaded with sexual associations!*) The temple was described with feminine features—*a giant Eve!*—and when the divine presence indwelt her, she made the land fruitful.[17]

Eve is similarly constructed as a holy place. God "builds" (*banah*)

Eve—whereas he "forms" (*yatsar*) Adam—a construction term used for the building of altars, cities, and the temple itself (all sacred sites in the ancient world).[18] Eve's name means "Life," and she's named this because she would become "the mother of all the living."[19] Like the temple, she bears life-giving presence to the world.

As we've seen, Eve receives Adam's indwelling presence and bears his life to the world (on a *horizontal* level), similar to how humanity is designed to receive God's indwelling presence and bear his divine life into the world (on a *vertical* level). Sex is sacred not only for its *unitive* ability to bring the two halves of the temple together but for its *procreative* potential to bear the life-giving presence of God into the world.

Sex thus points to the purpose of creation. The temple was a microcosm of creation, a "small-scale image of the entire universe," in the words of theologian G. K. Beale. It held rich symbolism of sky, land, and sea. At its center was garden imagery, reminiscent of Eden. It was a miniature model of the cosmos-in-harmony, where heaven and earth were most intimately connected as one.

Marriage is a mini-temple, itself a microcosm of creation. You know those Russian dolls, with a small doll inside a bigger version of the same doll, within an even bigger version of the same doll? Creation is the "big doll," which you open to discover the temple inside as a "medium doll," a smaller replica. When you open that "medium doll" of the temple, you find a husband and wife inside as an even smaller replica. They represent the world.

You were made for God. This temple theme points to God's purpose for you, and for all creation: to be filled with the indwelling presence of God and bear his life to the world. Even if you're single, marriage reveals the intimacy and covenant loyalty you were designed for with God, as a mini-temple displaying God's faithful love and fruitful presence in the earth.

You were made for beautiful union.

"Same Same but Different"

Adam and Eve are compatible but not identical. We've explored how they're the same (they're *human*). Let's look further at how they're different (as male and female). This is expressed in the word *suitable* (*kenegdo*) used multiple times in Genesis 2 for Eve: she's someone *suitable* for Adam.

What does suitable mean?

My grandmother used to always say, "Mejito" [a Spanish term of endearment], "we need to find someone *suitable* for you." She had a long list of criteria in mind: a college degree, respectable family background, and shared future goals. That's not at all, however, what Genesis is talking about.

The Hebrew word *kenegdo* is actually hard to translate into English. It's literally a combination of two smaller words: *ke* ("same as" or "like") and *neged* ("opposite of" or "against"). So the literal meaning is that Eve is both "the same as" Adam and "the opposite of" Adam. She is his synonym and his antonym, a counterpart who is both just like him and juxtaposed against him.

What in the world could that mean?

It reminds me of a popular phrase I've often seen when traveling in Cambodia: "Same Same but Different." This idiom shows up on bumper stickers and T-shirts and is sort of a national inside joke. In Khmer (the Cambodian language), the word *same same* actually means "different." So it's a play on words, combining associations of both sameness and difference.

The word *kenegdo* is doing something similar, telling us Eve is both *the same* as Adam, yet *different* from him. The surrounding story explains how.

Compatibility Test

God gives Adam a job: name the animals. The man has to decide what to call each of the critters. Now, was this just busywork? A zoological task to kill some time? No, the text hints God had a secret agenda in mind.[20] Imagine Adam watching a lion and lioness walk by: *How nice, they each have a pair!* Next, a doe and buck graze together: *Isn't that sweet? What a great couple.* Two gorillas share a banana: *How romantic! Wait a second . . .*

The epiphany kicks in: *What about me?*

Adam's awareness of his aloneness grows. All the animals have mates, but he's on his own. He's an isolated image bearer in the world. God puts words to the surfacing sensation and drops the bombshell: "It is not good for the man to be alone." *Boom!*

This was the secret agenda God had been planning all along. As my friend Hakeem likes to say, "God be sneaky like that!" Significantly, the "suitable" phrase sandwiches this scene. God gives Adam this errand just *after* declaring his need for someone suitable, and the scene wraps up with the observation that among the animals "no suitable helper was found."[21]

Adam's experience of his aloneness awoke an anticipation, built an appreciation, for who was about to arrive. It taught him an important lesson. We were made for relationship.

Important qualification: This doesn't mean you need to be married to experience deep relationships. Some of the loneliest people I know are married. Some single friends have richer relationships than spouses. In my college dorm, the loneliest people were often those sleeping around the most . . . with lives like a train wreck. You can be the best at sex and the worst at relationships, which (*surprise!*) actually means you're the worst at sex.

Adam wasn't just missing a lady friend; he was missing a *human.* Big picture: You were created for community, and community comes in all shapes and sizes.

Adam and Eve are, however, a particular *kind* of pair; they are sexually compatible. When Eve joins Adam on this pilot episode of *Animal Kingdom,* the surrounding story helps explain what *kenegdo* means. Eve is *the same* as Adam: She's a human being and not a cougar or a polar bear. Yet she is also *the opposite* of Adam: She's a woman and not a man. She stands shoulder to shoulder with him, as a coequal and complementary counterpart.

Preston Sprinkle, president of the Center for Faith, Sexuality, and Gender, helpfully summarizes the consensus of scholarship on this term:

> Eve is a human and not an animal, which is why she is *ke* ("like") Adam. But she's also a female and not a male, which is why she is different than Adam, or *neged* ("opposite him").[22]

Side note: This helps explain why bestiality's a bad idea. Ol' Bessie's not a "suitable" partner because she's not the same as you; she's not *human*. (Plus, it's not nice to your pets.)[23]

Adam and Eve's compatibility, however, means something more than they like each other's eHarmony profile (*We're so good together!*), or they share the same hobbies (*We both love hiking!*), or they're good for each other's financial future (*With our combined bank accounts, we could retire at forty!*). Rather, this passage speaks to something deeper and more primal: She's a female, he's a male.

They are sexually compatible.

Compatibility tests are popular, to discover whether that special someone's right for us. We want to know that our romantic crush is a good fit and won't be trouble down the road. This is good! I do a lot of premarital counseling and believe you should dig deep (*please!*) to discover whether someone's on the same trajectory with you before getting married.

It's worth observing, however, God's "compatibility test" here for that suitable someone is a lot simpler than ours. The Great Matchmaker's list is a lot shorter than my grandma's, with one major box to check.

The two can become one flesh.

Sex as Re-Union

Sex is more than simply a union, it is a *re*-union. It's a "getting the band back together," as the two sides of the icon—the corresponding halves of humanity—reunite as one. God's "splitting of the Adam" reveals an explosive backdrop to where the fireworks of sexual attraction come from. This creation story unveils why the sexes are drawn like magnets to each other. Why over half our pop songs are written about love, longing, or heartbreak. Why the highest-selling movies use romance to keep our eyes glued to the screen. Why we spend as much on weddings as on a college education.

It's because, Genesis would suggest, we came from union, and to union we long to return. As Old Testament scholar Gerhard von Rad points out, Genesis 2 provides an origin story for "the extremely powerful drive of the sexes to each other":

> Whence comes this love "strong as death" (Song of Solomon 8:6) and stronger than the tie to one's own parents, whence this inner clinging to each other, this drive toward each other which does not rest until it again becomes one flesh in the child? It comes from the fact that God took woman from man, and they actually were originally *one* flesh. Therefore, they must come together again, thus by destiny they belong to each other.[24]

We crave union because we came from union. Not only the union of our parents but, on a deeper level, we came from God. "Reunited and it feels so good," Peaches & Herb crooned in their classic 1970 song. And sex *can* feel good. Oxytocin is released into the bloodstream: the "love chemical" that promotes bonding and attachment with others, eases stress and heightens emotions, boosts generosity and solidifies social relationships. When diversity comes into union, it's pleasurable.

This hints that sexuality is about more than just sex. Our insatiable hunger for romance and connection, our irrepressible desire to transcend ourselves, the longing for ecstasy discovered in the embrace of the other, powerfully points to a deeper reality embedded in our humanity.

We were made for communion with God.

God's not shy about sex. After creating Eve, we're told he "brought her to the man." This phrase has sexual and marital connotations in Genesis: Rebekah is "brought . . . into" Isaac's tent to consummate the marriage; Leah is "brought . . . to" Jacob's tent on their wedding night to do the same.[25] God is the Great Matchmaker, who brings Eve unto Adam, so their diversity can be rejoined into union: to delight in one another and start a family together.

Do you wonder whether God feels skittish about sex? Whether he's bashful about your body, dismayed by your desire for intimacy and romance? *No!* God loves sex; he invented it. God created sex by his good pleasure, for our good pleasure. God designed sex to reveal his love in technicolor—his love for *you.*

You can have a sex-positive vision of your body and sexuality, without caving to the reductionistic visions of our culture (that may tout themselves as positive but end up becoming negative distortions of the icon in the long run). The love of God is the endgame of the icon, which you are invited to reflect in your embodied life.

God is pro-sex. He chose it as the providential instrument through which to create the human race. This instrument is part of a symphony that, when played properly, sings to his deeper heart for the world, belting out a melody that runs through the center of the universe . . .

God is love.

Genesis 2:24 (NASB) says it is "for this reason" (the Adam and Eve story) that couples get married and become one flesh. The author is saying this wasn't just a one-off event but a prototype for marriage. Adam and Eve's union becomes the basis for ours. The two can become one, because from one the two became. We all arose from our parents' union. Sex is a return to a type of center we've come from, a participation in the primordial pattern from which the miracle of our own existence has arisen in the world, a bouncing back upon the archetypal launchpad—*the trampoline!*—that first catapulted us out.

This diversity-in-union is, as we've seen throughout this book, a window into greater realities: creation, salvation, the Trinity, and the kingdom. This means sex is sacred. It involves the *uniting* of lives (as the two become one flesh), and the *generation* of life (as the vehicle through which flesh and blood is formed to fill the earth). The two-becoming-one is an icon of the broader diversity-in-union our world was made for.

Do you treat sex as holy? Do you see it as something sacred? You should, because this beautiful union unlocks the true purpose of the world: to be filled with the life-giving presence of God.

When a man leaves his father and mother to be united to his wife, he is departing from the union that brought him into existence, like a neutron being fired out of the atom he's called home. As he clings to his bride and the two become one flesh, the neutron penetrates an atom to form their own new unit. And this union has the potential to fire out additional neutrons of their own to continue the most powerful chain reaction the world has ever seen.

The explosion of humanity upon the earth.

12

TRIUNE SYMPHONY

Harmony is powerful. There's something mesmerizing when multiple voices and instruments are working together in unison. I play guitar and have loved writing music over the years. You can hear the grandeur of harmony in even just the simplicity of a chord.

For those unfamiliar, a chord is comprised of three notes (the root, third, and fifth) called a triad. These notes work in perfect harmony together. The chord is one: When I strum it on my guitar, you can't tell where the three notes end and the one chord begins. Yet it is also three: harmonically comprised of these particular notes, mutually constitutive of one another. Three notes; one chord. This triune structure forms a foundation upon which a symphony of sound can be built.

Harmony is diversity-in-union.

What if I told you humanity was, similarly, meant to be a triune symphony? To sing of God's love not only with our voices but through the very structure of our being? That while sin has introduced discord, God is the Master Conductor restoring the melody?

We've already seen that the family is an icon of the Trinity (remember chapter 3, with the African statue?). That's my favorite idea in this book: that sexual love, through both its *unitive* and *procreative* dimensions, gives us a window, in some mysterious sense, into the inner life of God.

Some may wonder, however, whether this idea is truly biblical. In this chapter, I'd like to develop a thicker theological foundation for it. Let's take Herman Bavinck as our tour guide, the nineteenth-century Reformed polymath, who poetically reflected on the triune structure of humanity in Genesis 1–2:

> God made the two out of one, so that he could then make the two into one, one soul and one flesh. . . . The two-in-oneness of husband and wife expands with a child into a three-in-oneness. Father, mother, and child are one soul and one flesh, expanding and unfolding the one image of God, united within threefold diversity and diverse within harmonic unity. . . . [This three-in-oneness] constitutes the foundation of all of civilized society. . . . Their unity [is] the threefold cord that binds together and sustains all relationships within human society.[1]

Harmonic unity; three in one. Don't worry if some of that flew overhead; we'll unpack it here piece by piece. Big picture: The family has a triune shape, the foundation upon which the symphony of humanity can be built.

The Family as Icon

When Bavinck says "God made the two out of one," he's referring to the Genesis 2 story we just looked at in the previous chapter, where God created Eve from Adam's side, as "bone of [his] bones and flesh of [his] flesh." They are two persons, sharing one substance. This is significant, as we've seen, because it means all humanity is one, sharing a primordial unity in Adam. We all proceed from our founding father, our substance originating like a tree from this singular seed. Or to use the musical analogy, Adam is like the root note, from which Eve proceeds as a complementary second note in harmony.

They are two; yet they are one.

God made the one into two, Bavinck continues, "so that he could then make the two into one." He's still riffing on Genesis 2, which says *this is why* man and woman are able to come back together as one flesh. The two can become one, since from one the two became. Man and woman are compatible counterparts, a complementary pair made with and for one another, able to reunite their diversity into union.

Husband and wife become "one soul and one flesh," Bavinck says. Now, Genesis doesn't use the phrase "one soul." This is Bavinck's way of affirming that sex is more than just skin-on-skin; it's the uniting of persons, the "mingling of souls" (to borrow a phrase from pastor Matt Chandler), designed for the covenant of marriage.[2] The term *one flesh*, however, *is* explicit in Genesis. As we've seen, it's more than just a cute metaphor; it refers to a true union God has joined together.

Husband and wife share a two-in-oneness.

This "two-in-oneness," Bavinck continues, "expands with a child into a three-in-oneness." Male and female can "be fruitful and multiply," Genesis 1:28 declares, the *unitive* aspect of sex generating its *procreative* dynamic. Children are the "flesh and bone" of their parents, in biblical idiom, generated by their existence, sharing in their nature, and reflecting their image into the world. They are a "third" person who is of "one" substance with their mother and father.

To continue the musical analogy, the child is like an additional third note who arises to join the harmony of her parents.

Now, Bavinck says the child is "one soul and one flesh" with their parents. His gist is right (he's speaking quick and loose about the "oneness" of the family), but his language is sloppy. Let's correct it for more biblical precision. Scripture never speaks of children as one flesh with their parents (this language is reserved for the sexual union of the husband and wife relationship) but rather as the "flesh and bone" of their parents (which still gets at the foundational unity Bavinck is trying to express). This retains a distinction between the marital and filial relationships, yet still makes the same broader point.

Father, mother, and child share a three-in-oneness.

The family is made for harmony. Maybe your family didn't feel very harmonious growing up. Maybe it felt more like discord and clanging cymbals—or even screamo music with the dial cranked up to 11. Maybe your family didn't come anywhere close to reflecting the love of the Trinity. My heart goes out to you; your pain is important to God. We'll get to that more in a minute.

Yet this design is still important. It points to the life you were made for with God, a life of belonging and love. A life that God is out to restore, drawing out your own distinct notes to participate in the redemptive symphony of the whole.

The family's unity is like that African statue we saw earlier (in chapter 3), only rather than concrete and plaster, the family is united by a *substance* of flesh and bone—a shared *human* nature. And rather than an immobile sculpture, the family is comprised of living, breathing persons, intended to coordinate the movement of their lives together. This deep unity of substance and nature (which are Trinitarian categories) means the family is one.

Expanding the Adam

Bavinck next makes a striking claim: The family "expands" and "unfold[s]" the "one image of God." What's he talking about? We tend to see *individuals* as bearing the divine image but not *humanity* as a collective whole. "I" am the image; not "we" are the image. Genesis depicts this, however, as a both/and rather than an either/or. This can be seen clearly in the "image of God" poem at the climax of Genesis 1:

So God created *the Adam* in his own image,
    in the image of God he created him;
    male and female he created them.

Now, I've used "the Adam" where most translations use "man" or "mankind," as a more literal translation of the Hebrew term (*ha adam*). Translators face a challenge in English: Does "the Adam" refer to Adam the *person* (the first human) or Adam the *human race* (corporate mankind)?

The answer: "Yes!" It's not an either/or but a both/and.

The Hebrew term *adam* can refer to both (and is used both ways in Genesis).[3] The reason most translations use "man" or "mankind" is to correctly emphasize that all humanity is in view here. It would be a bummer if English readers thought God only made the *first* human in his image and not the rest of us too.

Yet something gets lost in translation: "Mankind" loses its narrative relationship to *Adam*, our original ancestor. Humanity is *named* Adam because we come *from* Adam. Think of it like the term *Israel*, which can refer to both the *nation* of Israel and the founding *father* from whom the nation came. These two meanings are not unrelated: It is *because* the nation came *from* Israel (the person) that it is *named* Israel (the nation).

This is common in many indigenous languages around the world, where the tribe's name is frequently taken from their first ancestor in their creation stories. We use last names similarly today: I'm called *Butler* because I come from a long line of Butlers, traced back through my father's line across the generations. Families around the world generally take their name from their "founding fathers."

Adam is the founding father of humanity.

So when the apostle Paul says all humanity is in Adam, he's not making this stuff up; he's reading Genesis 1. The New Testament takes this to mean humanity shares a foundational unity in the substance of our being, corrupted in our flesh through Adam yet redeemed in Christ through the Spirit.

Humanity was made to reflect the image of God *together*, through the symphony of our shared life, revolving around the melody of divine love, performed in collective concert into the world.

The One Image

So back to Bavinck's claim that humanity is "the one image of God." The image of God is *corporate*, not just *personal*. This was a major theme for the early church.[4] Over the first few centuries, the image of God was emphasized as a corporate concept. God made humanity one, with a foundational unity in Adam, to image God not only *to* one another but *with* one another into the world.

One of the chief marks of sin, the church fathers continued to elaborate, was a fracturing of this unity. Saint Augustine saw humanity as something like a china doll—with a unity both precious, yet fragile—thrown to the ground by sin, fragmenting the human social body into hostile members, competing factions, and warring parties. Sin dismembers the human social body, dividing the one divine image.

Discord has been introduced into the symphony, in other words. The band members are battling against each other on the stage of creation. We're throwing drum sticks at each other, trying to smash one another with our guitars, blasting our own volume to drown out each other's sound—all in rebellion against the Master Conductor. In this battle of the bands, some bands of nations are trying destroy other bands of nations, in a quest to delete their music from the playlist of humanity so that only their own soundtrack can be played.

The symphony's been shattered.

Jesus has come, however, to restore the symphony! He's out to put the human family back together and heal the image of God we were meant to collectively display. Jesus bore the discord of our sin in his body that he might reunite us as a human social body. What was lost in Adam is redeemed in Christ.[5] Jesus is out to make us one again, as he and the Father are one, that in the power of their Spirit we might image God accurately once more— together.[6] Jesus is restoring a communion-of-persons who perform the triune God's symphony of love into all creation.

So, when Bavinck refers to "the one image of God," he's not

imposing a foreign concept on the Bible (even if this theme is less familiar to us) but reclaiming something foundational to God's vision for humanity. We are one. At least, we're supposed to be. This oneness is not just an abstract, ethereal concept. It's embedded in our flesh and bone, the stuff of our existence, our substance and nature—generated through sex.

Sex is how *the Adam* gets built. The family expands and unfolds this one human race, generating other image bearers who share in the corporate image of God. It is through the sexual union of male and female that babies are made and the human social body grows upon the earth. *The Adam* is like a lumbering giant who rises up from the ground, his body enlarging beneath him through the sexual union of his citizens, increasing in size through the intermingling of his members, generating the birth of the nations like growing legs with which to stand upon the globe.

Family is how the "one image" expands and unfolds into the earth.

Animals have sex too, you might be wondering, *yet they don't bear the image.* Yes, to be clear: The claim being made here is not that *sex* is the image of God but rather that *humanity* is the image of God. Yet humanity is sexed in nature, a truth highlighted by Genesis in the context of the image. Sex is *related to*, not *equated with*, the image.

It's also worth observing that human sexuality is (ideally) different from that of most animals, driven not by simple instinct or a desire to reproduce, but rather as a loyal covenant love and mutual pleasure between persons that—as we've seen throughout this book—uniquely reflects the divine character. What's more, humanity's triune structure as the "image" does not preclude other elements of creation from bearing a similar structure. You could argue—and many have—that creation itself bears the marks of the Trinity.[7] Humanity as the "image" unlocks this insight like a key.

Unity and Diversity

Bavinck goes on to speak of the family as "united within threefold diversity and diverse within harmonic unity." The family is harmonic diversity-in-union. That sounds beautiful, but is it biblical? Yes. Check out the last two lines of that Genesis 1 poem:

> So God created *the Adam* in his own image,
>   in the image of God he created *him* [unity];
>   male and female he created *them* [diversity].

In Hebrew poetry like this, the first line states the big idea while the last two lines unpack that idea from different angles. So the big idea is God creating mankind in his image. Line two then emphasizes our *unity*, while line three emphasizes our *diversity*. There is both unity and diversity in the one image of God.[8]

Diversity-in-union is central to this poem. In Hebrew, that word "him" is singular, while "them" is plural. Yet they both refer to the same object. *The Adam* is both a "him" and a "them," both a singularity and a plurality.

How does the "him" become a "them"? Keep reading. Shortly after this poem, Genesis 2 goes on to address how *the Adam* is "split" into male and female. The singular becomes plural, as the father of the human race is joined by the mother of all the living.[9] Through diversity-in-union, Adam and Eve will bring forth humanity—when the two become one flesh—multiplying and expanding the image of God into the world.

The "threefold" diversity Bavinck speaks of appears in the "be fruitful and multiply," which follows immediately on the heels of the poem. This location is no coincidence. Union gives birth to life. Children are the "third," generated by the two-in-oneness of male and female. Father, mother, and child are the "threefold diversity" by which the one Adam expands into the earth.

Bavinck refers to this as a "harmonic unity." Family members are like musical notes, a triad distinct yet united as participants in a symphonic whole. The triune God reveals that the melody we are designed to revolve around is love.

The family "constitutes the foundation of all of civilized society," Bavinck concludes. This is a common observation: Parents make babies, babies make families, families make nations, and nations make civilizations. Babies are like Legos: the building blocks that build up humanity.

What is unique to Bavinck's observation, however, is this: The triune structure of the family means there is a Trinitarian structure undergirding humanity as a whole. The family is, he says, "the threefold chord that binds together and sustains all relationships within human society." Humanity is a communion-of-persons who, in the diversity of our members, shares one substance of human nature. The family is both a microcosm of this communion and the organic means by which the communion itself is generated.

The Adam has a triune foundation.

The family mediates between the *personal* and *corporate* dimensions of the image of God. You bear the image as a *person* because your family has welcomed you into the *corporate* human race. There's no contradiction between many *individuals* bearing the image and all humanity *collectively* bearing the image, because the family is the mediating vehicle that holds these dimensions together. It is precisely through the family's triune structure that these dimensions are mediated.

If we are to image the triune God accurately, these social relations within the one human family are to be characterized by love. Humanity is made to image the triune God.

Genesis 1 is all about diversity-in-union. Earlier in this book, we saw how male and female are a window into the complementary pairs of heaven and earth, land and sea, night and day, which bring beauty and life into the world. Here in the climactic poem of Genesis 1, we see that diversity-in-union is an icon of something much more: not only the structure of creation but the identity of our Creator. The human family is mysteriously wrapped up somehow, this poem suggests, with the image of God.

Genesis 1 does not come right out and explicate a full-on doctrine of the Trinity. But it does give us a relational vision of humanity, as a communion-of-persons created in the divine image, that is surprisingly compatible with robust Trinitarian doctrine. This is precisely the type of picture we should expect, if humanity is created in the image of a triune God.

Reminder: The Greek word for *image* is "icon." In the ancient Greek translation of Genesis 1, popular in Jesus's day, humanity is created as an "icon of God." This icon of God is formed through sexual love, which bonds husband to wife, generates children, and forms the family as a communion-of-persons.

This bolsters the central thesis of this book from one more powerful angle, related to the very identity of God: Sex is iconic.

The Power of Belonging

Loneliness is epidemic in our culture. Millions of people live with sparse human contact, in what poet Emily Dickinson called "the horror not to be surveyed."[10] This is devastating, for we crave connection. Rich relationships are associated with better physical and mental health, and a longer, richer life. There's a reason: We were made by a triune God.

You were made relationally by a relational God. You were made to know and be known, to give and receive love, to be built up in healthy, secure community. God built this into creation, through the family, a witness to the power of belonging.

Our brains confirm this. When children grow up with secure attachment, research shows their neural pathways form with healthy patterns.[11] Your primary caregivers shaped your experience of *being known*. It's much more than just the words you heard, it's your experience of eye contact, tone of voice, facial expression, body language, healthy touch, and more.

As a child, your body was soaking in your whole relational environment—for better or worse—impacting your mind's development. Ideally, these relationships are loving, reflecting the love, security, and belonging of the Trinity. But we live in a broken world with broken families. At one level, all of our families are imperfect, interrupted by the discord and clanging of sin; we've all been impacted.

But no matter how difficult your upbringing was, here's the good news: There's healing in healthy relationships. I think this is why Jesus calls the church to be a *redemptive* family—not a biological family but a divine one—"the household of God."[12]

When you are known in deep friendships and healthy community, it actually rewires your brain! Did you know when a person tells their story to someone who listens with empathy—where they are truly heard and understood—both the person telling their story *and* the listener undergo changes in their brain circuitry? It begins to reroute your neural pathways. You begin to experience decreased anxiety and to feel a greater sense of emotional and relational connection and a greater awareness of and compassion for others.[13]

You begin to be shaped by the power of belonging.

This is why Christian psychiatrist Curt Thompson says that, when it comes to healthy relationships, "Our Creator has formed us in such a way that there is nothing more crucial to our long-term welfare."[14]

When you experience harmony with others, receiving the music of those around you and contributing the notes you were meant to play, rejoining the symphony of humanity, your life can be reorchestrated by the Master Conductor around his melody of love.

This power of belonging is not only with others but ultimately with the triune God. This is the most powerful form of belonging. It's no surprise that Jesus defines *eternal life* as a relationship: "that they know you, the only true God, and Jesus Christ whom you have sent."[15] Not only know *about* God but *know* God. In your very bones. In relationship. Indwelt by the Spirit, united to Christ, in the home of the Father.

In beautiful union.

The family is iconic of this greater reality. Some worry today about *idolizing* the family. For sure, this can and does happen (though I suspect this is a stronger temptation for traditional cultures than for the contemporary West). There's always the danger of turning a good thing into an ultimate thing, of elevating your spouse or child or relatives over God.

But there's also the danger of diminishing the sacred significance of the family, of not recognizing or honoring the powerful value God has invested in it. In my experience, some of those who most loudly decry the idolization of the family today seem to suffer from the opposite error: no longer seeing its sacred value or wanting to honor God's beautiful vision.

We are not called to *idolize* the family, but we are called to *honor* it.[16]

For it is a gift of the triune God made to sing of his love.

Triune Remix

Let's wrap up with a triune remix of Adam and Eve's creation story. A remix keeps the core of a song, yet uses fresh instrumentation to explore it from a new angle. Let's see how the Trinity's harmony draws out powerful sounds often unheard in the lyrics of this original track. For Genesis 2 sings of the first human family in a way that powerfully resonates with classical Trinitarian theology.

The Procession of the Beloved

Eve proceeds from Adam, a second to his first. She shares his *nature:* as a human who is like him and unlike the animals surrounding them. She shares his *substance:* built from his side as "bone of [his] bones and flesh of [his] flesh." Similarly, the Son proceeds from the Father, a second to his first, proceeding from his "side" and indwelt by his life, sharing in his divine nature and substance, distinct from all creation.[17]

Triune Symphony

181

Eve is distinct from Adam, yet shares an integral union with him as the one from whom her existence has arisen. Similarly, the Son is both distinct from, and shares an integral union with, his Father.

Wait a sec, you might be asking, *is Jesus the Son or the Spouse? Does this imply incest?* Great question. Remember, this is an analogy. The metaphor doesn't imply anything inappropriate, any more than when Israel is called both God's covenant bride and his firstborn son, or the church's identity as both the bride of Christ and children of God. There is mystery in the inner life of God that these metaphors point to but cannot contain.

Every analogy breaks down at some point—even the analogy of "Son" for the second person of the Trinity[18]—so there's a danger in reading too much into them.[19] The language of Father and Son speaks, at its heart, to a relationship of origination and procession, similar to how Eve proceeds from Adam.[20]

Now, Eve is unique. Women are generated by their parents, not their husbands. My wife was not created from my side. Yet Genesis 2 tells us that is why husbands and wives get married and become one flesh. In other words, Adam and Eve's story is presented not as a one-off event but as a prototype for every human marriage. So, how do wives "proceed from" their husbands?

If we take the one-flesh moment as the starting point for marriage—in the consummation of conjugal union—every wife emerges from this union like a new Eve split from the side of her Adam, penetrated by his indwelling presence and arising to stand face-to-face with him.[21] The beloved proceeds from her lover.

Eve is every wife.

The Procession of Love

Next, "Adam knew [Eve]," returning their diversity back into union, "and she bore a son and called his name Seth." That word *knew* is interesting. Adam doesn't just know facts and figures *about* Eve, he *knows* Eve. This is intimate, relational knowledge, which leads to generation.[22] Similarly, a husband and wife don't just know *about* each other, they *know* each other—and this knowledge can lead to generation, bringing forth a third from their union.

Seth is distinct from his parents as a third person, yet also shares their nature and substance as their flesh and bone, bears his father's image and likeness, and is named by his mother. Similarly, in the creational design of the family, the child emerges like a new Seth, proceeding *from* the lover, *through* the beloved, as the fruit of their love who bears their image and extends their life into the world.

Love gives birth to life.

In the words of the Nicene Creed, the Spirit proceeds "from the Father and the Son."[23] While the Son proceeds more immediately from the Father as a "second," the Spirit proceeds from them both as a "third." The Spirit is shared between them as the bond of love who completes the expansive circle of their communion.

Hold on, you might wonder, *you can have lots of kids, but there's only one Holy Spirit. Is this a problem for the analogy, suggesting more than one Spirit?* Another great question, dear reader. Consider this: Each child proceeds *directly* from their parents, not *through* their siblings. I have four brothers (I'm the oldest, thank you very much), but we all came straight from Mom and Dad—we're all a "third" in relation to their union. So we can think of the "third" as a category rather than a quantity.[24]

It's also helpful to remember, the Spirit is associated with fruitfulness in the biblical story, empowering the blessing of numerical expansion in large families and abundant harvests. So the category of "third" (on a human level) is able to grow abundantly by the power of the "third" (on a divine level).[25]

The family analogy also helps address a recent problem: Some have begun using the Trinity to argue for polyamorous relationships. *God's got three persons in his communion-of-love; why can't I have more in mine?* Somebody tried using this recently with a friend, to justify his open marriage. Sorry, Don Draper, the third person of the Trinity doesn't support your fling with the sexy receptionist. The category of "third" finds its correspondence in the addition of children, not of spouses.

No Lonely Lover

There's a major difference between Adam and the Father, however, worth observing. Before the rest of his family arrives on the scene, Adam is alone. Yet the Father has never been alone. The Son is *eternally* begotten, always present at the Father's side.[26] "There was never a time when he was not," Trinitarian orthodoxy rightly proclaims. There was never a time when the Father was all by himself.

This makes sense of what happens next. "It is not good," God declares, "that the man should be alone." Sin has not yet entered the world, but something is not good: loneliness. The *not goodness* of Adam's aloneness points to something profound: God is no lonely Lover. God is no solitary God, no isolated monad.

The one true God is a communion-of-love, and humanity is not complete until the I comes face-to-face with a Thou. We don't need romance, but we do need community.

Within the Trinity, the Lover without his Beloved and Love would be "not good"—for then God would cease to be the triune God he is, which is by its very nature an impossibility. Like Adam singing over Eve and welcoming Seth, the Lover eternally delights in his Beloved and rejoices over the Love they share between them.

This remix amplifies a powerful truth: Every biological family is an icon of the Trinity.

Give and Receive

As we resolve this chapter, I want to leave you with a beautiful takeaway: The Son and Spirit give what they receive. They take what they receive within the *inner* life of the Trinity and turn around to give it in their *outward* relations with us in salvation.

The Son is the Beloved in the inner life of God (in what we

might call the "bridal" relation), yet he turns around in the economy of salvation to become the Lover to his church (in the "groom" relation). The One who has received God's life-giving presence within himself from all eternity turns around to impart his life-giving presence within his bride in time. The second person in the communion of God becomes the first in his communion with his people.

The Beloved of God becomes the Lover of his church.

The Spirit, meanwhile, is Love in the inner life of God (in what we might call the "child" relation) yet turns around in the economy of salvation to empower the Beloved's fruitfulness (in what we might call the "maternal" relation). The Spirit brings forth children of God with new life from above and raises us up to maturity in life with Christ. The third person in the communion of God becomes the second in the communion of salvation.

The Love of God gives birth to children of God.

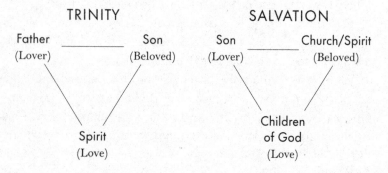

The Son and Spirit "pay it forward," to use a modern idiom. They take what they receive in the inner life of God and turn around to share it with us in salvation. This means Beloved and Love speak not only to the identity of God in eternity but to who God makes us—in Christ and through the Spirit—to be. Sexual love is a sign not only of who God is but of who he's destined us to become in him.

The triune shape of salvation flows from the triune identity of God.

Jesus is the Master Conductor, who takes the bent and broken instruments of our lives—even *people* who've been tossed aside and discarded—and transforms us to become instruments of his Spirit, attuned to the melody of love belting out from the voice of his Father.

Jesus invites you into *his* family, where each member has a part to play. He can turn even the parts of your life that feel like discord into something like cellos and flutes and trumpets in the crescendo of the triune God's symphony for the world. You're invited to follow the lead of our Master Conductor to belt out this eternal song.

The triune harmony of love.

A River Runs Through It

My kids are currently researching our family history for a school project. They've called the grandparents, asking for stories from their lives. They've traced the generations back as far as they can. And guess what picture they're using to trace these ancestral connections? A family tree. This is our most popular image for tracking your ancestry across generations.

The family tree image makes sense. Your ancient ancestors sprung roots up from the deep, with the trunk of your modern descendants stretching up toward the sky, all the way to Grandma Ethel and Grandpa Humphrey sprouting that branch you're sitting on today . . . sipping that cup of coffee, reading this book, spinning atop this cosmic rock we call earth.

Interestingly, the Bible makes a different image central for this life-giving power of sex.

A river of life.

River from Eden

The Garden of Eden had a mighty river, Genesis 2 tells us, bringing life to the world:

A river watering the garden flowed from Eden; from there it was separated [*parad*] into four headwaters. The name of the first is the Pishon; it winds through the entire land of Havilah. . . . The name of the second river is the Gihon; it winds through the entire land of Cush. The name of the third river is the Tigris; it runs along the east side of Ashur. And the fourth river is the Euphrates.[1]

Imagine the scene: a mountaintop garden, with a river rushing down the mountainside to water the surrounding lands below. Eden was located atop "the mountain of God": depicted as a holy place, a temple space where heaven and earth met.[2] Upon exiting Eden's garden, this mighty river "separated" (*parad*) into four rivers that spread into four regions. Havilah was associated with Egypt, the Tigris with Assyria, the Euphrates with Babylon, and the Gihon with Jerusalem in Israel—the mighty civilizations of the biblical world.

Eden's river is bringing life to the nations.

Eden is depicted here as a "cosmic mountain," in the words of biblical scholars, whose river brings life and gives rise to the population centers of the ancient world.[3] This picture makes sense. Ancient civilizations were built along rivers. They provided drinking water and agricultural abundance that could support large populations on the surrounding land. God blessed the nations with a river of life.

A River of Nations

So what's this have to do with procreation? Check this out. When the river *separates* into four rivers, that word "separated" (*parad*) is one of those hyperlink words we talked about earlier that connects concepts in the Bible.[4] It shows up a bunch for procreation.

In the Table of Nations (Genesis 10), for example, Noah comes down the mountain with his three sons, from whom the nations were "separated [*parad*] into their lands."[5] The passage repeats this one more time for emphasis: "Out of these the nations were *separated* on the earth after the flood."[6] The context is a genealogy, a family tree, only the echo of Eden sets this up as a "river of nations" who flow forth from Noah's progeny.

Noah is depicted like a new Adam: He tends a garden (after the flood), atop a mountain (where the ark lands), and he falls into sin (with the fruit of the vine).[7] Then Noah's family comes streaming down the mountain like a mighty river, his sons branching out like three additional headwaters, flowing out to fill the earth with people. Genesis 10 echoes Genesis 2.

The nations arise from this river of life.

More examples follow. Three chapters later, Abraham and Lot look down from a mountain to choose their respective dwelling places in the land below. They then "separate" (*parad*) and descend, parting company to settle with their families into the lower plains.[8] A generation later, Jacob and Esau wrestle in their mother's womb as twins, and she's given a prophecy of what it means: "Two nations are in your womb, and two peoples from within you will be separated [*parad*]."[9] The brothers will divide like headwaters, branching out from a common river in different directions.

Moses sings how "the Most High gave the nations their inheritance, when he *separated* all mankind, he set up boundaries for the peoples."[10] The song is packed with water imagery, flowing to dry and thirsty lands to fill them with God's abundant provision. Humanity is fruitful and multiplying, branching into tributaries of tribes and streams of nations.

Genesis depicts Adam's family as a mighty river—whose origins are in a sacred space, where heaven and earth meet—rushing down from the cosmic mountain of God to fill the world with life. This river from Eden is an icon of procreation. And sex is how the river moves forward.

Sex is a vehicle for life.

A Vehicle for Life

Growing up, our family drove a big red Volkswagen van. We went everywhere in that feat of German engineering. All seven of us would pile in and head to the mountains for camping, the beach for surfing . . . we even drove it cross-country once, from Oregon to Georgia and back again. Its wheels were a transport to adventure, carrying our family forward to a future destination. Similarly, sex is a vehicle for existence, carrying the human family forward to the future.

Sex is a big red Volkswagen.

Sex is what generates the generations. Procreation produces population. The two becoming one flesh is how new flesh is formed to fill every nook and cranny of the world.

It's always amazed me that God entrusts the miracle of making the human race to us. When God says, "Be fruitful and multiply," he's essentially saying, "Go have sex and make babies."[11] (*Who says God's a cosmic killjoy?*) God creates the first two, then passes the baton to us. God pulls Eve from Adam, then pulls the rest of us from their union. God created us not only *for* diversity-in-union but *from* diversity-in-union.

Mankind is manufactured in the factory of marital union.

Sex is also a vehicle for something much more: the work of the Spirit. "All creatures look to you," the psalmist rejoices. "When you send your Spirit, they are created, and you renew the face of the ground."[12] The Spirit is seen here to animate both *animal* life ("all creatures") and *agricultural* life ("the face of the ground"). God's presence is at work in procreation, empowering the fruitfulness of creation.

God's Spirit is the Giver of Life.

The Spirit is identified with the river of life. Jesus refers to the Spirit as *living water,* an ancient term for rivers. Unlike the standing water of puddles and ponds—stale and stagnant, filled with leaves, animal feces, and disease—river water is *alive:* rushing, moving, and bringing life to everything along its path. Similarly, the Spirit of God is like a river from Eden, causing crops to thrive and population centers to arise.

The river of life is the Giver of Life.

Wait a sec. Are we created by sex or by the Spirit? Yes. It's not an either/or but a both/and. God creates us *through* sex. In Acts 17,

Paul grabs the mic at Athens and drops a little Sex Ed on the masses: "He made from one man every nation of mankind."[13] The "one man" is Adam: the original headwater from whom the human race flows. Don't miss the shock here, though: *God made.* Our Creator is the primary agent in procreation, making the human race.

Sex is a conduit for his creation.

We tend to think we're making the little munchkins on our own, while God waits shyly in the living room for us to finish our dirty business. Far from it. God's getting the job done, making nations. Our Creator's at work when we're working it. When Mom and Dad snuck into Mr. Wilson's science classroom after hours, they weren't just experimenting with *biology* but *theology*— God was the Master Chemist concocting an explosive mixture. And when the smoke cleared . . . *you* were the result revealed on the lab table.

Sex is how God makes nations.

Children build families, families build tribes, and tribes build nations that fill and flood the earth. God makes the human race through the intimacy of intercourse; it's built into the blueprint of his original architectural design. We are together a temple, constructed to be corporately indwelt by the presence of the living God. Sex is a vehicle for family, the foundation of civilization.

Your origins are in a sacred place. You received life from the mighty river of God's Spirit. Whatever the circumstances of your birth, God brought you forth in love. Your parents, whatever their motives, were merely a medium for your Maker. You didn't make yourself; your life is a gift. So you don't have to earn it, you can simply receive it. Your immeasurable worth flows from the mighty current of an infinite God. You can rest in the river of his life.

River vs. Tree

The river has some advantages over the tree, as an icon of procreation. While a tree grows *up*, a river moves *forward*. The river thus speaks to the future-orientation of children. Families don't ascend *up* into the sky but rather move *forward* into the future. Our progeny are like postcards we mail to the future, and Genesis tells us the postal service carries them there by boat.

Also, while a tree simply *is* fruitful, a river *empowers* fruitfulness. This speaks to the Spirit's role in procreation. The Spirit of God empowers human fruitfulness, like a river nurturing the soil we're planted in. Crops don't grow in the water but in the soil that the water has saturated and prepared for fruitfulness. The river thus points beyond itself to the Spirit of God, who empowers the fruitfulness of creation.

The river and tree share similarities too. Both speak to the *unity* of the nations. A river comes from a single source, a point of origin, similar to how the whole tree is contained within the seed. The unity of the human family is like zooming out on a satellite map to discover the various streams, lakes, and ponds are all connected as one larger body of water. Adam is our original headwater in Eden, giving rise to the various tributaries and channels of the nations downstream. We're all connected like one large family tree.

Only by water rather than bark.

Rivers and trees are also both *expansive*. Like a tree's branches, which spread and stretch upward toward the sky, a river also expands wider and wider as it progresses farther downstream. The nations similarly spread as they march through history, like an army expanding into vast new terrain, crossing fields and plains until at last we cross the threshold of the horizon's golden shores into eternity.

We fill the earth.

The river does have one more advantage though: It's liquid. Life moves forward through liquid means. The man's procreative presence goes forth in intercourse to water the soil of the woman's womb. Inversely, the woman moistens in the exchange to make way for this aquatic channel between them. They are like two sides of a canal opening, to share this river of life. The fruit of their love, if conceived, is nurtured within a liquid womb, until the water breaks and the newborn emerges through a river of life.

When it comes to sex, a river runs through it.

The river is an icon of procreation. It speaks to the fruitfulness of creation, the rise of the nations, and the work of the Spirit. Sex is how the river moves forward when it comes to humanity. God shares his life with us through his Spirit, and we share his life with our children through sex. God is at work in this expansion of the human family, carrying us forward into the adventure of the future.

The Holy Spirit is driving the big red Volkswagen.

The Pain of Infertility

All this talk of children can be painful for those struggling with infertility. One in ten couples faces this difficult journey.[14] Some might worry that emphasizing procreation will simply pour salt on the wound, yet I've found the opposite to be true: A biblical framing can help name the pain and legitimate the struggle.

If infertility is part of your story, you're not alone. It's a common experience not only in the church today but also in the Bible. Let's see how an iconic vision of sex speaks into it.

Not the Way It's Supposed to Be

Infertility is not the way it's supposed to be. This is the first thing to recognize. Barrenness first appears in Genesis 3, after the Fall. The man's curse involves the barrenness of the ground, while the woman's curse involves the barrenness of the womb.

The woman will face "sorrow in conception [*heron*]," we're told, a Hebrew euphemism for infertility.[15] Some English translations are misleading here, rendering the phrase as "pain in childbearing," which makes us think of a woman in the hospital *giving* birth. But the Hebrew word *heron* means "conception" (this is its clear meaning every other time in Scripture).[16] Genesis is speaking to the *sorrow* that comes from being unable to conceive a child.

God affirms the pain of infertility.

The next part of the woman's curse moves to childbirth: "In pain you shall bring forth children."[17] This is now speaking to the groaning of labor pangs in the delivery room nine months later. In other words, the curse includes both ends of the pregnancy spectrum: conception and birth. Both getting pregnant and giving birth have become difficult, impacted by the weight of the Fall.

The womb and ground share a correspondence. The man's curse involves *barrenness* in relation to the land, similar to how the woman's curse involves *barrenness* in relation to children. The soil will now require "painful toil," and only yield its food by "the sweat of your brow."[18] That word "toil" (for the man) shares the same Hebrew root as "sorrow" (for the woman).[19] In other words, the ground and womb are both designed for abundance but now provoke struggle and pain in our world's distance from God.

Fruitfulness has been frustrated by the Fall.

Infertility and famine are major themes in the story that follows. Sarah, Rebekah, Rachel, and Leah all face infertility, while Abraham's family is driven down to Egypt twice by famine . . . and that's just in Genesis. As Exodus opens, Pharaoh oppresses the men with painful toil and the women by murdering the fruit of their womb. In other words, he's depicted as an agent of the curse, an ally of the serpent, who is an obstacle to the redemptive purposes of God.

What does this mean? Infertility is not the way it should be. It's a tragic reality of our fallen world. To say it again, the Bible names the pain and legitimates the struggle.

The Bible also confronts myths about infertility. It confronts the lie that *it must be your fault*, honoring stories of childless couples who are "righteous before God, walking blamelessly in all the commandments and statutes of the Lord."[20] This corrects the misconception that you must have done something wrong, or God must be angry with you. It confronts the bad advice of friends who say hurtful things like, "If you just had more faith," or "There must be a sin you need to repent of." No; that's just not true. God is with you in compassion amid the tragic realities of our fallen world.

The Bible also confronts the lie that *you shouldn't be sad*. Our culture is not good at grief. We're encouraged to toughen up. Put on a happy face. Focus on the positive. Soldier on. If you can't have children, you might feel the pressure to stuff your emotions and pretend the pain isn't there. Yet grief and lament are everywhere in the Bible. Hannah is so upset by her infertility that she "wept and would not eat," as she cried out to God in the temple. She endures the cruelty of a rival who would mock her barrenness and "provoke her grievously to irritate her," and the ineptitude of a religious leader who mistook her wailing for drunkenness.[21]

Yet Hannah faces her *sorrow in conception* head-on—and God hears her cry. It's okay to be sad. It's healthy to make space for grief, even if well-meaning friends tell you otherwise. God is a comforter, who hears your cries and can draw close to you in your heartache. Far from a *lack* of faith, bringing your tears before God is a *sign* of faith. It's a sign you believe he's good enough to invite grief, and strong enough to care for you in it.

A Fruitful Life

Infertility doesn't have to have the last word on living an abundant life. Fruitfulness is so much bigger. Jesus didn't have kids and lived the most fruitful life in history. Some of the most life-giving people I know are childless. As professor and author Karen Swallow Prior reflects on her own childlessness:

> Even though God has not fulfilled my longtime desire to have children, he has filled my life with so many other gifts that my greatest struggle has been to be a faithful steward of so much abundance. . . . I can't help but wonder how different the church and the world would look if infertility were viewed not as a problem to be solved but a calling to serve God and meet the needs of the world in other ways.[22]

My friends Nam and Anna have longed for kids but say God has used their childlessness to bring forth other kinds of fruitful-

ness. They work with hundreds of the world's most impover-
ished villages, equipping churches to holistically transform their
neighborhoods and disciple leaders to walk reliant on the presence of God.

You don't need to be a globe-trotter, though, to experience
this abundant life. Some couples step into foster care or adoption,
becoming a redemptive family for children who've lost theirs.
Others pour increased energy into their vocation or ministry,
cultivating the abundance of God's world and hospitality of his
family in a variety of ways.

If procreation is iconic, then you can have the reality it points
to: life in the Spirit. This is accessible to us all, in Christ. The
abundant life of the kingdom is what the sign ultimately points
to, rooted in the very life of God.

The Ground of Resurrection

The ground of resurrection is barren. When Abraham's body
"was as good as dead," the apostle Paul says, and "Sarah's womb
was also dead," they received a child "against all hope."[23] Paul
presents God's opening of Sarah's womb as a witness to the God
"who gives life to the dead and calls into existence the things that
do not exist."[24] This is a foundation story for both the Jewish and
Christian faiths.

While sometimes God "opens the womb" in the Bible, theologian J. Todd Billings observes that this was not the normal experience:

> The Israelites did not expect God to overcome infertility
> in the vast majority of circumstances. Rather, in the cases in
> which God reverses death by providing children to the in-
> fertile, God offers testimony to his unique power to reverse
> death.[25]

God's overcoming of Sarah's barrenness is a sign of resurrection. The acclaimed Jewish scholar Jon Levenson sees such events

in the Hebrew Bible as a sign that God will ultimately conquer death and restore his people.[26] He describes the filling of Sarah's womb as a "restorative action of God" that "opposes the natural course of things" by reactivating the "powers within nature—principally the power to procreate—that had shriveled and virtually disappeared before God's new intervention."[27]

That's something we all need.

This means infertility is itself iconic, in its own way. Infertility is a window into our larger barren estate in a parched and war-torn earth. The infertile thus have a gift for the church, something to teach us all, in the heartfelt longing for a child that is a sign of our deep collective longing for new creation. We live under the conditions of the Fall, and getting honest with our barren condition—which, in one way or another, we all find ourselves in—can cultivate in us a thirst for the rushing river of God's life-giving presence.

Our hope is exercised in barren places.

Abraham and Sarah looked to the God of resurrection in their barrenness, Paul says, the same God "who raised Jesus our Lord from the dead."[28] At one level, we are all like Abraham and Sarah—barren people in a famished land. We can look to the God of resurrection who has raised Jesus from the grave, whose river of life is coming to renew and restore the world.

Infertility reveals our condition; children display our hope.

My friends Sebastian and Catherine struggled to conceive for over a decade. Then one day, my wife had a dream where God said he was going to give them a child that year. She woke up, told me, and recorded it in her journal. We did *not* tell them this (*generally a good principle with predictions of marriage or babies*) but instead prayed for them that year.

Later that year, when it came true and their child Luke was born, we shared the news with them and showed them Holly's journal. Sebastian laughed out loud and said God had told him the same thing around the same time! We rejoiced in this sign of God's power.

God still "opens the womb" today. Such stories are good news for us all—even if you're not the one who gets the child! As C. S. Lewis observed, such miracles are not exceptions for the lucky few but rather a sneak preview for us all of what's to come:

> If [these miracles] have occurred . . . they have occurred because they are the very thing this universal story is about. They are not exceptions (however rarely they occur), not irrelevancies. They are precisely those chapters in this great story on which the plot turns. Death and Resurrection are what the story is about.[29]

Catherine and Sebastian's pregnancy, like Sarah and Abraham's, was a signpost of new creation, an icon of hope for a dying world. Infertility is a window into the barren condition of us all, but its overcoming is a sign of the coming kingdom.

We can rejoice in such events, whatever our circumstances, for they are ultimately a witness to Jesus's victory. They speak to the God of resurrection, of Christ who was buried in the desolate ground of an accursed world, yet raised for our justification by the life-giving Spirit of God, and who will ultimately overcome the barrenness of our lives and of the world—in all its various forms.

Temple Streams

The river of life will flow again, like streams from the temple of God. Israel's temple was envisioned as a new Eden, with God's life-giving presence emerging from its sanctuary like a rushing river of living water bringing abundance into the land. When the streams of God's Spirit went forth from the temple, flowers would burst into bloom, trees would bear abundant fruit, and harvests would be huge—the land would be renewed.[30] God's presence would bless "the fruit of your womb and the fruit of your ground."[31]

What gave the temple this life-giving power? Beautiful union. It was the "hot spot" of God's presence, where heaven and earth intersected and God dwelt in intimacy and power with his bride. The Most Holy Place was like the bedroom, where this union was most powerfully consummated. God's presence penetrated the temple, and from this center brought life and abundance into the land.

Union gives birth to life.

Life-Giving Presence

The temple was associated with the female body. The Bible describes its architecture with personified human features—having a face, shoulders, and ribs—using a variety of hyperlink words from the "building" of Eve in Genesis 2.[32] Eve is a prototype of the temple to come, which was constructed as an iconic representative for Israel as the bride of Yahweh, in covenant union with her King.

The temple was also associated with fertility. At its dedication, Solomon recognized God's indwelling presence would bring *literal* fruitfulness: causing the surrounding crops to be plentiful and the land to flourish. It would also bring a *metaphorical* fruitfulness: The nation would experience peace and be protected from hostile invasion, with justice established in the land. Wrongdoers would find forgiveness and the poor would feast, as God's abundance reigned.[33]

Turn off the faucet, however, and the tap stops dripping. If union was interrupted, Solomon continued, the land would dry up—barren with famine. If the nation rebelled, thorns and thistles would overrun the once fertile ground now absent of God's indwelling presence. Injustice would run rampant, enemies invade, and the people be carried off into exile. The garden would wither into a wasteland, the nation unravel in desolation.[34]

The temple's dedication brought an important public service announcement: Divine presence brings fruitfulness; absence brings barrenness.

God tells Solomon he will enter the temple. On condition of their faithfulness, he will "dwell among" and "not forsake" his people (that's marital imagery).[35] The temple is prepared like a body to receive God's indwelling presence. The sanctuary is like a womb: receiving the word and presence of God and bearing his life to the world.[36] When God enters and fills her, abundance springs forth like streams of living water. The river of life flows down Mount Zion once more, making the land fruitful.

God's union with his bride brings forth the life of his kingdom.

Similarly, Christ's union with his church is fruitful. A living temple, she conceives children of God through the river of his Spirit and bears new life into the world. When Jesus famously meets a Samaritan woman at a well, she is symbolically depicted as a representative of his bride. The well is not only an ancient fertility symbol but also a famous setting in the Bible where the groom first meets his bride.[37] Like the church, the Samaritan woman is part Jew, part Gentile. Like the church, she has a scandalous past. Like the church, she encounters Jesus as one who has come from a distant land (ultimately, heaven to earth) to meet her. Like the church, she is radically transformed through the encounter, telling everyone to "Come and see!"

Like the church, Jesus brings living water to her—and through her to the world.

God's goal is not only to dwell intimately *with* you as his bride but to bring his abundance into the world *through* you. We are indwelt by the life-giving presence of God, which makes us fruitful.

The Church as Temple

The church is the bridal temple of Jesus. We are "God's building," the New Testament says, built with "living stones," constructed together to become "a holy temple," "a dwelling in which God lives by his Spirit."[38] We receive not just a part of Jesus but "the fullness of him who fills everything in every way."[39] We are united to him to bear his life to the world.

Israel's sanctuary in the Old Testament points to the church's power in the New. Jesus says he and his Father will "come to" those who love him, and "make [their] home" with them (that's temple language).[40] They will not only abide *with* us but *in* us—through their Spirit's divine presence—and when they do we will "bear much fruit."[41]

We are a living temple.

Body, bride, and temple are not three disconnected metaphors for God's people. They are brought together by this Old Testament background: You were made to be a bridal temple for God's indwelling presence, united with him in covenantal union as his body.

"Come to me and drink," Jesus invites all who are thirsty, with the provocative promise: "Out of his belly will flow rivers of living water."[42] Guess where Jesus is standing when he says this? In the temple. Also vital is *when* he says it: the climax of a national festival where the people cried out in front of the sanctuary for God to bring the river of life rushing forth from the temple again.

What's this river represent? John makes it crystal clear. "This he said about the Spirit."[43]

Jesus is turning on the firehose once more, to bring life rushing forth to the world. Jesus loves to walk to the side of his house, unkink the garden hose, and crank on the faucet: to bring resurrection rivers gushing to all the neighborhood. The only requirement to drink is that you're thirsty.

Also, did you catch that word *belly* above? It could be translated "womb" (its most frequent meaning in the New Testament).[44] That's where the waters are flowing from. Rivers rushing forth from our womb, as from the inner sanctuary of the temple, bearing his life-giving presence to the world.[45] Our union with Christ makes us fruitful.

There is a Trinitarian dimension to sex. If salvation is union with Christ, the kingdom is the abundant life that flows from his Spirit. If marriage points to the work of Jesus, children point to the labor of the Spirit. The *unitive* dimension of sex points to your union with Christ; the *procreative* dimension points to your life from the Spirit. Procreation is an icon of the abundance of the kingdom.

Jesus gives his river of life to you, and you bear his life to the world. "The water I give them will become in them a spring of water welling up to eternal life."[46] Jesus fills us up as his bride to overflowing, pouring his presence into you like water into a pitcher until it spills out all around. Jesus's goal is not simply to give himself *to* you but to pour himself *through* you, like streams of living water into a barren and thirsty land.

God wants to make you fruitful. He wants to bring forth *the fruit of his Spirit*—"love, joy, peace, patience, kindness, goodness, faithfulness, gentleness, self-control"—saturating your soil with his presence until such produce comes bursting off your branches.[47] The way to produce this fruit is not by striving in your own strength, not muscling it up like a tree in famished soil, but rather by saturating in his Spirit, soaking in his power. Receiving the presence of God produces the character of God.

Such fruit is a sign of the coming kingdom.

Resurrection River

"Where the river flows everything will live."[48] The prophet Ezekiel sees a coming day when the river will flow from God's holy mountain once more, rushing down from the temple—like a new Eden—bringing abundance to everything in its path. This river's water is so strong, we're told, that the trees along its banks will bear fruit every month (not just every year), because "the water from the sanctuary flows to them."[49] *That's some powerful H_2O!*

The river has procreative power.

Even the Dead Sea will teem with life. Now that's saying something. There's a reason they call it the Dead Sea: *Nothing can live there!* It's chock-full of salt. If Dasani bottled water there, customers would soon die of dehydration. Yet the river of God will be so powerful, it even "makes the salt water fresh."[50] Move over LaCroix; this water's got kick!

That word *fresh* is the same Hebrew word for *healed:* The river of God heals creation. The trees that grow along its banks are for "the healing of the nations."[51]

This is a resurrection river. The Spirit will saturate even the Dead Sea's saltiness, till its banks overflow with the life-giving abundance of God. God can bring your dead things back to life. That marriage you thought was hopeless. Your innocence that was stolen. The health you'd given up on. Those desires you thought were snuffed out for good. The river of God's presence can restore you.

We find the fulfillment of this river at the end of the biblical story, in Revelation 22, where the river flowing through God's city is the Spirit of God, who rushes forth from the throne of God and the Lamb, to turn graveyards into gardens and give birth to a country of resurrection.

"No longer will there be any curse," we're told. No more thorns and thistles; no more barren land. The age of sin and death is over; the era of life and love has come. The Spirit of Jesus "comes to make his blessings flow, far as the curse is found."[52] Joy to the world, indeed. For the river of the divine presence will flood the earth with the glory of God.

There is life in God's kingdom, for a river runs through it.

We can dock our vessel here, for this riverboat journey has come to an end. The river of life that began in Eden long ago shall wind its way through the course of our history until reaching its destination in the city of God. What began on the banks of creation shall end in the life of the kingdom. From this vantage point, we shall be able to gaze back upon the winding course of our years and perceive its common thread in the Giver of Life, who gives rise to the fruitfulness of the nations, lavishes his abundance on creation, and makes bountiful the kingdom of God.

14

ROYAL WEDDING

We love royal weddings. Nearly two billion people tuned in to watch Prince Harry and Meghan Markle make their vows (*that's 25 percent of the world!*). The star-studded spectacle took place at St. George's Chapel in Windsor Castle, in the presence of six hundred guests, including the Queen. Even in America, where we've long since thrown off the yoke of the monarchy, every media outlet ran endless stories in anticipation of the upcoming royal nuptials. It seemed to be all anyone was talking about. Try as we might to break free from tradition . . . we're still enchanted by the fairy tale.

A royal wedding is at the center of the most erotic book in the Bible. In the Song of Songs, King Solomon is united with his bride. The book is packed with sexual imagery.

There's a debate today, however: Is the Song of Songs about love human or divine? Historically, Israel and the church have seen this epic love song as an allegory for God's relationship with his people. Yet many modern critics argue this undermines the song's basic celebration of human love and betrays a religious prudishness about sex. (*Ew. Sex can't be in the Bible; let's make the book about God instead.*) Academics can be experts at missing the point. This is a false dichotomy.

It's not an either/or but a both/and. As the renowned Jewish scholar Jon Levenson observes, the royal wedding of Solomon and his bride is *both* a focus of the Song *and* a symbol of God's greater relationship with his people as King. When Jewish and Christian figures interpret the Song of Songs allegorically,

> they're *raising* the significance of sex, they're not *denying* it. They're raising it by connecting it to the most enduring and significant romance in history [God's relationship with his people]. . . . It's not that the larger relationship is some-how sexless or bodiless or has no erotic dimensions, it's the other way around: it's that in order to understand the mean-ing of those bodily relationships you have to understand what the higher relationship is that they symbolize . . . within this biblical and Jewish and Christian framework sex is about a much larger thing which is a more enduring and encompassing relationship.[1]

Just so. Properly understood, divine and human love *enhance* one another, rather than *detract* from each other. The Song of Songs' celebration of human sexual love *magnifies* the intimacy of union we were created for with God. And as a sign of the church's union with Christ, this masterpiece *intensifies* the meaning and delight packed into the marital bliss of lovers in embrace.

There's a reason we love the fairy-tale romance: It echoes a greater, transcendent reality. As we prepare to land the plane on this book, the Song of Songs is a great runway to touch down on, for it places our central theme front and center . . .

Sex is iconic.

We Are a Temple

The woman in Song of Songs has some strange features. One art-ist attempted a literal depiction: eyes like doves, hair a flock of goats, teeth like freshly shorn lambs, a nose like the tower of Lebanon, her temples pomegranate slices, with lips a scarlet thread dripping milk and honey, a neck like the tower of David hung with a thousand shields, her breasts like two fawns feeding among the lilies, the fragrance of her garments like the fragrance of Lebanon, her navel a round goblet, with a belly like a heap of wheat . . . [2]

Not the most attractive figure—LOL!

Until you realize she is Israel. The goats, sheep, and fawns evoke the pastoral scene of the countryside; the tower of David with its thousand shields echoes the city center of Jerusalem; the lips dripping milk and honey call to mind the Promised Land as a "land flowing with milk and honey"; the prominent appearance of pomegranates, apples, figs, and grapes elicit the fertile produce of the land.

Jerusalem is prominent in the woman's description. She is "lovely as Jerusalem," regularly calls out to the "daughters of Jerusalem" (an Old Testament term for the towns and villages surrounding the royal capital), and is described prominently as a vineyard and fig tree, both significant biblical images for Jerusalem.[3]

The bride is Jerusalem.

Furthermore, the *temple* in Jerusalem looms largest in her description. The bride's pomegranates recall the high priest's garments and the four hundred decorative pomegranates in the temple.[4] Her wheat and goblet elicit the grain and wine offerings of the sacrificial system, while the king's banqueting table evokes the Bread of the Presence in the Most Holy Place on Yahweh's table—where Yahweh as king feasted with his bride.

Reference to the cedars of Lebanon elicits the renowned timber from which Solomon's Temple was made.[5] "The beams of our house are cedar," the bride declares, "our rafters are pine."[6] The temple is conceived as a home where the groom and bride dwell together, and in which they consummate their marriage.

The bride is like a palm tree and her breasts are "clusters" of fruit, evoking the imagery from Solomon's Temple of palm trees and fruit carved into its cedar panels.[7] Similarly, the "lilies" referenced throughout the Song evoke the capitals of the pillars, which were lily shaped.[8] Apples, raisins, pomegranates, and fruit appear prominently in the Song, like the garden decorations adorning the temple, with primordial allusions to Eden.

The bride is described as a "paradise," a "garden locked, a fountain sealed," a "well of living water" with "flowing streams"—like the temple, which was envisioned as a new Eden, a restoration of the paradise garden once lost.[9]

Her dark skin is described as "like the curtains of Solomon," evoking the dark curtains that formed a veil to the Most Holy Place in Solomon's Temple.[10] Purple and scarlet, the colors of her hair and lips, recall the colors of fabric used throughout the temple—purple was associated with royalty; the "scarlet yarn" was associated with priestly cleansing rituals—both colors were prominently prescribed for the house of God.[11]

She has "no blemish," a phrase regularly used for the priests and sacrifices, which were expected to have "no blemish" in the temple system.[12] The "fragrance of [her] garments," alongside repeated references to myrrh and frankincense, recall the anointing oil and incense regularly used in the temple, rising up as a pleasing aroma to God.[13]

The point: Solomon's bride is Israel personified. He is not giving a *literal* depiction of her, rather an *iconic* one loaded with temple imagery. Like a bride today representing the church, so here Solomon sees his bride as representing something much grander and cosmic in scope: Israel prepared to receive God's indwelling presence, as a social body in covenant union with her king.

The bride of the King is a temple.

We are a temple. The Song of Songs points to your identity as the bride of Christ the King. You were made to be a holy place filled with his presence, washed and cleansed by his sacrifice, now with "no blemish," dressed in the finest of garments, adorned with the richest of fragrance, brought to his table to dine with him, and to rule and reign with him forever. Do you desire to live into this calling? This is your destiny as the bride of the King.

God Is a Lover

As the bride represents Israel, so Solomon represents God. The groom's primary title in the book, "my beloved," is used twenty-six times—the Hebrew gematria for Yahweh—a Jewish literary way of identifying the groom with Israel's God.

He is also described with temple imagery. His head is gold, his arms are rods of gold set with jewels, his body is polished ivory with sapphires, his legs are alabaster columns on bases of gold, his appearance is like the cedars of Lebanon—all prominent features in the construction of Solomon's Temple, where Yahweh dwelt with his bride.

Interestingly, the Song tends to associate the "firmer" construction elements with Yahweh (gold rods, ivory walls, alabaster columns), and the "fertile" garden elements with the bride (like a garden within a temple)—though not in a rigid hard-and-fast way (there is subtle crossover between the elements in each figure's description).[14] Together, they are the house of God.

Allusions to the temple can also be seen in the groom's association with the sweet smell of herbs and spices (evoking the incense in the Holy Place), liquid myrrh (recalling the anointing oil used to light the lampstand in the Holy Place), his "banqueting house" (like the table with bread in the Holy Place), and a full pool and streams of water (like those emerging from the temple).[15]

Solomon composes this song to celebrate his marriage as king, seeing it as a window into a greater reality: the King of the universe come to make his home with his people. Like a groom today representing Christ as to his church, so here Solomon is presented as a type or picture of Yahweh entering royal union with his bride.[16]

Solomon sings over his bride in the Song, like a new Adam rejoicing over a new Eve. They consummate their marriage in a garden—echoing Eden once more, where the greater divine marriage is consummated in a garden temple. This is iconic of God as King singing over us as his bride and restoring paradise with us.

Our deepest desires are fulfilled in God, where we can declare,

"I am my beloved's and my beloved is mine." "I am sick with love," the bride declares, expressing her deepest longings for her groom. "Let him kiss me with the kisses of his mouth." "Let my beloved come to his garden, and eat its choicest fruits."[17] Christ fulfills this foundational longing of the human heart.

Sex is an icon of salvation.

You were built for love. You were not made to do this life alone; you were made to find your deepest longings fulfilled in God. What would it look like to reach out to him as the only One who can truly satisfy your soul? To find your heart captivated by the glory of his affection? To become intoxicated with his presence in punch-drunk love?

You may not feel like royalty, but in Christ you are. You are the bride of the King. What would it look like to live into that true identity? To know yourself as the beloved of God? To desire him above all others?

Foreskins and Hymens

Our bodies are iconic. They're designed to point to greater things. The Song of Songs makes this clear. You want to know one more shocking place I discovered this powerful truth? Circumcision.

Circumcision is a sexual symbol. It's not only Israel's temple that involved sexual symbolism but circumcision as well. That may sound sacrilegious at first, for a ritual so central to Israel's identity. Yet consider these five observations.

First, circumcision is performed on the male genitals, involving the removal of the foreskin from the sexual organ of the penis. This location is strongly suggestive of sexual symbolism.

Second, circumcision is associated with procreation, as a sign of God's covenant to make Abraham the fruitful father of many nations. In the ritual's foundation story, God overcomes Abraham and Sarah's barrenness, enabling them to conceive a miracle child in their old age against all possible odds. Circumcision marks Israel as the fruitful result of God's faithfulness to this promise.[18]

Third, circumcision involves the removal of a symbolic obstacle. One day, the prophets proclaimed, God would circumcise not only Israel's genitals but their hearts. The stubborn exterior of their uncircumcised heart of stone would be removed, giving way to a soft and receptive circumcised heart of flesh beneath.[19] In Hebrew, a hardened heart is literally an "uncircumcised heart." This is why Pharaoh refused to let Israel go: He was unreceptive to allowing the divine word and presence to penetrate his heart.

The foreskin is, similarly, a symbolic obstacle to fruitfulness—a blockage to be removed. Obviously, Israel did not see this blockage as literal (they knew uncircumcised Gentiles were reproducing like jackrabbits). Yet circumcision was a sign, loaded with sexual symbolism, that pointed toward a receptive and fruitful relationship with Yahweh.

Fourth, circumcision is a seal of the covenant. In the Old Testament, it was a sign that one belonged to Yahweh, included within Israel as his covenant people. Marriage imagery, as we've seen, was foundational to this covenant relationship. The performance of circumcision upon the genitals reinforces this marital symbolism with Yahweh as proper to the covenant being sealed.

Fifth and finally, circumcision involved the shedding of blood. Its foundation stories associated the ritual with sacrificial imagery.[20] Zipporah circumcises her son in a fascinating scene and declares Moses "a bridegroom of blood to me," an act that saves him from judgment.[21] That phrase "bridegroom of blood" is repeated twice in the short passage for emphasis, and tied explicitly to both Passover and circumcision themes.[22] As Moses is a "bridegroom of blood" to Zipporah, so circumcision points to a greater reality.

Yahweh is a "bridegroom of blood" to Israel.

In light of all this, let me propose a suggestion: The male foreskin functions symbolically in circumcision similar to the female hymen on a wedding night. Follow me for a moment. When a woman consummates her marriage on the wedding night—ideally, in the biblical vision, as a virgin—this consummation is associated with the breaking or tearing of the hymen, which is:

1. an act upon the genitals;
2. associated with procreation;
3. penetrating a "hardened" obstacle to fruitfulness;
4. sealing the covenant;
5. with the shedding of blood.[23]

Both consummation (for the female) and circumcision (for the male) involve the penetration of an exterior surface on the genitals, an experience which is often painful, yet which opens up an interior soft and receptive (symbolically in circumcision) to the covenant partner. Both acts seal the covenant with a shedding of blood, involving one's identification as belonging to their covenant partner. Both acts are associated with procreation, involving the potential to make one fruitful.

The foreskin and hymen are analogous to one another.

With circumcision, Yahweh is the outgoing partner while the Israelite male is the receptive partner. With consummation, the husband is the outgoing partner while the wife is the receptive partner. An Israelite male's torn foreskin was an embodied sign of his covenant union with Yahweh, similar to a wife's torn hymen as an embodied sign of her covenant union with her husband. The Israelite male functions in the "bridal" relationship to Yahweh, reinforcing the bridal imagery for the entire people of God—men and women—in both Old and New Testaments.

Such symbolism reinforces this book's central theme: Our bodies are iconic. The horizontal relationship between a husband and wife is designed to mirror the greater vertical relationship we were made for with God as his people.

This also reinforces the temple themes we've observed in this book. Israel saw sexual symbolism at play in the temple, as the Song of Songs makes clear. Similarly here, like consummation, the inner sanctuary was entered by the parting of the veil through the shedding of blood. The blood was shed just outside the veil upon the altar, in order to gain entrance and pass through the curtain into the Most Holy Place, where Yahweh dwelt most intimately with his bride and made her fruitful.

Circumcision, like consummation and the temple symbolism, involves the shedding of blood to gain entrance through the veil into the Holy Place. Both also thus point ultimately to Christ's sacrifice: the ultimate shedding of blood, by which entrance is gained into the holiest place, as the veil is torn and the covenant is sealed with his church, and his bride filled with his presence and made fruitful.

Circumcision and consummation are prophetic signs of the gospel.

The Sexuality of Scripture

When Paul says *one flesh* is iconic of Christ and the church, he's not making up a new theme but riffing on an ancient one. The Song of Songs is important because it confirms we—like Paul—are reading the biblical story rightly. There is a sexuality to Scripture, which reads the grand drama we find ourselves in as a divine romance.

The Divine Romance

The Song of Songs sings the whole story of the Bible in a sexual key. Chapter 1 recalls Israel's slavery in Egypt: The bride's skin is burnt because she was made to work harshly by her relatives in a vineyard not her own. Yet her beauty is outstanding among the mares of Pharaoh's chariots. Chapter 2 moves to Exodus imagery: The groom calls to her, "Arise, my love, my beautiful one, and come away."[24] He brings her to his banqueting house and garden (with images from Sinai, the tabernacle, and the Promised Land), where they "catch for us the little foxes" that spoil the vineyard (like the conquest that dealt with enemies spoiling God's good garden).[25]

Once in the land, chapter 3 alludes to Israel's cycles of rebellion and restoration: The bride awakes to find her lover no longer in bed with her (like idolatrous Israel finding God's presence has departed, a common theme in books like Judges), so she rushes out to search for him until they are reunited (like Yahweh returning in faithfulness to his people). She clings to him when she finds him and won't let him go.

This leads to Solomon's arrival at the climax of chapter 3 for the wedding (like Solomon's dedication of the temple in 1 Kings 8) and the consummation of the wedding in chapter 4 (like the filling of the temple with God's glory).

Chapter 5 alludes to Israel's subsequent rebellion: When she doesn't receive the lover at the door, she finds him gone. While searching for him, she is beaten by the city watchmen, has her veil taken away, and is filled with longing for their reunion (themes resonating with Israel's exile). They are reunited in chapters 6–8 (a sign of future hope), where they delight in and rejoice over one another for the remainder of the Song.

This epic song celebrates God's romance with his people. To be quite frank, modern scholars who dismiss such a reading don't know what they are talking about. Far from an imposition upon the Song, it is rather the obvious point, running clearly with the grain of the text. The author intends us to see this royal wedding iconically intertwined with the great divine romance between God and his people.

Far from a prudish denigration of human sexuality—*au contraire!*—it elevates romantic love to unprecedented levels of transcendent meaning. The divine level does not lessen the human level; it heightens and loads it with power.

Solomon's epic song reads the biblical story rightly, for it centers on the union of the King of the universe with his people as his bride. The significance of sex is propelled upward as from a trampoline—to return to a theme we opened with—the earthly icon proclaiming a heavenly reality . . .

God loves us.

The Point of the Pentateuch

The Song of Songs is building on an even earlier theme, the meaning of the Pentateuch. The first five books of the Bible—known as the Pentateuch—were for Israel more like one big book (with five *long* chapters). The Pentateuch is structured as a chiasm—a literary style popular in Hebrew writing—with mirrored bookends that work their way inward toward a climax in the middle. If you want to know the main point of a chiasm, look at its center.

So what's the center of the Pentateuch? The Day of Atonement (in Leviticus 16). This is the view commonly held by biblical scholars, given the structure of the Pentateuch. This was the annual day when the Most Holy Place of the temple could be entered through sacrifice. According to Michael Morales, a renowned biblical scholar, this structure means the central point of the Pentateuch is this: *union with the presence of God through the shedding of blood.*[26] That's the heart of the Pentateuch.

Union with God through the shedding of blood.[27]

Sex is iconic of this center. As we've seen, sex points toward union with God through the shedding of blood. That's not to say *sex* is the main point of Scripture. Rather, it is to say sex is *a sign of* the main point of Scripture. And a central one at that. The point of the Pentateuch becomes the point of the biblical story as a whole, fulfilled in Christ and the church: union with God through the shedding of blood. Sex is a sign of this destination, from the outset of the biblical story.[28]

When the Song of Songs says the romance between Yahweh and his bride is consummated in a temple garden, this isn't revisionist history but rather reading the story of Scripture rightly—with the grain of the text itself.

How do you see Scripture? A legalistic rule book? A dry list of dreary commands? Far from it. Scripture is more romantic, more filled with longing and desire—as I hope this book has made clear—than we've often been trained to think. Once you have eyes to see, the imagery is everywhere. These GPS coordinates are set from the start of the biblical story and embedded in the heart of its continuing narrative, until arriving at this destination in its final pages—in the royal wedding at the consummation of history.

Become the Bride

The gospel invites you to a royal wedding. This invitation is for men *and* women, young *and* old, single *and* married. This is for all of us.

But you're not simply invited to *attend,* you're invited to become the bride. God's not looking for you to be a spectator, an outside observer, flashing pictures with your camera while straining your neck to try and get a glimpse of the action. No, God's inviting you to encounter him as the great Lover of your soul, to know yourself as his beloved, to stand with him before the eyes of the watching world, and be united with him in covenant forever.

What would keep you from saying, "Yes!"? Why wouldn't you enter into union with the King?

"Let me hear your voice!" the king calls out to his bride at the end of the Song, to her who "dwell[s] in the gardens." "Make haste, my beloved," the bride calls back to her groom, looking up to "the mountains" with longing, like the bride of Revelation crying out "Come, Lord Jesus!"[29] Jewish interpreters saw this as a messianic cry, of longing for God's return. The couple is one flesh, yet separated and longing for reunion. The day will come when he will descend from the mountains to reunite with her in the garden.

Their longing—nay, our longing—will be fulfilled at the end of the world.

15

THE END OF THE WORLD

The end of the world is a wedding. It's not the sun burning out as the earth freezes over. Not the apocalyptic fire and smoke of a Cormac McCarthy–esque wasteland. No, it's the wine and feasting of a royal wedding, the laughter and celebration as Christ and his church are united together forever.

Weddings celebrate union, and this wedding is no different. The wedding of Revelation 21–22 celebrates the union of *heaven and earth* (as God and humanity dwell together forever), the union of *east and west* (as the nations come streaming into God's holy city), the union of *weak and strong* (as the tears of the suffering and the glory of kings are received by Jesus), and the union of *good folks and bad folks* (who together belt out the song of the Lamb once slain, redeemed by the grace of God).

Our end is beautiful union.

A Bridal City

The wedding of Revelation draws heavily on the Song of Songs imagery that we explored in the previous chapter. Fascinatingly, the bride is not a *person* but rather a *city:*

I saw the Holy City, the new Jerusalem, coming down out of
heaven from God, prepared as a bride beautifully dressed
for her husband.[1]

That may sound strange at first (*Jesus is marrying a city?*), until
we realize the city is his church. She is "the wife of the Lamb,"
whose twelve gates are identified with the twelve tribes of Israel,
and twelve foundations with the twelve apostles of the church.[2]
This is a city where the streets have no name, for its residents are
still building and burning down love. This bridal city is the people
of God.

The city's shape is a perfect cube: the shape of the Most Holy
Place in the temple, only now expanded to the size of a massive
continent (*the city's dimensions are huge!*).[3] The Most Holy Place
has become a city; the city has become a sanctuary that covers the
earth with the glory of God as the waters cover the sea. Like the
Most Holy Place, where God's presence dwelt most intimately
and powerfully with his people, so a voice now shouts from the
center of the city, "Look! God's dwelling place is now among the
people, and he will dwell with them. They will be his people, and
God himself will be with them and be their God."[4]

There is no *building* for a temple, for "the Lord God the
Almighty and the Lamb are its temple."[5] The divine presence is
no longer contained in brick and mortar, for he permeates his
people—the bridal city, a temple built with living stones. God's
indwelling presence is so strong that it radiates from his bride:
"[The city] shone with the glory of God, and its brilliance was
like that of a very precious jewel."[6] God's presence makes his people shine.

The city is "adorned with every kind of jewel." The list of
twelve specific jewels evokes the twelve gemstones on the high
priest's breastplate, which he wore into the Most Holy Place to
represent each of the twelve tribes.[7] Like the high priest, this city
represents the people of God, glittering in radiant glory.

The city is a temple is a bride.

The New Jerusalem does not *contradict* the old Jerusalem with its temple; she *fulfills* it. The temple was always eschatological, pointing forward, representing the bridal identity of God's people and anticipating the consummation of their union in a building "not built by human hands."[8] This destiny is fulfilled in Revelation's royal wedding at the end of the world.

This wedding will bring life to the land. "Behold, I am making all things new," the One on the throne declares.[9] His river of life rushes through his bride, making her gardens abundantly fruitful. The trees by the river bear twelve different kinds of fruit, monthly rather than yearly, with leaves for "the healing of the nations."[10] Christ's union with his church heals creation, as the tree of life is restored.

Together, they bring fruitful life to the world.

This end is, more truly, a beginning. The age of sin and death will be over, the dawn of new creation begun. Joy to the world! God and his bride will share their life-giving presence far as the curse is found. "Death shall be no more, neither shall there be mourning, nor crying, nor pain anymore, for the former things have passed away."[11] Their faithful love brings forth the abundance of the kingdom.

This is your destiny, O church: to be the fruitful bride of God who reigns with him in his kingdom forever.

Throne, Lamb, River

The Trinity inhabits this temple. God is described with three major images: a throne, a lamb, and a river. John sees the

river of the water of life, bright as crystal, flowing from the throne of God and of the Lamb through the middle of the street of the city.[12]

This is Trinitarian imagery. The throne belongs to God the Father, who now reigns on earth as in heaven. The Lamb is Christ the Son, whose sacrifice has made this reconciliation possible. The river is the Spirit, who rushes out to share their life-giving presence with the world.

These are also temple images. The Throne was associated with the Most Holy Place, where the ark of the covenant served as God's footstool. The image was of God as King of the universe, sitting upon his heavenly throne, with his feet touching down here to rest upon the earth. Now, in Revelation, that heavenly throne has itself come down to rest upon the earth, as God reigns from the center of the new creation.

The Lamb is also a temple image. The sacrifices were made just outside the Most Holy Place, on the altar, where blood was shed to atone for the people's sin and reconcile them to God. The Passover Lamb was an archetypal sacrifice, which had facilitated the people's deliverance from slavery into freedom with God. Now, in Revelation, the once-for-all sacrifice has been made: Christ has atoned for his people's sin, delivered them from slavery, and brought them into the freedom of God's holy presence.

The River is a temple image as well. The prophetic hope was for these waters to rush out from the temple's sanctuary and down the mount—like that ancient river from Eden—bringing life to the land once more. Now, in Revelation, that prophetic hope is fulfilled by the Spirit, who goes forth from Christ and the Father to rush through the city of his people and make their land fruitful, healing the nations and restoring creation.

This bridal city is indwelt by the triune God.

As "Lover, Beloved, and Love" speaks to the *immanent* Trinity (God as he is in himself from eternity), so "Throne, Lamb, and River" speaks to the *eschatological* Trinity (God as he will come to indwell creation at the consummation of history). This temple imagery draws upon the iconic meaning of sex to point to future hope. You and I were made for the love of the Trinity: the Spirit within us, Christ before us, the Father over us.

The end of the world—the goal for which it was made—is to be indwelt by the triune God. The end is love, for God is love.

Our end is found in God.

The Hope of the World

You were made for God. That is your highest calling, your deepest purpose, where your greatest longings will be fulfilled. What would it look like to live into this reality? To prepare for this destiny? To make Christ your highest priority, the love above all loves, the greatest excellency above which none else can compare?

This is how you prepare for the end of the world. Not by hunkering down in a bunker with stockpiles of canned food and ammo. Not by doomsday predictions on sandwich board signs spouting vitriol with disdain. No. Such fear and hate are antithetical to the hope of the gospel. You prepare for the end of the world by becoming a lover of God.

You might feel like hope is lost. Like the world is too far gone. War and rumors of war. Poverty, tyranny, and global instability. The raging dumpster fire of the daily news. The unraveling in your own life. But the gospel says you can lift your eyes in hope. A wedding is coming, and it's a wedding that will heal the world.

Weddings are beautiful—the flowers and music, the feasting and dancing—but they are nothing without the one who stands at the center: your spouse. Christ stands at the center of the wedding at the end of the world, the wedding that is waiting for you. The glory of the new creation is the glory that radiates from his face, the glory of his great love for us.

On that day, we shall no longer be a bride eagerly anticipating our wedding day. We shall be "the wife of the Lamb," who has entered the fullness of our communion with the One we were made for.[13] We shall be wrapped in the divine embrace, declaring "I am my beloved's and my beloved is mine," rejoicing in the radiance of the love that arises between us.[14] We shall shine with his indwelling presence, streaming forth from us to fill the earth with glory.

This wedding is the end of the world but in another sense its true beginning. For it shall inaugurate the end for which the world was made, the goal of our existence: to be embraced within the faithful love of God. This love shall bring forth the abundance of his kingdom, as we delight in the communion of the Trinity. The icon shall give way to the reality it pointed toward all along.

We shall be united with God.

CONCLUSION

_____

The Divine Flame

Elijah and I were right to be enchanted by the mystery as kids. That trampoline above his bedroom held the secret of where we had come from and where we were going, the meaning and purpose behind the world.

Sex explains everything. Sort of. It's a sign of the structure of creation, the nature of salvation, the abundance of the kingdom, and the identity of God.

Sex points to greater things. To the wondrous intimacy of Christ and the church, the glorious complementarity of heaven and earth, the mysterious communion of the triune God, and the life-giving presence of the Spirit.

Am I crazy, or is this a better vision? Am I losing my marbles, or is God's vision for sex way more beautiful and compelling than anything else on offer? You don't need to apologize for the Christian sexual ethic or be bashful about it, any more than you'd apologize for owning the *Mona Lisa* or living in the Taj Mahal. While it may be countercultural, it can stand on its own—outshining all lesser competitors.

God's beautiful vision unlocks the true. It explains the problem with divorce (it violates union), gay sex (it violates diversity), premarital sex (it violates covenantal love), adultery (it violates faithful love), pornography (it violates the unitive dimension of sex), and abortion (it violates the procreative dimension of sex).

Yet every such *no* is embedded within a richer, all-encompassing *yes*. Yes to generosity, hospitality, and life. Yes to faithfulness, sacrifice, and commitment. Yes to diversity-in-union. Yes to the future. Yes to love. Yes to Christ.

What would it look like for you to say yes to such greater things? To say yes to Christ and live with faithfulness and integrity to his vision for the world? You can say yes because he's worth it, and because his vision is good, true, and beautiful.

We need a new sexual revolution. One driven not by the freedom to do what we want but the freedom to reflect who God is. Not by the dry legalism of rule keeping but the deeper human vocation of image bearing. Not by the objectifying use of the other for self-love but the sincere giving of the self in a communion-of-love.

This revolution is for all of us. Single or married, male or female, divorced or widowed, rich or poor, from a loving family or a broken home. Whatever your history, your heartbreaks, your suspicions, your circumstances, your inclinations, your longings, this vision is for you because Jesus is for you. You can have the reality—with or without the sign—for the message contained in sex is available in Christ to all who would receive him.

God's vision points us to the good, and you can live into these good, larger, spacious realities that sex is designed to point to. Ultimately, they are rooted in the death-defying love of God, as celebrated in the high point of the Song of Songs:

> For love is strong as death,
>   jealousy is fierce as the grave,
> Its flashes are flashes of fire,
>   the very flame of Yah.[1]

The passion of human romance, the Song is saying, is lit by a divine flame. The "flame of Yah" is shorthand for the flame of

Yahweh, the very fire of God. It's not only the uniting of bodies, this epic poem declares, but the desire beneath—the desire that drives the two toward becoming one—that is iconic of God's divine desire for his people. This divine flame that burns through the center of the universe can ignite your heart to burn for him too.

Christ's desire is for you as his bride. His love for you is stronger than death. His jealousy for you is fiercer than the grave. His passion for you was poured out on the cross. His holy affection for you burns with resurrection power stronger than sin, death, and hell, which he willingly entered and overcame in order to be united with you forever.

The desire of love is a sign of the gospel. Your heart is a wick; his love is the flame. You were made to burn for him.[2]

What would it look like for you to live into this vision? To find your own story wrapped up in this greater story? In the love that is behind and underneath and around all our stories? In the eternal affection of the triune God?

What do you need to give up, to let go of, in order to make space for these greater things that lead to life? What do you need to reach out for, to cling to, in order to wholeheartedly embrace and say yes to the One who's already drawn close to embrace you?

You were made for love. For *this* love. That is the heart of the iconic vision. You were made for a love that is faithful, strong, and true. You were made for the security of the divine embrace. You were made for holy affection and intimate care. You were made for belonging, not dependent on your performance or striving, where you are known as you truly are. You were made for a fruitful life, bringing generative abundance into the world around you.

Don't settle for anything less; reach out for the something more that your heart was made for—reach out for Christ himself. You were made to know yourself as the beloved. As *his* beloved.

You were made for beautiful union.

Big Thanks

A big thanks to . . .
Jenni Burke, the best literary agent in the world (seriously), and the whole Illuminate Team, for helping to refine and champion this project.

The whole team at WaterBrook and Multnomah. I'm so humbled to work with such an amazing crew! A special shout-out to Paul Pastor, you were a literal answer to prayer as editor, exponentially improving this project with your wisdom and craft.

Redemption Tempe. It's an honor to serve as your pastor; this book was forged in the trenches of our shared life together. To the leadership team: I can't imagine a better (or funner) crew to run with in ministry. A special shout-out to Tyler Johnson, Jim Mullins, and Luke Simmons for all the encouragement and support.

The many friends whose brilliant insights and meaningful conversations are threaded between these pages. Luke Hendrix, you've shaped me into the man I am today. Ben Thomas and Paul Ramey, our cord of three strands is not easily broken. Jesse Lusko, our midnight conversations via cell phone through the neighborhood have been a highlight. Brett McCracken, Preston Sprinkle, and Jamin Goggin: Your feedback on early versions of the manuscript was invaluable. Tony Scarcello, for sharing your story and becoming a friend. Eric and Amy Ludwig, for refreshing cabin retreats where reflection was experienced and many words written. Rick McKinley, Paul Metzger, and Gerry Breshears: for pastoral and theological formation. Tim Mackie, for some great conversations that alerted me to important themes. The Searock crew, for all the encouragement and support. The cohorts who endured rough draft versions of these ideas and refined them through our lively conversations. Sebastian and Catherine Rogers, and Maurice and Leslie Cowley: for being there through it all. Luke and Jillana Goble, and Paul and Bethany Richter: for walking the foster/adoption journey with us. Liz Martin, Emma Tautolo, and Natalee Anderson: for formative conversations on singleness. Peixoto, Provision, and Lux: for the coffee and ambience where many of these words were written.

Mom and Dad, for giving me life and building me up. Grandma and Grandpa Valdez, for imaging Christ and the church. My band of brothers, for always having my back. Felina and Francisco, for trusting us to be in life together. My extended family: You're the tree; I'm a branch.

Holly, Aiden, James, and Jacob: my tribe, my one flesh and my flesh and bone, my icon of adoption and new birth, my window into the Father heart of God and his eternal communion-of-love . . . I love you.

Above all, God—Father, Son, and Holy Spirit—Creator and Redeemer, from whom I've come and where I'm going, my life and my longing, my joy and salvation, my king and my friend: "I am my beloved's and my beloved is mine." Soli Deo Gloria.

NOTES

Introduction

1. Obviously, there is diversity within the historic Christian vision of sex. I love Saint Augustine but disagree with him on some significant points, and I'll critique some aspects of the recent purity culture movement later in this book. There are, however, broad brushstrokes to the historic Christian vision, as we'll see in the pages that follow. When I use terms like "the traditional Christian sexual ethic," it is this broader consensus that I am referring to.

2. This icon is from Saint Catherine's Monastery, Mount Sinai, Egypt (public domain). The first image was originally posted by carulmare at Flickr, "ICONS, Sinai, Christ Pantocrator, 6th century," November 23, 2006, www.flickr.com/photos/8545333@N07/4124982761. The second image, with mirrored composites from the left and right sides of the icon, was created by JustinGBX in Photoshop on October 3, 2014, https://en.wikipedia.org/wiki/Christ_Pantocrator_(Sinai)#/media/File:Composite_christ_pantocrator.png.

3. Alex Morris, "Tales from the Millennials' Sexual Revolution," *Rolling Stone*, March 31, 2014.

Chapter 1:
Sex as Salvation

1. Ephesians 5:31–32, NIV, though I've translated *proskollao* as "cleave" to match the Genesis 2:24 translation we'll be using later.

2. Some take "one flesh" to be about marital union more broadly (rather than consummation specifically), but Paul is able to use the phrase for sex with a prostitute (1 Corinthians 6:16), where marriage is not in view. Others take it to refer simply to kinship, but this arises from a conflation of "one flesh" with "flesh and bone" (as we'll see in chapter 3). "One flesh" refers to sexual union; the case for this will be developed throughout this book.

3. This temple imagery is not just poetic license; we'll see later in this book (particularly chapters 11–15) how temple imagery is interwoven with sexual themes.

4. See endnote 2 just above.

5. Coleman Hell, "2 Heads," track 6 on *Summerland*, Columbia Records, 2016. The lyric is likely an adaptation of Shakespeare's "making the beast with two backs" in *Othello*, an Elizabethan street-phrase used by the playwright to accentuate the coarse character of Iago, the speaker.

6. Preston and Jackie Hill-Perry, "Pornography and Marriage: Part One," April 2, 2019, in *Thirty Minutes With the Perrys*, podcast, https://thirty-minutes-with-the-perrys.simplecast.com/episodes/pornography-marriage-part-one-AGdq_bPi.

7. Emily Nagoski, *Come as You Are* (New York: Simon & Schuster, 2021), 218–46.

8. Mark Regnerus, *Cheap Sex: The Transformation of Men, Marriage, and Monogamy* (New York: Oxford University Press, 2017), 22–26.

9. Sheila Wray Gregoire, *31 Days to Great Sex* (Grand Rapids: Zondervan, 2020), 135–36.

10. C. S. Lewis, *The Great Divorce* (New York: Simon & Schuster, 1996), 95.

11. Revelation 17–22.

12. While both women and men are *victims* of rape, the offending perpetrators are virtually always male. In those exceedingly rare cases where a woman is the rapist (using coercion to *be* penetrated), there is usually an extreme power dynamic at play, such as a teacher with

an underage student. Similarly, while men as well as women can be prostitutes, a male prostitute generally plays the "feminine" role in the equation. You get paid to *be* penetrated, not to penetrate. The point: There is a gendered dynamic to rape and prostitution, as inversions of iconic design.

13. Acts 20:35.

14. This should go without saying, but consent is still vital in marriage. Wives: You have the right to say no. Sexual assault within marriage is a real thing, and it's wrong. We're not talking about *frequency* here (how often sex should happen in marriage can be negotiated in ways that are unique to each couple) but rather an overall *posture* between spouses (the divine design is ideally reflected in mutual self-giving and reciprocity).

15. Ruth 3.

16. Joshua Ryan Butler, *The Pursuing God* (Nashville: Thomas Nelson, 2016).

17. According to Scripture, church tradition, and the best historical evidence we have, Jesus never had sex.

18. 1 Corinthians 7.

19. Mark 10:29–30. Notice how Jesus speaks not only of "the age to come" but "now in this time."

20. See Sam Allberry's excellent book, *7 Myths About Singleness* (Wheaton, Ill.: Crossway, 2019), 120.

21. Carl Trueman, *The Rise and Triumph of the Modern Self* (Wheaton, Ill.: Crossway, 2020), 22.

22. The 242 phrase count includes the variations: *en Christo* ("in Christ"), *en kyrio* ("in the Lord"), *en Christo Iesou* ("in Christ Jesus"), and *en auto* ("in him"). The phrase shows up 216 times in letters attributed to Paul and 26 times in those attributed to John.

23. In ancient imagery, the husband and wife are one body, with the husband as head. Scripture also uses this imagery, which we'll explore later in this book.

24. Acts 11:26; 26:28; 1 Peter 4:16.

25. Romans 5:5; Ezekiel 11:19; 36:26; Luke 22:20; cf. Jeremiah 31:33; Hebrews 8:10.

26. *International Standard Bible Encyclopedia*, ed. James Orr (Chicago: The Howard-Severance Company, 1915), s.v. "loins."

Chapter 2:
Why Sunsets Are Beautiful

1. Genesis 1:27.

2. Day 1 involves the separation of light from dark (associated with the passing of time in verse 14), Day 2 the vertical dimension of heaven from "the waters that were above" (a reference to ancient cosmology; verse 7), and Day 3 the land from "waters under the heavens" (or, sea; verse 9). Days 4, 5, and 6 involve the filling of these respective spaces. I've summarized these pairs here as heaven and earth (vertical), land and sea (horizontal), and night and day (temporal).

3. Peter Kreeft, in "Understanding Man & Woman" (Ecce Films: 2016), the third in the *Humanum* video series, available at www .eccefilms.com/humanum.

4. Brett McCracken, "Where Water Meets Rock," *The Gospel Coalition*, August 10, 2017, www.thegospelcoalition.org/article/where -water-meets-rock.

5. This is known as the "edge effect" in permaculture design.

6. Shakespeare, *Romeo and Juliet*, act 2, scene 2.

7. Ezekiel 28:13–14.

8. Acts 17:28.

9. Matthew 6:10.

10. Genesis 1:27, NIV.

11. N.T. Wright, "From Genesis to Revelation," in *Not Just Good, but Beautiful: The Complementary Relationship Between Man and Woman*, eds. Helen Alvaré and Steven Lopes (New York: Plough, 2015), 87–88.

12. People with intersex conditions are created fully in the image of God. Intersex conditions do not disrupt the male/female binary as a "third" sex (a description commonly rejected by intersex persons) but rather combine characteristics from both sexes (though in the vast majority of intersex conditions one's biological sex as male or female is still clear). For an introductory discussion, see Preston Sprinkle, *Embodied: Transgender Identities, the Church, and What the Bible Has to Say* (Colorado Springs: David C. Cook, 2021), 113–26.

13. Tsui-Ying Sheng, "The Union of Yin and Yang," in *Not Just Good, but Beautiful*, 141. Male and female are distinct yet interdependent,

like the broader reality of nature they are embedded within. We need both to exist, literally. (It's how you were born.)

14. For example, its absence of a Creator with a corresponding philosophical dualism.

15. This means God did not create us out of loneliness or boredom, or to meet some unmet need within—like a codependent lover constantly texting to make sure things are okay. No. God has perfect relationship within God's own triune life and created us from an overflow of that divine love, to lovingly share his life with us. Our Maker did not make us to get something from us but to give himself to us. God is love and this love is rooted in the mystery of the Trinity.

Chapter 3:
Lover, Beloved, Love

1. The African statue photo is by Abbi Alivizatos.

2. On the identification of the Father as Lover, Son as Beloved, and Spirit as Love, see for example: Matthew 3:17; 17:5; Luke 20:13; John 3:35; 5:20; 17:24; Colossians 1:13; Romans 5:5; Galatians 5:22. The context in such verses is obviously not sexual, but it is deeply relational and familial. In the pages that follow, you'll see how the metaphor of sexual love works by analogy.

3. Again, while it is powerful to recognize this design in the structure of human relationships, this should not be used to imply that marriage or childbearing is the only or most blessed state of life for Christians. Rather, for all of us, it points to the *generative* nature of divine love, and how God has coded that into the life and reproduction of humanity.

4. See, for example, Jesus's discourse in John 14–17, where the persons of the Trinity each seek to lift up and glorify one another.

5. See chapter 12 for an exploration of the biblical foundations for this reading of the image of God.

6. Christopher West, *Theology of the Body for Beginners* (Westchester, Pa.: Ascension Press, 2009), 8.

7. This reading of the Trinitarian analogy is supported by the *filioque* clause, that the Spirit proceeds from both the Father *and* the Son.

8. As the mature Christian tradition has recognized, all our language for God is analogical, not univocal. This is because God is Creator,

distinct from creation. Every analogy breaks down at some point. When we call God our Rock, it doesn't mean he's literally made of granite. The mountain is a metaphor for our Maker. Yet it speaks to something true: God's firm reliability. Similarly, things of this world—like the family—can speak by analogy, even if not univocally, to the reality of God.

9. For example, the Trinity has one will, whereas a father, mother, and child have three. While it's worth recognizing this tension would have been less felt in the ancient world, when the household was generally conceived to have a type of singular will—as a household unit, at least—originating in the father, this doesn't change the fact that, on a deeper anthropological level, regardless of social convention, family members have always had multiple wills in a way that is disanalogous from the Trinity. Chapter 12 will explore further questions and qualifications with the analogy.

10. See chapter 12 for a fuller exploration of the family's relation to the image of God.

11. Genesis 29:14.

12. Judges 9:2.

13. 2 Samuel 19:12.

14. The most influential advocate for this argument is James V. Brownson, in *Bible, Gender, Sexuality* (Grand Rapids: Eerdmans, 2013), 85–109. The problem with this reading is that it conflates these two phrases that are related yet distinct. While "flesh and bone" is regularly used for kinship, it is never used synonymously with "one flesh." And Paul is able to use "one flesh" for sex with a prostitute (1 Corinthians 6:16), where covenant and kinship are clearly nowhere in view. We'll unpack the background and significance of these two terms more in chapters 11 and 12.

15. The Hebrew phrase is a *metonymy*, where a part of something is used to stand in for the whole. Flesh represents the outside of the person (your surface or exterior), while bone represents the inside (the architecture of your interior). So calling family members your "flesh and bone" is a way of saying, "We're made of the same stuff, you and I, inside and out!" The terminology is related to generation, and first appears in Genesis 2:23 for Eve who was pulled from Adam's body, her existence uniquely generated from his, similar to how their children will later be pulled from her body. (See chapter 11 for a detailed discussion of Genesis 2.)

16. Etymology Online, s.v. "kin," www.etymonline.com.

17. Furthermore, the reason the Trinity shares this oneness is because the Son and Spirit "proceed from" the Father. The Son is "begotten" (like a child), "not made" (like a painting). Like a child who proceeds from their parent, the Son is "of one being" with the Father because he shares of his nature. The Son and Spirit share the same substance with the One from whom they proceed. While the oneness of the family analogy does break down around the will (the Trinity has one will, whereas a father, mother, and child have three), there is a strength in the analogy when it comes to procession, substance, and nature. Chapter 12 will develop a thicker foundation for this analogy, with appropriate qualifications.

18. Abha Bhattarai, "Millennials Are Picking Pets over Children," *Washington Post*, September 23, 2016.

19. Bhattarai, "Millennials Are Picking."

20. Bhattarai, "Millennials Are Picking."

21. Neil Postman, *The Disappearance of Childhood* (New York: Delacorte Press, 1982), xi.

22. Genesis 5:1–3.

23. Pete uses this truism frequently in his trainings based on his book, *Emotionally Healthy Spirituality* (Grand Rapids: Zondervan, 2017).

24. This is not to say God is absent in the image-making process (Karl Barth's critique in *Church Dogmatics*, III.1), delegating it off to sex to avoid getting his hands dirty. Rather, God is at work in a couple's embrace, like a king exerting the strength of his mighty arm through the stamp of a royal insignia, impressing his royal signature upon the life of every child through sex. God has ordained a couple's union as the vehicle through which he impresses the sign of his identity and authority upon us. God gifts his image not *in spite of* sex, but rather *through* it.

25. Romans 5:5.

26. Galatians 5:22.

27. See chapter 13 for more on infertility and procreation.

28. The ecstatic moment is not iconic on its own, in isolation from the communion-forming event. It's thus worth noting that masturbation and pornography fall short of the *unitive* dimension of sex, even if one achieves a state of orgasm on one's own. Similarly, contraceptive sex intentionally shuts union off from the *procreative* di-

mension. Even if contraception is permissible to steward the size of one's family, this is different from a couple being permanently closed off to the fruitfulness of their love (see my article, "The Ethics of Contraception," available on my website, www.joshua ryanbutler.com). The fullness of the icon is oriented toward the formation of a biological family, in joy, as a tripersonal communion-of-love.

29. See chapter 12 for clarifications and qualifications on the metaphorical nature of this language.

Chapter 4:
Wedding on a Mountain

1. For just a few examples from some inconspicuous places, check out Nehemiah 9:17; Jonah 4:2; and Lamentations 3:22.

2. Psalm 33:5; 36:7.

3. Deuteronomy 7:9; Psalm 136.

4. Genesis 40:14; Joshua 2:12–13; Ruth 1:8; 2 Samuel 9:3.

5. Ephesians 5:25.

6. I believe I heard Pastor Tim Keller say this in a talk, but I was unable to locate the source of the quote.

7. Galatians 5:22.

8. This language comes from Gary Thomas, *Sacred Marriage* (Grand Rapids: Zondervan, 2015). Such language should not be used to justify abusive relationships (as we'll see in chapter 6). Also, this is not to pit holiness against happiness. True, deep happiness comes through our sanctification, as a byproduct of holiness.

9. Francis Sutherland explores this semantic shift in his essay "Why Making Love Isn't What It Used to Be," in *Challenging Change: Literary and Linguistic Responses*, ed. Vesna Lopicic and Biljana Misic Ilic (Newcastle upon Tyne, UK: Cambridge Scholars Publishing, 2012), 15–22.

10. Anthony Trollope, *He Knew He Was Right* (Leipzig, Germany: Bernhard Tauchnitz, 1869), 259.

11. Linda Waite et al., *Does Divorce Make People Happy? Findings from a Study of Unhappy Marriages* (Institute for American Values, 2002).

12. Zephaniah 3:17.

13. See Jeremiah 11:15; 12:7, NRSV.

14. Deuteronomy 33:3, NRSV; this term *habab* means "love" or "make love" in Aramaic. On the later rabbinic tradition, see Michael L. Satlow, *Jewish Marriage in Antiquity* (Princeton, N.J.: Princeton University Press, 2001), 234–35. Moses uses this term here to describe Israel; in light of the gospel, it is also appropriate to apply this term to the church.

15. Isaiah 54:5.

16. Raymond C. Ortlund, Jr., *Proverbs: Wisdom that Works*, Preaching the Word (Wheaton, Ill.: Crossway, 2012), 100.

17. For example, Isaiah 54:5; Jeremiah 3:20; Ezekiel 16; Hosea 2.

18. Jeremiah 31:32, NIV.

19. While this connection is less clear in English translations, the Hebrew words *tannin* and *rahab* are both terms for a sea monster or dragon. See *Strong's Expanded Exhaustive Concordance of the Bible* (Peabody, Mass.: Hendrickson, 2009), s.v. "tannin," "rahab." Both terms are used in association with Egypt and God's Exodus act of deliverance. See Isaiah 30:7; 51:9-11; Ezekiel 29:3; 32:1-3; Exodus 7:9-12; cf. Psalm 74:13; 87:4; 89:10; 148:7; Genesis 1:21; Job 26:12–13.

20. Exodus 19:4-6, NIV.

21. Exodus 19:3–8.

22. See "Covenant: God's Law and the People's Consent," in *The Jewish Political Tradition, vol. 1: Authority,* eds. Michael Walzer, Menachem Lorberbaum, Noam J. Zohar (New Haven, Conn.: Yale University Press, 2000), 5–46. Later generations of Israelites saw themselves as present at Mount Sinai, in their ancestors, giving their consent as a people to willingly enter this covenant.

23. Kyle Harper, *From Shame to Sin: The Christian Transformation of Sexual Morality in Late Antiquity* (Cambridge, Mass.: Harvard University Press, 2016). What Harper traces is much greater than simply consent in marriage. He traces a transformation in ancient society's moral framework for sexuality as a whole, which radically elevated the agency of women, slaves, children, and the poor.

24. Traditional Jewish wedding ceremonies do not have vows; the commitment is seen as implicit in the covenant. Yet the Ten Commandments here perform a similar function, setting the parameters of

expectation, by outlining a framework for the covenant relationship and setting boundaries for the commitment being entered into.

25. Some of this wording is taken from my previous book, *The Pursuing
    God* (Nashville: Thomas Nelson, 2016), 35.

26. Law and love are not contradictory. As Jesus taught, the heart of
    the law is love (Matthew 22:36–40). Marriage's legal aspect estab-
    lishes a common foundation for a couple building their future to-
    gether. God brought his beloved to the mountain, however, not
    simply to give her the law but to give her himself. Similarly, the
    goal of marriage is not to simply avoid having an affair but to live
    into intimacy and communion as you build a life together. What
    you are committing to in your vows is a life based on love.

27. Why the husband and not the wife? It may not seem very equal to
    modern sensibilities, yet women were much more vulnerable in the
    ancient world, so a formal commitment on the man's part served to
    protect wives from mistreatment. This was a "women's rights"
    document, with the goal of protecting the more vulnerable partner
    in the relationship. You can envision the daughter's parents saying,
    "We want prenup! We want prenup!" If the dude broke his promises
    down the road, their daughter would bear the disproportionate
    impact—so this public commitment was reinforced by their sur-
    rounding community. Civil society was to have their back.

28. Tim Keller makes this observation in *The Meaning of Marriage*
    (New York: Penguin, 2011), 90–91.

29. Exodus 25–31.

30. Hebrews 13:5. See also Deuteronomy 31:6–8; Matthew 28:20; John
    14:18; Genesis 28:15; Joshua 1:5–9; 1 Chronicles 28:20; Psalm 94:14.

31. 1 John 4:18.

32. See Psalm 136, which repeats this refrain twenty-six times. In
    many ways, this is the central theme of the entire book of Psalms.

Chapter 5:
Brace to Be Born

1. John 17:24.

2. Michael Reeves unpacks this powerful observation in his excellent
   book, *Delighting in the Trinity* (Downers Grove, Ill.: IVP Academic,
   2012), 19–38.

3. Todd Wilson, *Mere Sexuality* (Grand Rapids: Zondervan, 2017), 97.

4. John 3:3–4.

5. My friend Riccardo Stewart inspired this paraphrase in his Easter sermon at Redemption Tempe on April 1, 2018.

6. John 3:5–8. Jesus also references water: being born "of water and the Spirit," or "water, namely the Spirit" (an alternate rendering of *kai*). The former rendering suggests a sacramental association with baptism, the latter rendering an association with the "river of life" image (which we'll explore in chapter 13).

7. 1 John 3:1, 9, NIV. I rendered the word *seed* in verse 9 in the original Greek.

8. *Strong's Expanded Exhaustive Concordance of the Bible* (Peabody, Mass.: Hendrickson, 2009), s.v. "sperma." *A Greek-English Lexicon of the New Testament* (New York: Harper, 1894), s.v. "sperma," 4690.

9. 1 John 3:7, 9, 13, 16, 18; 4:7; 5:1, 4, 18.

10. See chapter 13 for these "river of life" associations.

11. Matthew 13:38. Those exact words are found in the King James Version and other translations.

12. 1 John 3:24, NIV; 1 John 4:13, NIV.

13. The association of semen with the river of life is not creative license; see chapter 13 for a fuller biblical exploration of this connection.

14. Romans 8:19, NIV.

15. Romans 8:22, NIV. Paul connects this travail to the Fall, when creation was "subjected to futility" and "bondage to corruption" (verses 20–21).

16. Romans 8:21, NIV.

17. Romans 8:23. Paul mixes metaphors here, using imagery from both natural childbirth (for creation's groaning) and adoption (for our identity as children). Generally, when it comes to our identity as God's children, Paul emphasizes adoptive imagery while John emphasizes natural birth imagery.

18. *Strong's*, s.v. "stenazo." *A Greek-English Lexicon*, 4727, from the root *stenos*.

19. Romans 8:18, NIV.

20. Acts 2:24. I've added "birth" to "pangs" as a more literal rendering of *odin*. The Greek term means "birth pangs," though it's obviously working metaphorically in this passage.

21. Colossians 1:18; Romans 8:29, NIV; cf. 1 Corinthians 15:22.

22. Thomas Andrew Bennett, *The Labor of God* (Waco: Baylor University Press, 2017).

23. Jesus also compares his disciples to a mother in labor (John 16:20–22), to describe how their anguish (at his crucifixion and death) will turn to joy (in his resurrection) like a mother beholding her newborn child. Once more, the little bundle of joy is the victorious Son of God.

24. Tish Harrison Warren, "The Church Made Vagina Sculptures Long Before Nadia Bolz-Weber," *Christianity Today*, February 26, 2019.

25. Warren, "The Church Made Vagina Sculptures."

26. Andrew Wilson, "God Always Heals," *Christianity Today*, November 4, 2014.

27. Jesus's resurrection has actually *induced* labor on the old world. Jesus refers to "end times" events (a reference to the church era on the other side of his victory) as "the beginning of birth pangs" (Matthew 24:8, NIV); Paul uses this language ("labor pains") too (1 Thessalonians 5:3). In other words, Christ's resurrection has sparked a pivotal shift in the epochs. His victory has converted the tomb into a womb, our final destination into a transit station.

28. 2 Corinthians 5:17.

29. Ezekiel 16 describes the Exodus using both birth and marriage imagery. The newborn is female here, rather than a "firstborn son," because Ezekiel develops the analogy to highlight Israel's marital relationship to Yahweh. Yet in the Exodus, Israel's primary descriptor is God's "firstborn son."

30. Alastair J. Roberts and Andrew Wilson, *Echoes of Exodus* (Wheaton, Ill.: Crossway, 2018), 44.

31. The first word, *chazaq*, means "to seize, strengthen, or harden." Earlier in Exodus 4, God has Moses "seize" a snake that's chasing him, "strengthening" his grip around its tail, as the serpent "hardens" into a staff in Moses's outstretched arm. This first use of the term in Exodus is a foreshadowing of what's to come: Pharaoh will chase Israel down like a snake (the text identifies him with the serpent), but God will "seize" (*chazaq*) Pharaoh, turning the tyrant's slippery arrogance into a hardened tool in his outstretched mighty

right hand—like the staff Moses will wield at the Red Sea, as God's iconic representative—to the display of his divine glory. God "seizes/hardens" the slippery serpent.

The second word, *kabad*, means "heavy, or glory." Earlier in Exodus 5, the term first appears when Pharaoh "hardens" Israel's labor, making their enslavement "heavy" (forcing them to make bricks without straw), oppressing them to increase his own "glory." When the same term is used shortly thereafter, for God's hardening of Pharaoh, it's as if God is saying: "You made life heavy for my people; now I'm going to make life heavy for you." Pharaoh sought to increase the weight of his own glory by pushing God's people down, so God brings the weight of his divine glory by pushing the oppressor down—to deliver his people from their oppression. God makes himself "heavy" upon the oppressor.

The third word, *qashah*, is the term with childbirth resonances I describe here, which appears in Genesis 35:16–17 (Rachel's labor), Exodus 7:3 (God's action toward Pharaoh), and Exodus 13:15 (Pharaoh's action toward Israel).

32. Genesis 35:16–20. This scene signals the completed emergence of the twelve tribes of Israel, followed by a genealogical account of each son's line by their particular mothers.

33. Exodus 7:3; 13:15.

34. Exodus 1 emphasizes Israel's fruitful multiplication, in fulfillment of God's promise to Abraham.

35. Israel's identity as God's "firstborn son" (4:22) and Pharaoh's refusal to "let my people go" (5:1; 9:1) are common themes in the first half of Exodus.

36. Romans 5–8 traces these themes, drawing heavily on Exodus's imagery of slavery, sonship, and coming deliverance. It's worth recognizing: In Exodus, Egypt is a *recalcitrant* mother; whereas in Romans 8, creation is an *expectant* mother (who eagerly awaits the revealing of God's children). Egypt's recalcitrant posture mirrors other New Testament passages, such as Matthew 24:8 and 1 Thessalonians 5:3, where the birth pangs come upon a rebellious world. Romans 8, however, emphasizes the broader scope of God's good creation (groaning under the futility and bondage of sin). The distinction is likely between the imperial political powers and a world in rebellion under judgment, and the good created order groaning beneath their weight.

37. Exodus 14:16, 22, 28.

38. Numbers 11:12, NIV; Deuteronomy 32:10–14, NIV. Moses's vocation, told to carry the people in his arms like a nurse, has priestly overtones as a representative of God's actions on behalf of his people.

39. Ezekiel 16. The newborn is female here, rather than a "firstborn son," because Ezekiel develops the analogy to highlight Israel's marital relationship to Yahweh.

40. See, for example, *b. Yoma* 75a; *Sifre Num.* 89; *Exod. Rab.* 1.12; *b. Sota* 11b.

41. 1 Thessalonians 2:7.

42. 1 Corinthians 3:1–2, NIV.

43. Hebrews 5:12–14, NIV.

44. John Calvin, *Institutes of the Christian Religion,* ed. John T. McNeill, trans. Ford Lewis Battles (London: Westminster John Knox, 1960), 1012–16 (4.1.1 and 4.1.4).

45. James 3:1.

46. Galatians 4:11, 19.

47. This raises a question for the maternal analogy of the church: Is Christ the Son in the husband/father relation (the second person of the Trinity), or God the Father (the first person of the Trinity)? At face value, these can seem to contradict each other. Two observations. First, it's a metaphor! There's a danger in pushing the imagery too far. Second, the biblical stress is on Christ in the groom relation to the church as bride, and the Father in the paternal relation to us as children. These do not contradict each other, so long as we keep in mind the metaphor is working on different levels. Some of the deeper logic for the analogy, as it relates to the persons of the Trinity, will be explored at the end of chapter 12.

48. Matthew 6:9.

49. Ephesians 2:19.

50. 1 Timothy 5:1–2.

51. Timothy Keller (@timkellernyc), Twitter, February 3, 2015, 9:05 a.m.

52. Galatians 4:6, NIV; cf. Romans 8:15.

53. Richard Bauckham, *Jesus* (Oxford: Oxford University Press, 2011), 65.

54. The body is a central New Testament image for the church's identity as family (cf. 1 Corinthians 12:12; Romans 12).

55. 1 Corinthians 12:21.

56. 2 Peter 1:4.

Chapter 6:
Civil War Amputees

1. John 3:17.

2. The American Institute of Stress, www.stress.org/holmes-rahe -stress-inventory.

3. Frank Olito, "How the Divorce Rate Has Changed Over The Last 150 Years," *Insider*, January 30, 2019.

4. Matthew 19:3, NIV.

5. Matthew 19:4–6, NIV.

6. Some say Jesus never said anything about same-sex sexual activity (a topic we'll address in the next chapter), but it's worth noting here: Jesus goes out of his way to include the diversity of male and female when defining what marriage is. This is an implicit rejection of same-sex unions, which Jesus roots not in culture but the structure of creation. There would be no need for Jesus to address this directly in a context like first-century Israel, where it was not controversial, as there would be later for the apostles in the epistles, in the context of the Gentile mission where such ethical expectations were no longer taken for granted.

7. Mike Miller, "Gwyneth Paltrow Calls 'Incredibly Painful' Divorce from Chris Martin the 'Most Difficult Thing I've Ever Done,'" *People*, June 1, 2017.

8. Malachi 2:16, NRSV and NIV.

9. The most literal rendition of Malachi 2:16 is "to cover one's garment with cruelty," which sparks the image of blood-stained clothes from the spouse you battered.

10. Renee Peltz Dennison, "Are Children of Divorce Doomed to Fail?," *Psychology Today*, August 2, 2014.

11. Matthew 19:13–15.

12. Jesus makes a concession for adultery in Matthew 19:9, and Paul for abandonment in 1 Corinthians 7:10–16. Regarding abuse, the logic

is similar to that of abandonment: When a pattern of abusive behavior makes it dangerous for the spouse or children to remain at home, there is a need for separation in the interest of safety because of the perpetrator's recalcitrant sin. If after a period of discernment it is determined reconciliation will not be prudent or safe, the separation may need to become permanent through divorce. Violence and abuse are the culprits here that ultimately break up the marriage, not the spouse and/or children who need permanent protection.

13. Matthew 19:8.
14. Matthew 19:10.

Chapter 7:
The Great Exchange

1. Tony Scarcello shares more of his story in *Regenerate: Following Jesus After Deconstruction* (Eugene, Ore.: Wipf & Stock, 2020).

2. A shout-out here to my friend Preston Sprinkle's excellent book, *People to Be Loved: Why Homosexuality Is Not Just an Issue* (Grand Rapids: Zondervan, 2015), that explores many of the key biblical passages relevant to this conversation.

3. Unfortunately, we haven't always lived up to this. The AIDS crisis of the 1980s was one tragic example, when, rather than rallying to love and serve people (particularly gay men) who were being struck by a confusing, terrifying, and deadly illness, many resorted to public talking points that were cold, judgmental, and cruel. This was not the way of Jesus, and we must own such failures for what they are.

4. James 1:19; 3:5–6; Matthew 5:43–48; 16:24.

5. A note on language. One challenge when people talk about *homosexuality* is they can mean so many different things by the term. Are we talking about *desire:* that someone is attracted to the same sex? Or *identity:* that someone identifies as gay, lesbian, or bisexual? Or *action:* men having sex with men or women having sex with women? All three are important areas worthy of discussion, but for the purposes of this chapter we'll focus more simply on the third realm of *action.* I'm using the phrase *gay sex* to refer to this—men having sex with men, or women having sex with women—because it's awk-

ward and lumpy to keep repeating *same-sex sexual activity* over and over.

6. Romans 1:26–27, NIV.

7. Romans 1:20, 25.

8. Genesis 1:26–27, NIV. I've replaced the NIV's gloss "creatures" with "reptiles," a more literal translation of both the Hebrew *remes* and Greek Septuagint's *herpeton*. Though Genesis 1 was originally written in Hebrew, these are the terms used in the Greek Septuagint version of the Old Testament, prominent at the time the New Testament was written.

9. Romans 1:22–23, 26–27, NIV. I've used "in the likeness of" and "mankind" (in place of the NIV's "to look like" and "human being") to highlight the similarities with the English translation of the terms in Genesis 1.

10. Robert Gagnon, *The Bible and Homosexual Practice* (Nashville: Abingdon Press, 2002), 159–83; Richard B. Hays, "Relations Natural and Unnatural," *Journal of Religious Ethics* 14 (1986): 184–215; Bernadette Brooten, *Love Between Women* (Chicago: University of Chicago, 1998), 241–49.

11. As the classicist Kyle Harper observes in his respected work, *From Shame to Sin* (Cambridge, Mass.: Harvard University Press, 2016), 93–99, "For Paul, same-sex attraction symbolized the estrangement of men and women, at the very level of their inmost desires, from nature and the creator of nature."

12. See, for example, the non-Christian classicist Thomas K. Hubbard's summary analysis in, *Homosexuality in Greece and Rome: A Sourcebook of Basic Documents* (Berkeley: University of California Press, 2003), 5–8; and William Loader, a proponent of same-sex marriage and renowned expert on sexuality in the ancient world, in *The New Testament on Sexuality* (Grand Rapids: Eerdmans, 2012), 84, 323–24, 496. See also Gagnon's discussion in *The Bible and Homosexual Practice*, 347–61.

13. Paul's inclusion of women and his use of "one another" for men both highlight mutuality in this sexual activity (female same-sex relationships were not marked by the same exploitative dynamics as many male ones in the ancient world).

14. Romans 1:23.

15. Romans 1:25.

16. This symbolic significance doesn't mean gay sex is morally insignificant; it's clearly prohibited in Scripture. The point being made here is simply that Paul focuses on this prohibited practice in Romans 1 because it is symbolic of something bigger within his broader argument in the passage.

17. Romans 3:23.

18. Rachel Gilson, *Born Again This Way* (Charlotte, N.C.: The Good Book Company, 2020), 42, 38.

19. Andrew Wilson makes this point in *God of All Things* (Grand Rapids: Zondervan Reflective, 2021), 67.

20. Please see chapters 12 and 14 for more on the Trinity and temple themes.

21. Psalm 72:14, NIV.

22. There may be some who, because of a disability, cannot consummate their marriage as husband and wife in bodily union. This is tragic yet different. They are still able to represent male and female in covenantal union, which is distinct from a male/male or female/female union. They are still iconic of humanity's diversity, in a situation more akin to infertility (which we'll explore in chapter 13), where for reasons beyond the couple's control, they are unable to reach the natural ends of marriage: the *procreative* end in the case of infertility; the *unitive* end in the case of such a disability.

23. Romans 1:24, substituting "desire" for "lust," to avoid restricting *epythumia* to the sexual connotations of lust, when a broader sense of sinful desire is likely in view here, as discussed in this section.

24. The word is also associated with the sacrificial system, where the connotations include not only moral impurity but physical uncleanness from contamination by things associated with death. See L. Michael Morales, *Who Shall Ascend the Mountain of the Lord* (Downers Grove, Ill.: IVP Academic, 2015), 153–66.

25. In Romans 1:28, *edokimasan* and *adokimon* carry a similar root and meaning in Greek, evoking a play on words in the original language.

26. Romans 1:28–32, MSG.

27. Strong's *Concordance* describes the *mind* (*nous*) as involving not only "the faculties of perceiving and understanding," but also those of "feeling, judging, determining." *Strong's Expanded Exhaustive Concordance of the Bible* (Peabody, Mass.: Hendrickson, 2009), 563.

28. Romans 2:1–3, NIV.

29. Romans 3:23.

30. Tony Scarcello shares more of his story in *Regenerate.*

31. John Calvin, for example, called this "the wondrous exchange made by his boundless goodness," using marital imagery to describe the effect of our union with Christ as his bride: "Everything which is his they may call their own," *Institutes of the Christian Religion*, ed. John T. McNeill, trans. Ford Lewis Battles (London: Westminster John Knox, 1960), IV.17.2. Similarly, Martin Luther called this a "happy exchange," whereby "all that is the husband's is also the wife's," so "we cannot be condemned for our sins . . . [since Jesus] has been pleased that these should be imputed to himself as if they were his own," and now as his bride, his kingdom "can no more be taken from us than from him," *The Freedom of a Christian (De Libertate Christiana)* (1520), c.12. WA7.

Chapter 8:
Sex Isn't Cheap

1. Jennifer Warner, "Pre-Marital Sex the Norm in America," WebMD, December 20, 2006.

2. Katelyn Beaty, "Joshua Harris and the Sexual Prosperity Gospel," *Religion News Service*, July 26, 2019.

3. Olga Khazan, "Fewer Sex Partners Means a Happier Marriage," *The Atlantic*, October 22, 2018; Nicolas Wolfinger, "Counterintuitive Trends in the Link Between Premarital Sex and Marital Stability," *Institute for Family Studies*, June 6, 2016.

4. Marina Adshade, "Does Marriage Really Make Us Healthier and Happier?" *The Institute for Family Studies*, November 6, 2019; Jay L. Zagorsky, "Marriage and Divorces Impact on Wealth," *Journal of Sociology* (December 2005): 406–24.

5. Particularly the detailed list of sexual laws in Leviticus 18. As New Testament scholar Scot McKnight summarizes, "If you double-click on the Greek term *porneia* for a definition, it sends you to Leviticus 18," in "What is Porneia to a 1st Century Jew?" *Jesus Creed* (blog), April 4, 2014. What virtually all those laws have in common is sex outside of marriage (with the exception of the prohibition on having sex with one's wife while she's bleeding on her period, which is probably still a good idea and kind to one's wife).

6. Matthew 5:27–30, 15:19; Mark 7:21–22; cf. 1 Corinthians 6:9.

7. Acts 15.

8. Ephesians 5:31, NIV, using "cleave" as an alternate translation for "be united" (*proskallao* in Greek; *dabaq* in the original Hebrew).

9. Unfortunately, a major problem in the biblical story is that God's people *do* leave him, betraying the covenant to go after other gods. Deuteronomy 28:20; 29:25; 31:16; Judges 2:12, 13; 10:6, 10, 13; 1 Samuel 8:8; 12:10; 1 Kings 9:9; 11:33; 18:18; 19:10, 14; 2 Kings 17:16; 21:22; 22:17; 1 Chronicles 28:9; 2 Chronicles 7:19, 22; 12:1, 5; 13:11; 21:10; 24:18, 20, 24; 28:6; 29:6; 34:25; Ezra 9:10; Isaiah 1:4, 28; Jeremiah 1:16; 2:13, 17, 19; 5:7, 19; 9:13; 16:11; 17:13; 19:4; 22:9; Ezekiel 20:8; 23:8; Daniel 11:30; Jonah 2:8; cf. Joshua 24:16, 20; 2 Chronicles 15:2; Psalm 119:87; Isaiah 65:11.

10. Deuteronomy 10:20; 11:22; 13:4; 30:20; Joshua 22:5; 23:8; 2 Kings 18:6; Psalm 63:8; 119:31.

11. Deuteronomy 11:22.

12. Deuteronomy 31:6, 8; Joshua 1:5; 1 Kings 6:13; 1 Chronicles 28:20; Isaiah 41:17; 42:16; cf. 1 Kings 8:57; Nehemiah 9:17–19, 31; Psalm 9:10; 16:10; 37:28.

13. The "leave and cleave" language introduced at the beginning of the Pentateuch (in Genesis 2) is used most frequently for God with his people at the end of the Pentateuch (in Deuteronomy). So Genesis 2 is setting you up to understand God's covenant relationship with his people as like a marriage, at the climax of the Pentateuch.

14. Shoutout to my friend Jesse Lusko, the originator of this great one-liner.

15. Mary is present at the Crucifixion. Before dying, Jesus entrusts her to the care of his beloved disciple (John 19:26–27). In Mary's bereavement, the prophecy she had received at Jesus's birth is fulfilled: "A sword will pierce through your own soul also" (Luke 2:35).

16. Matthew 27:46, 50; cf. Philippians 2:5–11.

17. Mark 14:24.

18. John 19:30. This is often rendered "It is finished," which is correct, but the root *teleo* speaks more specifically of consummation. *Strong's Expanded Exhaustive Concordance of the Bible* (Peabody, Mass.: Hendrickson, 2009), 5055; "HELPS Word-Studies," by Helps Ministries, Inc. 1987, 2011.

19. Saint Augustine, *Sermo Suppositus*, 120:3.

20. A. R. Cirillo observes, "This concept of union may be seen as the

basis of many of Donne's *Songs and Sonnets* . . . the moment of union is preceded by ecstasy, or a love-death, in which the two lovers are said to be dead, to die to life that they may live to love," in "The Fair Hermaphrodite: Love-Union in the Poetry of Donne and Spenser," *Studies in English Literature, 1500–1900*, vol. 9, no. 1 (Winter 1969): 81.

21. Jean Danielou, *From Shadows to Reality: Studies in the Biblical Typology of the Fathers* (Jackson, Mich.: Ex Fontibus, 2018), 48–56.

22. Tertullian, *De Anima*, 43; P.L. 723B.

23. Fight the New Drug offers a wide variety of up-to-date research on the harmful effects of porn: www.fightthenewdrug.org.

24. Mark Regnerus explores how hi-res porn, modern contraception, and online dating have acted as "market disruptors," lowering the "cost" of sex in the modern relationship market, in *Cheap Sex: The Transformation of Men, Marriage, and Monogamy* (Oxford: Oxford Univ. Press, 2018).

25. See my article, "The Ethics of Contraception," available on my website, www.joshuaryanbutler.com.

26. This is not to deny a strong ideological history behind the sea change; it's simply to note the technological catalyst that allowed this long-standing ideology—formerly more restricted to elites— to go viral as a popular movement. For an insightful and provocative account of the revolutionary ideology's deeper genealogical history, see Carl Trueman, *The Rise and Triumph of the Modern Self* (Wheaton, Ill.: Crossway, 2020).

27. Sally Lloyd-Jones, *The Jesus Storybook Bible: Every Story Whispers His Name* (Grand Rapids: ZonderKidz, 2007), 134, 173, 200, 227.

Chapter 9:
Cheating on God

1. Etymology Online, s.v. "adultery," www.etymonline.com.

2. Ezekiel 6:9, NIV.

3. Jeremiah 3:20, NIV.

4. Isaiah 57:5, 8, NIV.

5. Hosea 4:13, NIV.

6. Ezekiel 23:20, NIV.

7. Ezekiel 23:14–17, NIV.

8. Ezekiel 23:21, NIV.

9. Isaiah 1:21.

10. Cornelius Plantinga, *Not the Way It's Supposed to Be* (Grand Rapids: Eerdmans, 1995), 13–14.

11. Exodus 20:5; Deuteronomy 5:9.

12. Exodus 34:14, NIV. See also, Joshua 24:19; Nahum 1:2; Ezekiel 16:38, 42; 23:25.

13. Hosea 2:14–15, NIV. I've rendered "Achor" into its literal translation of "Trouble."

14. Genesis 39:9, NIV.

15. Genesis 20:6.

16. Psalm 51:4.

17. Genesis 38.

18. Anthony Phillips, "Another Look at Adultery," *Journal for the Study of the Old Testament* no. 20 (1981): 3.

19. Richard M. Davidson, *Flame of Yahweh* (Peabody, Mass.: Hendrickson, 2007), 348.

20. Proverbs 6:32, NIV.

21. Proverbs 6:27, 29, NIV.

22. Deuteronomy 22:22; Richard M. Davidson contrasts Israel's laws on adultery with those of the surrounding nations in the ancient Near East, in *Flame of Yahweh*, 347–49.

23. Deuteronomy 11:25.

24. In ancient patriarchal societies, women were often considered the "property" of the husband, not in the modern-day sense of "owning" a watch but in a social context that generally involved both rights and responsibilities, duties and privileges, yet entailed a power dynamic that placed women in a significantly more vulnerable position.

25. Jay Stringer, *Unwanted: How Sexual Brokenness Reveals Our Way to Healing* (Colorado Springs: NavPress, 2018).

26. This quote, often misattributed to G. K. Chesterton, actually comes from Bruce Marshall, *The World, the Flesh, and Father Smith* (Boston: Houghton Mifflin, 1945).

27. Hosea 2:16–20, NIV, substituting "take you as my wife" for "betroth" and "know" for "acknowledge."

Chapter 10:
Welcome the Children

1. Psalm 68:5–6, NIV.

2. Ephesians 1:3-6, NIV.

3. Matthew 1:1–17; Luke 3:23–38.

4. Galatians 4:4–5, NIV.

5. I was unable to locate the original source for this quote, but it is commonly quoted in adoption resources and easily found online.

6. Best practices in child welfare confirm this. Adopted children do better, studies have found, when they are able to stay connected with their biological families. Open adoption is now encouraged, where a child has access to information and, when safe and appropriate, the opportunity to build relationship with their birth parents.

7. Birth imagery is also used for our salvation (see chapter 5). Generally, the apostle John emphasizes *birth* imagery, while the apostle Paul emphasizes *adoption* imagery. While birth emphasizes our regeneration (made alive by the Spirit), adoption emphasizes our status (as full heirs with the Son).

8. Check out ProGrace, an organization with resources equipping Christians to support children and women while engaging the reality of abortion: www.prograce.org.

9. Wikipedia, "List of United States Cities by Population," last modified August 26, 2022, https://en.wikipedia.org/wiki/List_of_United _States_cities_by_population.

10. *Roe v. Wade*, 410 U.S. 113 (1973). In context, Blackmun is talking about an interpretation of intention in the U.S. Constitution, not about the personhood of the unborn more generally (philosophically, medically, and so on). Yet such an interpretation is only possible by excluding the unborn from the constitutional rights of personhood, similar to how slaves were treated as three-fifths of a person and excluded from the Declaration of Independence's ideal that "all men are created equal," until the Thirteenth Amendment.

As Martin Luther King, Jr., put it in his "Letter from Birmingham Jail," a law is only just when it "squares with the . . . law of God."

11. See, for example, Laurie A. Rudman and Kris Mescher, "Of Animals and Objects: Men's Implicit Dehumanization of Women and Likelihood of Sexual Aggression," *Personality and Social Psychology Bulletin* 38, no. 6 (February 28, 2012): 734–46; Phillip Atiba Goff et al., "Not Yet Human: Implicit Knowledge, Historical Dehumanization, and Contemporary Consequences," *Journal of Personality and Social Psychology* 94, 2 (2008): 292–306.

12. Luke 1:44, NIV.

13. Luke 2:12.

14. Luke 18:16, NIV.

15. I'm following the argument here of Nancy R. Pearcey, *Love Thy Body* (Grand Rapids: Baker, 2018), chapter 2.

16. Pearcey, *Love Thy Body*, 54. The embedded quotes are from: James Watson, "Children from the Laboratory," *Prism: The Socioeconomic Magazine of the American Medical Association* 1, no. 2 (1973): 12–14, 33–34. Francis Crick's comment was reported by Pacific News Service, January 1978. Peter Singer is quoted in Mark Oppenheimer, "Who Lives? Who Dies?—The Utility of Peter Singer," *Christian Century*, July 3, 2002, 24–29.

17. Rodney Stark, *The Rise of Christianity* (San Francisco: HarperSanFrancisco, 1997), 95–128.

18. Psalm 139:13–14; Isaiah 49:15–16, NIV.

19. John 8:44; John 10:10.

20. Cf. 2 Chronicles 28:1–4; 33:3–9; Jeremiah 32:32–35. I explore this in depth in my earlier book, *The Skeletons in God's Closet: The Mercy of Hell, the Surprise of Judgment, the Hope of Holy War* (Nashville: Thomas Nelson, 2014), 35–48.

21. Lee Edelman, *No Future: Queer Theory and the Death Drive* (Durham, N.C.: Duke University Press, 2004), 29. The title is taken from the song "God Save the Queen," by the Sex Pistols, and Edelman is responding to Pope John Paul II's characterization of same-sex unions as a "caricature" of authentic families, because by their very nature they can give no future to society. Edelman resists the claim that a future orientation is integral to the nature of sexuality.

22. Speech of Mother Teresa of Calcutta to the National Prayer Breakfast, Washington, D.C., February 3, 1994.

23. Barna Group, "5 Things You Need to Know About Adoption," November 4, 2013, www.barna.com/research/5-things-you-need-to -know-about-adoption.

24. Barna Group, "Three Trends on Faith, Work, and Calling," February 11, 2014, www.barna.com/research/three-trends-on-faith-work -and-calling.

25. Acts 3:15, NIV.

Chapter 11:
Splitting the Adam

1. This chapter's title is inspired by Richard D. Hess's essay, "Splitting the Adam: The Usage of *Adam* in Genesis I–V," *Studies in the Septuagint*, ed. J. A. Emerton (Leiden: Brill, 1990), 1–15.

2. Genesis 2:7, NIV.

3. Jamin Goggin and Kyle Strobel, *Beloved Dust* (Nashville: Thomas Nelson, 2014).

4. 1 Corinthians 11:12, NIV. In the Greek here, woman came "from" or "out of" (*ek*) man, while man is born "through" or "of" (*dia*) woman.

5. This is a major New Testament theme. Cf. Romans 5; 1 Corinthians 15. Contrary to popular assumption, mainstream science affirms monogenesis (the origins of the human race—genealogically, not genetically—from a single human parent couple), even in relatively recent history. See S. Joshua Swamidass, *The Genealogical Adam and Eve* (Downers Grove, Ill.: IVP, 2021).

6. 1 Corinthians 11:11, NIV. This statement is prefaced by "in the Lord"; Paul is emphasizing that Jesus is restoring the unity we lost in Adam, the wholeness we were made for together.

7. John Donne, "No Man Is an Island," *Meditation XVII: Devotions Upon Emergent Occasions.*

8. Romans 5; 1 Corinthians 15. On the compatibility of such texts with mainstream science, see endnote 5 just above.

9. 1 Corinthians 11:12, NIV.

10. Genesis 2.23, NIV.

11. They are each a *metonymy*, using one part as a stand-in for the whole.

12. Genesis 4:19; 6:2; 11:29; 12:19; 21:21; 24:3–4, 7, 37–38, 40; 25:1; 27:46; 28:1–2, 6, 9; 31:50; 36:2.

13. See *Strong's Expanded Exhaustive Concordance of the Bible* (Peabody, Mass.: Hendrickson, 2009), 6763. *Tsela's* overarching connotations are architectural and structural. The word can be translated "rib," but even here it carries the architectural sense of a "rib of the building." Its other possible translations ("chamber," "beams," "planks," etc.) also carry architectural associations.

14. Genesis 2:21–22, substituting "built" for "made" (to highlight *banah* as a construction term with architectural associations).

15. Thirty-seven of the thirty-nine other times the word appears in the Bible, it's in relation to the tabernacle or the temple. Within the Pentateuch, it *always* has this tabernacle/temple association. When I say it's a temple image, I'm including references to the tabernacle, which was a predecessor to the temple and carried the same associations.

16. Check out the amazing work my friends Tim Mackie and Jon Collins are doing at *Bible Project:* www.bibleproject.com.

17. See chapter 13.

18. The *forming* word used for Adam (*yatsar*) has sculpting associations, emphasizing his relationship to the ground he's made from. The *building* word used for Eve (*banah*), is associated with sacred architecture in the biblical story.

19. Genesis 3:20, NIV.

20. There are literary associations between this scene and Noah observing the animals entering the ark, in male and female pairs, for fruitful multiplication on the other side of the flood (Genesis 7:2–3, 8–9).

21. Genesis 2:18, 20, NIV.

22. Preston Sprinkle, *People to Be Loved: Why Homosexuality Is Not Just an Issue* (Grand Rapids: Zondervan, 2015), 32.

23. I don't like comparisons between bestiality and same-sex sexual activity when it comes to their *moral* significance. But it is worth recognizing there is a *logical* connection here between their prohibition in the Pentateuch. Bestiality violates the "sameness" of *kenegdo* (the sexual partner is not human), whereas same-sex sexual activity violates the "difference" of *kenegdo* (the partner is not one's male/female "other"). The Pentateuch is concerned with boundaries and distinctions ordered for beauty and life; these prohibitions fit within that broader concern.

24. Gerhard von Rad, *Genesis* (Philadelphia: Westminster Press, 1972), 84–85.

25. Genesis 2:22; 24:67; 29:23.

Chapter 12:
Triune Symphony

1. Herman Bavinck, *The Christian Family*, trans. Nelson D. Kloosterman (Grand Rapids: Christian's Library Press, 2012), 7–8. Original version published in 1908.

2. Matt Chandler, *The Mingling of Souls* (Colorado Springs: David C. Cook, 2015).

3. Cf. Genesis 5:1–3. Or Genesis 1:26, just prior to the poem, where God says, "Let us make *adam* [singular] in our image. . . . And let *them* [plural] have dominion." While some would argue from this that Genesis 1 should be read with the corporate meaning in mind, and Genesis 2 the individual, I would suggest this imposes a foreign dichotomy on the Hebrew text, which easily and more naturally holds the two meanings together in a manner similar to what I've described here in this chapter. This both/and meaning is more natural to Paul's reading of humanity's unity in Adam, and the early church's corporate understanding of the image of God in Adam.

4. See Henri de Lubac's magisterial study, *Catholicism: Christ and the Common Destiny of Man* (San Francisco: Ignatius, 1947).

5. See Romans 5.

6. See Jesus's high priestly prayer in John 17.

7. See, for example, Colin Gunton, *The One, the Three, and the Many* (Cambridge, UK: Cambridge University Press, 1993), and Peter Leithart, *Traces of the Trinity* (Grand Rapids: Brazos, 2015).

8. This is also seen earlier in verse 26, where God says, "Let us make *adam* [singular] in our image. . . . And let *them* [plural] have dominion." The image-bearing Adam is conceived as both singular and plural.

9. Genesis 1 raises a question that Genesis 2 addresses. It's as if Genesis 2 zooms in on this climactic poem of Genesis 1, then expands to give a whole story contained within its three verses. The heart

of the concept, however, is right there on page 1 of the Bible, packed into this three-line poem.

10. From Dickinson's poem, "The Loneliness One dare not sound."

11. Curt Thompson, *Anatomy of the Soul* (Carol Stream, Ill.: Tyndale, 2010), 109–34.

12. Ephesians 2:19.

13. Thompson, *Anatomy of the Soul*, xiv.

14. Thompson, *Anatomy of the Soul*, 109.

15. John 17:3.

16. Exodus 20:12; 21:15; Leviticus 19:3; 20:9; Deuteronomy 27:16; Proverbs 20:20; 23:22; Matthew 15:4–6; Ephesians 6:1–4; Colossians 3:20–21; 1 Timothy 5:4.

17. John 1:18 describes the Son as "at the Father's side" (literally "in the bosom [*kolpon*] of the Father"), proceeding from him back in eternity. Proverbs 8 describes Lady Wisdom—often taken to be an image for the pre-incarnate Christ—as at the side of God, brought forth back in eternity "before the beginning of the earth," and participating with him in all his works of creation.

18. The second person of the Trinity was not begotten by sexual union, for example, as human sons are (the Father did not have a divine consort back in eternity). The analogy speaks to origination and procession, with a shared substance and nature. This does not lessen his identity as a true Son. It is more accurate to say the Father and Son are the true prototype, with human parents and children being the replica designed to reflect something of the divine reality.

19. Scripture uses multiple metaphors to speak of the second person of the Trinity, such as the "Word" (a *vocal* analogy) and the "Light" (a *visual* analogy). Taken too literally, these metaphors conflict with each other (an audio wave, ray of light, and only-begotten child are three very different things—you can't be all three). Yet they all speak to *procession:* The second person of the Trinity proceeds from the first, like a word from a speaker, light from a source, and a child from its father.

20. For the theology nerds, this is not Eternal Functional Subordination (EFS). We are not imposing categories of *authority and submission* upon the immanent Trinity (which I believe is improper, unhelpful, and confusing) but rather discussing relations of *origina-*

tion and procession (which are Nicene categories at the heart of Trinitarian orthodoxy).

One set of categories is about "Who's in charge?" The other is about "How does life proceed?" Biblical categories like Son, Light, and Word all have to do with procession, not authority, when it comes to the immanent Trinity. The Son eternally proceeds from the Father: like light proceeding from a lamp, or a voice proceeding from the speaker. (Indeed, denying eternal generation is part of what's gotten some EFS theologians in hot water.) Personally, I find asking whether the light "submits to" the lamp, or the voice "obeys" the speaker, to just be a weird question.

While there may be an appropriate logic or taxis in the economy of salvation to the sending of the Son by the Father (to assume humanity) and obedience of the Son to the Father (according to his humanity) that corresponds to the eternal procession of the Son, this is different from imposing categories of authority and submission upon the immanent Trinity, which threatens to divide the one will of God.

21. The Hebrew term "one" (*echad*) in "one flesh" (Genesis 2:24) is the same term used in the Shema, the famous Old Testament prayer used daily by Israel, "Hear, O Israel: The LORD our God, the LORD is one" (Deuteronomy 6:4, NIV). As we've seen in this book, the Bible uses "one flesh" not as a metaphor but a literal descriptor for the reality of a true union, joined together by God and designed for inseparability (Matthew 19:6). The oneness of a marriage is powerful enough to bear witness, by analogy, to the oneness of God.

22. Genesis 4:25. Interestingly, the gospels emphasize the Son uniquely *knowing* the Father. (Cf. Matthew 11:27; John 7:29; 10:15.) Obviously, the context here is not sexual, yet it is still deeply relational, exclusive, and bound up with the inner life of the Trinity. The Son doesn't just know *about* the Father, he uniquely *knows* the Father and chooses to reveal the Father through the Spirit who proceeds from their union.

23. This is, of course, the *filioque* clause (affirmed by the Western tradition of the church, contested by the Eastern). Our reading here supports the veracity of the *filioque* clause.

24. Or, to be more specific, as a *qualitative* category, rather than a *quantitative* category, when it comes to the analogy.

25. Interestingly, the book of Revelation refers to the Holy Spirit as the seven-fold Spirit—literally, "seven spirits"—who surrounds God's

throne and is sent into all the earth (Revelation 1:4; 3:1; 4:5; 5:6). The number *seven* probably refers here (in apocalyptic symbolism) to the fullness of the Spirit's presence and the Spirit's identification with the seven churches of Revelation. Yet this still speaks to the *expansiveness* of the Spirit's presence, who shares God's presence with his people as the "spreading goodness" of God, to borrow a beautiful phrase from the eighteenth-century Puritan Richard Sibbes.

26. *Doesn't "begotten" imply a prior time of non-existence, before that "begetting" took place?* This is a point where the father/son analogy breaks down: its temporal nature. Unlike God, every father had a time they were not one (before their children were born).

Chapter 13:
A River Runs Through It

1. Genesis 2:10–14, NIV.

2. Ezekiel 28:13–16.

3. On "cosmic mountain" imagery in the Pentateuch, see L. Michael Morales, *Who Shall Ascend the Mountain of the Lord* (Downers Grove, Ill.: IVP Academic, 2015).

4. Thanks to Tim Mackie from *Bible Project*, who alerted me in a conversation years ago to *parad* as a hyperlink connecting the river imagery with the rise of the nations.

5. Genesis 10:5, NASB; cf. verse 32.

6. Genesis 10:32, NASB; cf. verse 5.

7. Other echoes include: God repeats to Noah the original blessing given to humanity to be fruitful and multiply in Genesis 1 (Genesis 9:1, 7), the animals' relation to Noah is described similarly as to Adam in Genesis 2 (Genesis 9:2, 10), and Noah is described as "a man of the soil" (*ish ha adamah*), a Hebrew phrase that echoes Adam being created from the soil (Genesis 9:20).

8. Genesis 13:9, 11, 14.

9. Genesis 25:23, NIV.

10. Deuteronomy 32:8, NIV, substituting "separated" for "divided." In addition to the song's more obvious imagery of water and provision, there is also the repeated description of God as the Rock. This title, in the context of the Exodus, is associated with God's provid-

ing a river of rushing water from a rock in the desert—a story with overtones tied to the earlier river from Eden and the later eschatological river from the Temple Mount.

11. Genesis 1:28.

12. Psalm 104:27, 30, NIV.

13. Acts 17:26.

14. "How Common Is Infertility?" National Institute of Child Health and Human Development, February 8, 2018, www.nichd.nih.gov/health/topics/infertility/conditioninfo/common.

15. This is my translation of *issebownek weheronek* in Genesis 3:16. See *Strong's Exhaustive Concordance of the Bible* (Peabody, Mass.: Hendrickson, 2009), s.v. "itstsabon," "heron."

16. Ruth 4:13; Hosea 9:11. See *Strong*, s.v. "heron."

17. Genesis 3:16.

18. Genesis 3:17, 19, NIV.

19. The root term is *itstsabon* (*Strong*, s.v. "itstsabon").

20. Luke 1:6–7. See also Hannah's story in 1 Samuel 1.

21. 1 Samuel 1:6–7.

22. This quote is a combination from two articles by Karen Swallow Prior, "The Hidden Blessing of Infertility," *Christianity Today*, July 29, 2014, and "Called to Childlessness," *The Ethics and Religious Liberty Commission*, March 6, 2017.

23. Romans 4:18–19, NIV.

24. Romans 4:17.

25. Exodus 34:19; J. Todd Billings, *The End of the Christian Life* (Grand Rapids: Brazos, 2020), 185.

26. Jon D. Levenson, *Resurrection and the Restoration of Israel: The Ultimate Victory of the God of Life* (New Haven, Conn.: Yale University Press, 2006), 110, 124–27, 180.

27. Kevin J. Madigan and Jon D. Levenson, *Resurrection: The Power of God for Christians and Jews* (New Haven, Conn.: Yale University Press, 2009), 146.

28. Romans 4:24, NIV. See verses 18–25.

29. C. S. Lewis, *Miracles* (London; Glasgow: Collins; Fontana, 1947; revised 1960), chapter 12.

30. Ezekiel 47:1–12; Zechariah 14:8.

31. Deuteronomy 7:13; 28:4 (compare the inverse in 28:18, echoing Genesis 3:16ff.).

32. Peter Leithart, "My Temple, My Bride" *Patheos* (blog), November 5, 2017. We'll explore this bridal-temple imagery in more depth in chapter 14.

33. 1 Kings 8, echoing the blessings of Deuteronomy 28.

34. 1 Kings 8, echoing the curses of Deuteronomy 28.

35. 1 Kings 6:13.

36. Regarding "the word," the Ten Commandments—or "Ten Words," in Hebrew—were stored in the ark of the covenant in the Most Holy Place of the temple's sanctuary.

37. Rebekah is found for Isaac at a well (Genesis 24); Jacob first meets Rachel at a well (Genesis 29); Moses rescues Zipporah at a well (Exodus 2). John 4:6–7, NIV, echoes specific details from these Old Testament stories: Jesus "sat down by the well" (cf. Exodus 2:15), and asks the woman to "give me a drink" (cf. Genesis 24:12–21). Arguably, Jacob's rolling the stone away (in Genesis 29) is a background echo to the resurrection (which will bring forth the "living water" Jesus promises).

   As the renowned Jewish scholar Robert Alter observes, this betrothal-type scene at a well involves the following elements (all included in John 4): (a) the future groom journeys to a foreign land (as Jesus does in John 4); (b) there he encounters a girl at a well (as Jesus does here); (c) one of them draws water from a well (as the Samaritan woman does here); (d) the girl then rushes to bring home news of the stranger's arrival (as happens here); (e) finally, the betrothal is concluded, after the groom has been invited to a meal (symbolically alluded to as Jesus is invited to stay in the woman's village). See Robert Alter, *The Art of Biblical Narrative* (New York: Basic, 2011), 62.

38. 1 Corinthians 3:9; 1 Peter 2:5; Ephesians 2:21–22, NIV; cf. 1 Corinthians 6:19.

39. Ephesians 1:23, NIV.

40. Compare John 14:23 with Exodus 25:8.

41. John 15:8.

42. John 7:37–38. I've rendered *koilia* as "belly," matching the King James Version and the most common definition of the term; *Greek-English Lexicon of the New Testament* (New York: Harper, 1894), "koilia," 2836.

43. John 7:39.

44. *A Greek-English Lexicon of the New Testament* (New York: Harper, 1894), "koilia," 2836.

45. The Greek is ambiguous whether "*his* belly" refers to Christ or his people. I believe this ambiguity is intentional on John's part; the linguistic flexibility allows the phrase to refer to both, consistent with the depiction of the Spirit elsewhere in John's gospel as the Spirit of Jesus and of his people.

46. John 4:14, NIV.

47. Galatians 5:22–23.

48. Ezekiel 47:9, NIV.

49. Ezekiel 47:12, NIV.

50. Ezekiel 47:9, NIV.

51. Revelation 22:2, NIV; cf. Ezekiel 47:12.

52. Revelation 22:3.

Chapter 14:
Royal Wedding

1. Jon Levenson interview, *On Script*, podcast, July 12, 2016; quote occurs between 35:00–36:00.

2. Song of Solomon (Songs), chapters 4 and 6. A quick search on Google Images for "Song of Solomon, Illustrated" will find the humorous image by Den Hart.

3. Song of Solomon (Songs) 6:4; 1:5; 2:7; 3:5, 10; 5:8, 16; 8:4. On these biblical images for Jerusalem, see Isaiah 5:1–7; Jeremiah 8:13; Matthew 21:33–35; Mark 11:12–25; cf. Judges 9:8–15; Isaiah 3:14; Jeremiah 12:10; Ezekiel 17:9–10; 19:10–14; Hosea 9:10–17; Micah 7:1.

4. Exodus 28:33–35; 1 Kings 7:42. For pomegranates as a significant feature of Israel's landscape, see Numbers 13:23; Deuteronomy 8:8.

5. 1 Kings 5:6, 9, 14; cf. Song of Solomon (Songs) 5:15.

6. Song of Solomon (Songs) 1:17.

7. Song of Solomon (Songs) 7:7-8; cf. 1 Kings 6:29, 32, 35.

8. Song of Solomon (Songs) 2:1-2, 16; 4:5; 5:13; 6:2-3; 7:2; cf. 1 Kings 7:19, NIV.

9. Song of Solomon (Songs) 4:12–15, substituting "paradise" for "or-

chard" in 4:13 (*pardes* is a Persian loan word used in the Septuagint for the Garden of Eden and the root of our word "paradise").

10. Song of Solomon (Songs) 1:5.

11. Purple and scarlet feature significantly throughout Exodus's prescriptions for the fabrics used in the tabernacle. On the "scarlet yarn," see its repeated use in the cleansing rituals of Leviticus 14, a use anticipated by the birth of Zerah in Genesis 38 and followed by the salvation of Rahab in Joshua 2, all likely associated with Passover themes.

12. Song of Solomon (Songs) 4:7, substituting "blemish" for "flaw"; cf. use of this Hebrew term *mum* in Leviticus 21–22, and elsewhere in the Pentateuch, in regulations for the priests and sacrifices.

13. Song of Solomon (Songs) 4:11.

14. My forthcoming book on gender will explore categories that help illuminate the significance of such themes, without letting them reduce to gender stereotypes.

15. Song of Solomon (Songs) 2:4; 5:10–16.

16. This association occurs not only in Solomon's composition of the Song but in his historical construction of the temple itself. The temple was not only designed to be a *building* but a *body*. Peter Leithart explores how the temple's architecture is described in 1 Kings 6–7 with personified human features (a "face," "ribs/sides," and "shoulders"), with multiple hyperlink words from Genesis 2 connecting its construction with the creation of Eve (such as "rib/side," "underneath," and "built"), and God telling Solomon at the temple's dedication he will enter it to "dwell among" and "not forsake" his people (that's marital covenant language), filling his house to make it fruitful; in "My Temple, My Bride," *Patheos* (blog), November 7, 2017. The temple is a feminine icon for Israel as God's bride.

17. Song of Solomon (Songs) 6:3; 5:8; 1:2; 4:16.

18. Genesis 17. Significantly, circumcision is given *in between* the Hagar story and the birth of Isaac. The Hagar story represents a "fall" of Abram and Sarai, attempting to fulfill God's promise through their own power and by unjust means. Circumcision is then given, involving a shedding of blood (with sacrificial associations), which reestablishes God's covenant with Abraham, a covenant that is thereafter fulfilled by God's power and through his righteous means. This is also the context in which their names are changed to Abraham and Sarah.

19. Deuteronomy 30:6; Jeremiah 31:33; 32:40; Ezekiel 11:19; 36:26; cf. 44:7–9 on Ezekiel's correlation of the "heart" and "flesh" (that is, genitals) related to circumcision.

20. Foundation stories in Genesis and Exodus foreshadow the coming Levitical sacrificial system, such as God's killing of an animal to clothe Adam and Eve (Genesis 3:21); the pleasing "aroma" arising from Noah's altar to God (8:21); and Abraham's near sacrifice of Isaac with a substitute provided (chapter 22). Such stories establish themes for the later temple sacrifices, to understand their meaning and significance. Two such stories that associate circumcision with sacrifice are, in particular, Abraham's "fall" with Hagar (see endnote 18 above), and Zipporah's "intervention" with Moses (Exodus 4:24–26, which connects to Passover themes).

21. Exodus 4:24–26. The Hebrew is unclear whether Moses or his son is in danger, and whether Moses or Yahweh is the "bridegroom of blood." I'd suggest this ambiguity is intentional, in order to allow a double meaning in which both readings are related. The second reading only further reinforces the primary point here: Circumcision is tied to Passover imagery and Yahweh is a "bridegroom of blood."

22. The Passover themes in Exodus 4:22–26 include the foreshadowing of the final plague just prior (verses 22–23), the angel of death motif (verse 24), and the covering with blood to avert judgment (verse 25).

23. From a modern medical perspective, there is not always a shedding of blood or a painful experience involved (even if these are still common); we are concerned here with the ancient understanding of the event more generally and its symbolic associations.

24. Song of Solomon (Songs) 2:10, 13.

25. Song of Songs 2:15, NIV.

26. L. Michael Morales, *Who Shall Ascend the Mountain of the Lord* (Downers Grove, Ill.: IVP Academic, 2015). Morales brilliantly connects this theme to the rest of the Pentateuch: Israel's covenant identity in Genesis and Deuteronomy, the deliverance and wilderness narratives in Exodus and Numbers, and the heart of the sacrificial and priestly system of Leviticus.

27. Union with God speaks to themes like the reconciliation of heaven and earth, filling with the Spirit, and indwelling divine glory. Shedding of blood speaks to themes like atonement for sin, the sacrificial system, and deliverance into the land.

28. It's suggestive that "leave and cleave" language is emphasized on the outer bookends of the Pentateuch, in Genesis (for human marriage) and in Deuteronomy (for divine marriage). Arguably, the "one flesh" consummation moment for the divine covenant occurs on the Day of Atonement, a covenant renewal ceremony where Yahweh and Israel are "re-united" through the shedding of blood.

29. Song of Songs 8:13, NIV; Song of Solomon (Songs) 8:14; Revelation 22:20.

Chapter 15:
The End of the World

1. Revelation 21:2, NIV.

2. Revelation 21:9.

3. Revelation 21:16–17.

4. Revelation 21:3, NIV.

5. Revelation 21:22, NIV.

6. Revelation 21:11, NIV.

7. Revelation 21:19–21; Exodus 28.

8. 2 Corinthians 5:1, NIV.

9. Revelation 21:5.

10. Revelation 22:2.

11. Revelation 21:4.

12. Revelation 22:1–2.

13. Revelation 21:9.

14. Song of Solomon (Songs) 6:3.

Conclusion

1. Song of Solomon (Songs) 8:6; I've rendered "flame of Yah" more literally from the Hebrew.

2. Shout-out to Housefires's song "The Wick" (2014), which this line is adapted from.

JOSHUA RYAN BUTLER serves as a lead pastor of Redemption Tempe in Arizona, is the author of *The Skeletons in God's Closet* and *The Pursuing God,* and is a fellow with the Keller Center for Cultural Apologetics. Josh loves shifting paradigms to help people who wrestle with tough topics of the Christian faith by confronting popular caricatures and replacing them with the beauty and power of the real thing. Josh and his family—his wife, Holly, daughter, Aiden, and sons, James and Jacob—enjoy spending time with friends over great meals and exploring the scenic beauty of the Southwest.

You can visit Josh at joshuaryanbutler.com, Facebook, Instagram, and Twitter.

Discover the Beautiful Invitation of Our Sexuality as God Intended It to Be

A provocative yet practical look at what God has to say about sex and what sex reveals about God.

Dig into the Bible's beautiful narrative about what our sexuality is intended to point us toward in this dynamic companion guide to the book.

MULTNOMAH

Learn more about Joshua's books
at WaterBrookMultnomah.com.